Christine Flynn Saulnier, PhD

Feminist Theories and Social Work:
Approaches and Applications

*Pre-publication
REVIEWS,
COMMENTARIES,
EVALUATIONS . . .*

"**T**his highly informed, comprehensive book linking feminist perspectives to social work is long overdue. Saulnier's introductory but systematic discussion of the major feminist frameworks–liberal, radical, socialist, lesbian, cultural, African-American, post-modern, and global–effectively acknowledges the many meanings of feminism that prevail in today's racially, ethnically, and politically diverse world. The thorough descriptions, balanced critiques, and sensitive application of the various feminisms to the key components of the social work curriculum make this well-written and accessible book especially relevant for practice, policy, human behavior, and research classrooms. The gender lens provided by the book is vital for the profession in which women predominate as clients and workers. Social work students and educators already interested in women's issues will love this book. It will also be a good read for anyone from any discipline broaching the topic for the first time."

Mimi Abramovitz, DSW
*Professor of Social Work,
Hunter College School
of Social Work, New York*

"**C**hristine Flynn Saulnier's book, *Feminist Theories and Social Work: Approaches and Applications,* makes a significant and unique contribution to the field. Although there is a growing body of work on feminist social work practice, Saulnier advances the knowledge base substantially by her readable and comprehensive analysis of feminist theories, encompassing liberal feminism, radical feminism, socialist feminism, lesbian feminist theory, cultural and ecofeminist theories, womanism or African-American women's feminist thought, postmodern feminist theory, and global feminism. What is even more significant in terms of this book's relevance to social work education is that Saulnier derives specific practice implications from each theoretical base for policy, community organization, administration, group work, case work, and research. Contrasting theoretical perspective are then brought to bear upon the social problems of alcoholism, battering, employment issues, and sex work. Throughout her critique of each theoretical perspective, she addresses issues of class and race.

This book is a unique integration of feminist theory and practice useful to a wide range of classes in social work, women's studies, and other human service fields. It is a gift–an essential reference to be read repeatedly–by all educators and practitioners who are eager to learn more about feminist theory and practice, but may be unable to carefully analyze and distill complex theories. I extend my admiration and respect to Ms. Saulnier for her skillful, insightful, and concise analysis of such complex theories."

Nancy R. Hooyman, MSW, PhD
Dean and Professor,
School of Social Work,
University of Washington, Seattle

"**D**r. Saulnier's work fills a significant gap in the texts currently available for teaching women's issues in the social work curriculum.

It provides a valuable resource for scholar or student in that the review of theories is comprehensive *and* very applicable to practice research and policy areas."

Kathleen E. Nuccio, PhD
Associate Professor,
University of Minnesota, Deluth

"**P**rofessor Saulnier has done an excellent job of reviewing historical and current literature on feminist theory and synthesizing this material with regard to its utility for social workers. Of particular importance is the care she has taken in describing the major categories of feminist theory and comparing and contrasting these perspectives. The book should be helpful to social workers in clarifying the extent of similarities and differences among the various perspectives on feminism, such as liberal, radical, socialist, lesbian, cultural, African-American, post-modern, and global.

Given Professor Saulnier's clear writing style, readers who have not studied this literature in depth should have a much better idea of how to articulate the various categories of feminist thought. This volume will be especially valuable to social work educators who are looking for a concise book that can be used in social work courses that are focused on feminist social work or have a module devoted to feminist social work. The applications to policy, administration, community organization, group work, case work, and research at the end of each chapter on a major school of feminist thought are especially useful in making the connections between feminism and social work practice.

Readers from related disciplines who want to develop an understanding of the many facets of feminist thought will also find this material useful."

Diana M. DiNitto, PhD
Professor, School of Social Work,
University of Texas at Austin;
Author, Social Welfare:
Politics and Public Policy

"**T**he author translates nine different feminist theories into plain English so they become readable and accessible. Each chapter presents a different theory in its historical context, a rich body of literature that captures the agreements and conflicts of its proponents, a critique of the theory, and applications of the theory for micro and macro social work practice and research. Dr. Saulnier's analysis sheds light on such contemporary issues as abortion, affirmative action, and pornography. There is much-needed emphasis given to African-American women's activism, thoughts, and contributions to theory development. The conclusion of the book provides a helpful comparison of the uniqueness and similarities of the theories in regard to defining specific social work problems, interventions, and solutions.

The Haworth Press, Inc.

Feminist Theories and Social Work
Approaches and Applications

HAWORTH Social Work Practice
Carlton E. Munson, DSW, Senior Editor

New, Recent, and Forthcoming Titles:

Feminist Theories and Social Work
Approaches and Applications

Christine Flynn Saulnier, PhD

The Haworth Press
New York • London

The Haworth Press, Inc., 10 Alice Street, Binghamton, NY 13904-1580

Cover designed by Monica L. Seifert.

Library of Congress Cataloging-in-Publication Data

Saulnier, Christine Flynn.
    Feminist theories and social work : approaches and applications / Christine Flynn Saulnier.
      p.   cm.
    Includes bibliographical references and index.
    ISBN 1-56024-945-5 (alk. paper)
    1. Feminist theory. 2. Social service–Philosophy. I. Title.
HQ1190.S265 1996
305.42"01–dc20

                                           96-4735
                                              CIP

To Becky and Jordan, with love.

ABOUT THE AUTHOR

Christine Flynn Saulnier, PhD, is Assistant Professor of Social Work at the University at Buffalo, SUNY, where she teaches courses in social welfare policy and in social work practice. Dr. Saulnier brings a feminist perspective to her teaching and her research. She is currently studying alcohol and drug service delivery systems in western New York; specialized alcohol interventions for women; and the health, mental health, and alcohol service needs of lesbian and bisexual women. Her social work practice experience consists of direct and indirect service delivery, including nine years providing disability services, and six years working in alcohol treatment and/or health care settings. She has published in the following journals: *Affilia: Journal of Women and Social Work, Alcohol Health and Research World, Journal of Applied Social Sciences, Journal of Drug Issues, Journal of Prevention and Intervention in the Community,* and *Substance Use and Misuse* (formerly *International Journal of the Addictions*).

CONTENTS

Acknowledgments

Ellen Lewin read the first (several) drafts when this was still a paper for my oral examination at Berkeley. Without her guidance, patience, and suggestions, the book would not have gotten off the ground. It was at her suggestion that I took the idea of *applying* the theories more seriously and expanded those sections.

Pat Morgan and Carol Stack convinced me that it was worthwhile to read broadly and try to keep up to date with many divergent theoretical developments. Pat also introduced me to the experience of doctoral students from different disciplines meeting regularly—for years—to discuss our work, to remind each other that the goal was social justice, and to ask ourselves constantly what our work had to do with achieving that goal. She also made us promise that when we finished our PhDs and went to other universities, we would continue the tradition.

And so I have. Most of the women who reviewed the chapters, and gave me suggestions about how to improve them, meet every other week to discuss theories, qualitative research, social justice, and getting dissertations done and articles submitted on a timely basis. The students include Vaune Ainsworth (psychology), Patty Kaiser (history), Pat Merle (social work, Columbia), Kathy Revelle (education) and Liz Wheeler (nursing). Lacey Sloan and Hilary Weaver (School of Social Work, University at Buffalo [UB]) joined us when they could and participated in the discussions and commented on the drafts.

Three other faculty in the School of Social Work at UB read and critiqued chapters: Jacqueline Gyamerah, Nancy Smyth, and Barbara Rittner. Their encouragement was as valuable as their comments.

I was also encouraged by reports from students and colleagues who attended conferences, encountered faculty from the University of New England, then returned to Buffalo to report "They want to know: Is it done yet?" It kept me moving!

Thank you all.

Introduction

I wrote this book for four reasons. First, I wanted to understand feminism better. I knew that if I were going to teach social work from a feminist perspective, I had better know what I was talking about. I knew feminist theory had a lot to offer social work and human services, and I wanted to add to the literature that was explaining the connections.[1] I started by writing a paper. As with many projects, it soon took on a life of its own.

Second, I was irked when I heard people complain that feminists contradict themselves all the time. I knew that was because feminists had different frameworks–all legitimately called feminist– from which they analyzed problems and formulated responses, but I did not feel I could articulate what those differences were, well enough to suit myself, or well enough to explain why it made no sense to search for a party line–a single, coherent *Feminism* with which every feminist would agree. I think I can explain that now.

Third, I was frustrated by trying to understand feminist books and articles that sometimes seemed almost purposefully inaccessible. Also, I was convinced that sophisticated, complex theory did not have to be incomprehensible to be worthwhile. I assumed I was not alone in my frustration. So I have tried to write a book that is

---

1. The list of feminist social work writers is lengthy and growing. Some of the names that come to mind are: Mimi Abramowitz, Paula Allen-Mears, June Axinn, Claudia Bepko, Sharon Berlin, Ruth Brandwein, Mary Bricker-Jenkins, Diane Burden, Bonnie Carlson, Barbara Collins, Lynn Cooper, Liane Davis, Diana DiNitto, Miriam Dinerman, Josephina Figuera-McDonough, Edith Gomberg, Naomi Gottlieb, Lorraine Gutiérrez, Jan Hagen, Ann Hartman, Nancy Hooyman, Diane Kravetz, Joan Laird, Monica McGoldrick, Carol Meyer, Ginny NiCarthy, Miriam Olson, Diana Pearce, Beth Glover Reed, Beatrice Saunders, Betty Sancier, Carol Stack, Mary Swigonski, Nan Van Den Bergh, Froma Walsh, Ann Weick, Natalie Woodman, and Janice Wood Wetzel. And those are only some of the better-known contemporary feminists in social work, not to mention historical figures such as Ida B. Wells, Mary Church Terrell, Jane Addams. . .

accessible to people who, like myself, prefer to have things said in plain words, when that is possible. I think of this book as a translation for people who do not have three years to spend wading through the literature, as I did, trying to figure out what these women were saying. They have *important* things to say, well worth the trouble of reading and re-reading, if you have the time. For those who do not, here are nine chapters of condensed theories and applications.

Finally, I was concerned that we, as feminists, were not always remembering that theories which contradict each other can sometimes lead to actions that are at cross-purposes.[2] Our contradictions can sometimes get us into trouble. I thought it was important to pay attention to that particular pitfall. I do not think it is necessary to choose one branch of feminism and base all your work on it. Different situations, different women, and different times call for different approaches. But, as we know, eclecticism can be both good and bad. It *matters* that some of these theories do not work so well together. My hope is that with a grounding in several feminisms and some practice with applying them, we can choose among the theories more wisely.

DIVIDING THE THEORIES

There are many ways to separate the theories. Common divisions are liberal, radical, and socialist, delineations that cover American feminism up through the early 1970s. Since then there have been some remarkable occurrences and several, though by no means all, of the more recent branches of feminist thought are presented here, including African-American womanism, cultural feminism, ecofeminism, lesbian feminism, global feminism, and postmodern feminism.

Not all the writers would agree with the way I classified their work, or with the list of only nine theories. Some theorists would

---

2. For example, while some feminists try to expand the definition of alcohol problems in women so that women have better access to services, others try to narrow the definition so that fewer women are pathologized by the label of alcoholic.

add more chapters, distinguishing socialist from Marxist feminism (e.g., Jaggar, 1983; Tong, 1989). Others would separate ecofeminism from cultural feminism (e.g., Braidotti et al., 1994). On the other hand, all of feminism is sometimes divided simply into radical versus liberal traditions. Although I have tried to base my chapters on relatively distinct philosophical and political approaches to problem definition and problem solving, most people probably draw on several theories for their work.

Some of the branches, such as radical and global feminism, are more clearly grounded in social movements and have more explicit prescriptions for activism. For example, it is not difficult to imagine what radical feminist activism would encompass. The practice of postmodern feminism, which emerged in academia, is not so readily defined.

The theoretical labels, for the most part, are applied by feminist academics. Probably few people would refer to themselves as cultural feminists although it is not unusual for radical and socialist feminists or for womanists to claim such identifications. Cultural feminism warrants a separate chapter because the theory and the solutions suggested by it are distinct. In any case, it is the reader and the practitioner who must decide if my divisions are helpful.

INCLUSIONS AND EXCLUSIONS

Because of the focus on theoretical distinctions and on social work, some important work is left out. Some of it is new work that is emerging out of more recent feminist movements, but has not yet formulated a cohesive theoretical structure, for example, feminist theories of disability. Because of their importance to social work, I added a bibliography of feminist writings that do not fit within any of the present theoretical divisions.

On the other hand, I did not include a well-developed branch of feminism–psychoanalytic feminist theory. This decision was a difficult one, based on much thought and many discussions with social work colleagues. I did not ignore either individual or group psychotherapy or leave out psychodynamic thought entirely. Where it was applicable, psychodynamic models were included in theoretical discussions and in applications. For example, Carol Gilligan and the psychodynamically oriented feminist theorists and clinicians at the Stone Center are all mentioned in Chapter 5 on cultural feminism.

The more specific theory, psychoanalytic feminism, was another matter. It became clearer to me when I searched for ways to apply the theory to the range of social work interventions, as I had with all the other theories, that I could neither find nor imagine how psychoanalytic feminism would guide macro-level policy, program administration, community organizing, or research methods. Finally, I decided that since the particular practice of psychoanalytic feminism–psychoanalysis–is unavailable to the populations social workers normally serve, it would be inaccurate for me to argue here that it serves a practical purpose for social workers. However, in recognition of the historical connections between social work and psychoanalytic thinking (Federn, 1992) and the potential interest of some readers, I have also included a bibliography on psychoanalytic feminism: Appendix A.

Throughout the book, there is heavy emphasis on the thought, writing, and activism of African-American women. In part, this is an acknowledgment that throughout feminist movements and theory building, African-American women have been contributors (hooks, 1984) even though it was not until comparatively recently that their works were widely disseminated. For reasons of access, favoritism, and sometimes blatant racism, the writings of women of color have often been discounted in favor of white feminists' writings. In academic settings and in the media, it is the most conservative edges of white liberal feminist theory that have received the bulk of attention (Faludi, 1991). Highlighting the work of African-American theorists does more than simply provide a balance to unwarranted selectivity, however. The juxtapositioning and interweaving of the work of white women and African-American women help to counteract the detrimental effects, intellectually and politically, of narrowness and exclusivity and provide a more accurate portrayal of feminisms.

African-American women are not the only women of color to have developed theories of feminism that are distinct from or interact with those developed by white women, but nowhere is the case for focusing on multiple systems of oppression argued so strongly as it is by black women. In addition, this theoretical development of feminist theories and activism have a long history, which is related to the practical reason for focusing on this work: African-American women's work is more readily available than the writings of other women of color.

THIS IS A CHALLENGE TO PRIVILEGE

Those who benefit from social privileges that are denied to others will be challenged by the material in this book. Men will be challenged to recognize how they gain from sexism. White women will be challenged to recognize how they are advantaged by racism. Heterosexual people will be challenged to recognize their heterosexual privilege. Despite efforts to present these theories in ways that would not offend or induce anger, it is not easy for us to recognize our privilege: white people benefit from racism, men benefit from sexism, and straight people benefit from heterosexism—*even though they may not agree with oppression.* We need to challenge these privileges. All of the theories described in this book constitute some threat to the current social order, and because of that, they are likely to raise our collective anxiety. I ask the reader to remain open-minded to the perspectives of the various theorists.

STRUCTURE OF THE BOOK

What follows is a review of nine branches of feminist theory: liberal, radical, socialist, lesbian, cultural, ecofeminist, womanist, postmodern, and global. The better-known branches, liberal, radical, and socialist are presented first, to lay the groundwork for related theoretical developments. Lesbian feminism, an outgrowth of radical feminism, follows. Next is cultural feminism, which is both a reaction to liberal feminism and an expansion of radical feminist thought. Womanism, both a completely new way of thinking and a reaction to liberal feminism, comes next, followed by postmodern feminism, which serves as a counterpoint to cultural feminist theory. The final chapter discusses global feminism, which is related to but more encompassing than socialist feminism. The chapters were written to be read in order.

Each branch is presented in a separate chapter,[3] with a brief overview of the philosophical and political contributions and contributors. This is followed by a review of the theory, then a critique of the theory's limitations and an assessment of its contributions. The chapters end with examples of applications of the theory to social work practice. Six areas of social work practice are covered in each chapter: social welfare policy, administration and/or organizational issues, community organizing, group work, case work, and social work research.

I need to point out here that feminists from different perspectives *talk to each other.* Regularly. Doing so, they influence each others' thinking. Overlaps are inevitable in theory, even more so in practice, so it was not always possible to find "pure" examples for the application of a particular theory. Hopefully, the examples will illuminate the theories, but the applications are often more muddied than the theories themselves; it is not unusual for feminist practice to draw simultaneously on several branches of theory.

The final chapter summarizes the nine branches, discusses common themes, then contrasts particular ways social problems could be defined and solved, using several different feminist theoretical approaches.

I want to emphasize that I made no attempt here to define *the* feminist theory. The opposite is true. I hope to show that a thorough grounding in feminisms will help those who work with and on behalf of women to consider many different frameworks. The chapters start with the branch that is probably most familiar and arguably the most influential: liberal feminism.

---

3. The exception is ecofeminism. Ecofeminist theorists write from at least two quite divergent perspectives. Some of that work is included under cultural feminism. More appears in the chapter on global feminist theory.

Chapter 1

Liberal Feminism

THE POLITICAL CONTINUUM

It is important to separate the traditional concept of liberalism, on which liberal feminist theory is based, from our current, common use of the term *political liberalism*, which is sometimes erroneously associated with left-wing political attitudes. In America, we *differentiate* liberal from conservative whereas in Europe, the original political philosophy of liberalism is *equated with* conservatism and differentiated from the left wing, or what Americans call the radical left. Adding to the confusion is the fact that Americans use the word liberal to describe those who advocate for government intervention, whereas historically "liberal" referred to people who opposed government interference with civil liberties (DiNitto, 1995).

We have a tendency, in America, to think of the political spectrum as going from liberal to conservative, but there is more to the continuum. Diana DiNitto (1995) has written an engaging account of terms used to refer to political ideologies. In it she described the political spectrum as follows:

radical	liberal	moderate	conservative	reactionary

We tend to lop off or cluster together the left half of the spectrum in our everyday language. It is helpful, in reading this book, to recall that liberal is to the right of radical and that, in general, the farther one moves to the left, the more fundamental the changes one is likely to support.

PHILOSOPHICAL CONTRIBUTIONS
AND CONTRIBUTORS

To situate the political philosophy of liberalism, it helps to consider its history. The liberal philosophers (John Locke [1632-1704] and Jean-Jacques Rousseau [1712-1778]), upon whose theories liberal feminism is based, were writing at a particular point in time. At least three ideas need to be considered before reviewing their tenets. The first is the influence of the Newtonian paradigm that the physical universe operates according to simple, rational, physical laws; that is, all significant events operate according to reason. Anything that does not operate in such a fashion was considered secondary, or "other" (Donovan, 1985). Donovan argued that for liberal male thinkers, many of whom questioned the extent of women's capacity to reason, women were included in this "other" category.

Second, it must be understood that Locke and Rousseau, in arguing for the "rights of man," were contesting the right of monarchs and aristocrats to rule the masses, not arguing for the rights of all people to exercise civil liberties. They argued in favor of political participation of *men* who were property owners (Eisenstein, 1983).

Third, Locke maintained that what made someone a "man" was his specifically human capacity to reason, unrelated to any physical characteristics or incapacities. The intrinsic dignity and worth of a man was grounded in the capacity to reason (Jaggar, 1983). Because of this devotion to rationality, liberals tended to value activities according to the amount of reason an activity required, so that physical labor was held in disdain and intellectual pursuits were prioritized (Jaggar, 1983).

Liberal concern with justice is based on a conception of society as composed of separate individuals, each competing for a fair share of resources (Jaggar, 1983). Liberals argue that individuals must be allowed to exercise their autonomy and fulfill their needs as they define them (Tong, 1989). This is complicated, however, by limited resources: as individuals attempt to secure as many resources as possible, it becomes difficult to create institutions that maximize an individual's freedom without detracting from the community's welfare (Tong, 1989).

Closely related to this notion, and the reason for the complication noted by Rosemarie Tong, is that liberalism's dedication to liberty means freedom from interference either by individuals or by the state (Jaggar, 1983), and so traditionally, liberals have attempted to limit the authority of the state. Of key importance to feminist theory is that a dividing line is drawn between the public realm, which the state is expected to regulate, and the private realm, which is expected to be free from state control (Jaggar, 1983).

There is also a split between (1) classical or libertarian liberals, those people who, in the United States, are now called conservatives; and (2) welfare or egalitarian liberals, those people who Americans currently describe as liberals. Classical liberals assign to the state two roles: first, the protection of civil liberties such as property rights, voting rights, and freedom of speech; and second, the provision of equal opportunity to individuals, *without interfering with the free market*. Welfare liberals, on the other hand, expect the state to regulate the market to the extent necessary to ensure some minimum level of economic justice. Welfare liberals assume that some individuals have more advantages than others and that the state must intervene by providing such programs as legal services, school loans, food stamps, low-cost housing, and government-funded health insurance (e.g., Medicare and Medicaid) to help people to obtain their fair share (Tong, 1989). Historically, in the United States, there has been a tendency in the direction of welfare liberalism in providing services and in taking steps toward redistribution of income, through somewhat progressive taxation (Jaggar, 1983). In the 1990s, however, a dramatic reversal of that tendency is occurring.

The traditional liberal values of independence (vs. interdependence), equality of opportunity (vs. equality of outcome), and individualism (vs. collectivism) are so ingrained in Western society that they are now accepted as standard social functioning rather than viewed as a particular ideology. These traditional liberal values are central to liberal feminist thought.

THE THEORY

Liberal feminists point out that society violates the value of equal rights in its treatment of women, primarily by restricting women as a group, rather than treating women as individuals (Jaggar, 1983). They argue that women should have the same rights as men.

Contributors to liberal feminist theory were many, including Mary Wollstonecraft,[1] John Stuart Mill, Harriet Taylor, and Elizabeth Cady Stanton (Eisenstein, 1981). Arguing liberalism from a racial as well as gender perspective were Josephine St. Pierre Ruffin, Anna Julia Cooper, Ida B. Wells, Frances E. W. Harper, Mary Church Terrell, and Fannie Barrier Williams (Donovan, 1985).

Theorists have continued to identify and clarify liberal feminist issues for the past two hundred years. In the eighteenth century, Wollstonecraft (1792/1967) attacked the barriers to women's educational and economic opportunities. In the nineteenth century, liberal feminists attacked the denial of access to citizenship rights by women (Eisenstein, 1981). Of key importance is that the liberalism inherited from Enlightenment times focused on equal treatment *outside*, rather than within, the family (Eisenstein, 1981). This dichotomy was not questioned by liberal feminists (Jaggar, 1983); while they challenged male bias in liberal theory, they accepted the division between public and private life (Eisenstein, 1981) and the notion that freedom of opportunity rested in the public sphere (Nes and Iadicola, 1989).

Twentieth-century liberal feminists followed suit, continuing to focus on changing public, rather than private realms. In the twentieth century, liberal feminists attacked women's lack of political equality and state interference in women's reproductive freedom, and more recently, they moved in the direction of welfare liberalism, arguing that women need access to certain social services to ensure equality between women and men.

Defining Gender as the Primary Issue

The debate over whether race or sex was the major source of oppression divided black and white women in both the nineteenth and twentieth centuries (Joseph, 1981), and it fostered divisions within several branches of feminist theory, including liberal feminism. The black women's clubs organized by Josephine St. Pierre

---

1. Some of Wollstonecraft's work fits more readily under radical feminism and will be discussed in that chapter.

Ruffin in the 1890s (Davis, 1990) worked toward racial and sexual equality and toward redefining the criteria of "true womanhood," carefully including all black women, rather than allowing class distinctions to divide women (Giddings, 1988). The same was not true for white liberal feminists. The difference between black and white women's organizations of the late 1800s was expressed by Fannie Barrier Williams as follows: "Among colored women the club is the effort of the few competent in behalf of the many incompetent. . . . Among white women the club is the onward movement of the already uplifted" (Giddings, 1988, p. 98).

This is not to say that all black women had a radical reorganization of America in mind.[2] White and black liberal feminists tended to support incremental change. Both the General Federation of Women's Clubs and the National Association of Colored Women (NACW) were composed primarily of educated, middle-class women who were committed to women's educational and economic progress, and members insisted on the importance of women's moral influence in the home. They shared a belief in the superiority of middle-class values (Giddings, 1988).

The Meritocracy and Women's Capacity to Reason

Early liberal feminists such as Wollstonecraft and Stanton noted that rights, status, resources, and rewards were ascribed by society based on the assumed capacity of an individual to reason, and they argued that women's reasoning capacity was similar to men's (Jaggar, 1983). The hierarchical structure between women and men, although it stood in opposition to liberalism's argument for a fair meritocracy[3] based on rationality and achievement, was allowed to continue because women's physical properties, rather than their intellectual capacities, were used to define women and their place in society (Eisenstein, 1981). Using John Locke's theory of the ratio-

---

2. Mary McLeod Bethune, for example, accepted the separate but equal policy for blacks and whites, placing enormous faith in the meritocracy of liberal philosophy and politics (Giddings, 1988).

3. A meritocracy is a system by which people are rewarded based on their individual accomplishments, such as educational attainment, rather than on group characteristics, such as ethnicity.

nality of humans, these feminists contended that the very real physical differences between women and men were unimportant since humans are *essentially* rational (Jaggar, 1983). Liberal feminists argued–then and now–that liberal values are violated when women are judged by physical rather then intellectual capacity (Jaggar, 1983). Instead, liberal values need to be extended to women by eliminating the inherent injustices and unfairness in the functioning of the meritocracy (Nes and Iadicola, 1989).

Education

Wollstonecraft (1792/1967) argued that if women and men were raised in a more androgynous atmosphere, and if women were provided access to educational opportunities similar to those afforded to men, distinctions between women and men would be eliminated. Following that line of thinking, early liberal feminists fought for equal education as the most effective means of social change (Jaggar, 1983). For black women, the education question was complex, and women were divided between Booker T. Washington's notion that blacks should focus on industrial education and W. E. B. Dubois' support of a " 'talented 10th,' a well educated cadre of Black leaders" (Giddings, 1988, p. 104). This talented tenth included college-educated black women who supported middle-class values[4] (Higginbotham, 1993). In either case, black liberal feminists supported women's as well as men's educational opportunities.

Economic Access

"Women's work"–child care, housework, and unskilled labor–is devoted primarily to the maintenance of the body. It lacks the prestige of work devoted to the rational mind. The definition of woman in terms of their reproductive and household roles follows women into the labor force and contributes to a sexual division of labor (Eisenstein, 1981).

---

4. Many black women pursued professional education and practiced law and medicine in the south well before the turn of the century (Giddings, 1988).

When women enter the workforce, they are still seen as caregivers, rather than as equal workers, and they tend to be shunted into caregiving roles and low-paying jobs. They are also paid less even when they perform the same jobs as men. Liberal feminists pointed out the inequality in such arrangements and insisted that women were entitled to the same access to jobs and to the same remuneration that is afforded to men. "Equal pay for equal work" became the slogan used by women trying to change this arrangement.

Citizenship Rights and Political Equality

Liberal feminists insisted on civic equality, but not all women approached citizenship in the same way: for example, in the matter of voting rights, white women tended to focus on *woman* suffrage while black women argued for *universal* suffrage (Giddings, 1988). Today, the liberal feminist fight for political equality between women and men has been extended to working toward better representation of women in public office. Liberal feminists also monitor electoral politics and support male candidates who favor women's issues (Jaggar 1983). They have amassed considerable money and power through organizations such as Emily's List, which provides financial support for women candidates, and The Fund for the Feminist Majority, which lobbies for legislation favorable to women. Other political achievements of liberal feminists include reforms in marriage, divorce, and child custody laws, which encourage more fair treatment of women.

The Equal Rights Amendment, the most far-reaching attempt to eliminate discrimination against women, has yet to pass, but of late, liberal feminists have not limited their antidiscrimination work to that proposal. Legal reform efforts to eliminate sex discrimination have been expanded and are now more likely to include supporting the rights of those who are denied equal opportunity because of discrimination based on race or sexual orientation (Nes and Iadicola, 1989).

Reproductive Rights

Throughout the more recent campaigns, liberal feminists have fought for women's right to control their own bodies. Access to sex education, women's control over contraception, and abortion rights have been key issues. The history of women's fight for control of reproduction has not always benefited all women equally. For example, the fight for birth control in the 1920s legalized contraception but evolved into a eugenics movement with the intent of keeping the "unfit"–which usually meant poor women, black women, and immigrants–from reproducing (Giddings, 1988).

Liberal feminists point out the sex discrimination inherent in limiting reproductive rights: although access to contraceptive information was "equally" denied to everyone regardless of sex, liberal feminists argue that since it is women who become pregnant and ultimately care for children, inadequate information and lack of contraception is more damaging for women than for men and therefore constitutes unequal treatment.

Social Services

Social structures favor men with power, prestige, and financial rewards (Tong, 1989). Unlike their nineteenth-century (and 1960s) predecessors who tended to argue along classical liberal lines of noninterference by government, more recent liberal feminists lean toward the welfare or egalitarian model of liberalism (Tong, 1989), promoting welfare state capitalism and a more equitable meritocracy (Nes and Iadicola, 1989). Liberal feminists demand that the state pursue social reforms that will ensure equal opportunities for women. They argue that to enforce equal rights, the state must make it economically possible for women to exercise those rights by funding crisis counseling services, shelters for battered women, services for incest survivors, and rape counseling. These services are now described as rights under the welfare state, and public funding is sought to provide them. This is clearly beyond the scope of the classical or libertarian liberalism supported by more conservative feminists who continue to argue for sex-blind equality (Jaggar, 1983).

Liberal Feminist Strategizing

Eisenstein pointed out the differences between women's and men's relationships to liberal law, which tends to protect men's domination and women's subordination (Eisenstein, 1981). Even when seeming to benefit women, laws such as protective legislation are often used to exclude women from better-paying jobs and to deny women promotions. Some liberal feminists argue for the elimination of all protective legislation since it excludes women from high-paying jobs (Jaggar, 1983). Others argue *against* eliminating those protections (Giddings, 1988) since in the short term, such legislation protects women, and they believe that it would be better, in the long run, to simply extend the protections to men than to take them away from women.

The dilemma is that providing any special benefits to women as a group leaves open the opportunity to charge that they are inferior. But if differences are denied, attention can be deflected from the disadvantages women face (Tong, 1989). Liberal feminists have to decide whether different yet equal is possible.

A pivotal case was described by Alice Kessler-Harris (1990). Sears Roebuck (department stores) was sued for sex discrimination in hiring and promotion. The case hinged on equality-versus-difference. Sears and Rosalind Rosenberg, a feminist historian who sided with Sears, argued that culture and socialization led to a fundamental difference between women and men that, in turn, caused women's lack of interest in high-paying, more demanding jobs. Therefore, sexual difference, not sex discrimination, had caused the objectionable work patterns that had been identified at Sears. Kessler-Harris, another feminist historian, claimed that historically, women did not choose to limit themselves to particular job categories, that economic need often overrode any socialization patterns, that women made individual choices in response to their individual needs, not because of their gender, and that it was hiring practices rather than employee choice that determined sex segregation patterns in the workplace. During the hearings, Rosenberg pointed out that although Kessler-Harris was arguing in the Sears case that women and men are the same, she had previously published work in which her arguments rested on differences between women and men (Scott, 1990). In explaining Kessler-Harris's seeming contradiction, Joan Scott noted that when studying labor history, Kessler-Harris's prior generalizations about women were justified because she was able to demonstrate that the term *worker* referred to man's rather than woman's experience and so, when Kessler-Harris had written about that history, she needed to discuss differences. But when faced with employment discrimination, Kessler-Harris's insistence on women and men's similarity and the need for Sears to make hiring decisions based on individual rather than group differences was appropriate. Sometimes, women were treated by employers as individuals and sometimes as a group. Feminist response was therefore dependent on circumstances (Scott, 1990).

ADDITIONAL CONTROVERSIES
IN LIBERAL FEMINISM

Abortion

One way of viewing acquisition of abortion rights is to call the legalization of abortion a success for feminists. Even George Bush capitulated in an election year and slightly loosened the "gag rule," which had banned federally funded clinics from dispensing information about abortion. It could be argued that liberal feminists have succeeded in making even a Republican president alter his campaign strategy to accommodate them.

Another view is that restrictions on economic access make choice ineffective for many women (Jaggar, 1983) and that abortion is still under the control of the medical profession, not pregnant women. In this view, restraint of trade imposed by a profession threatened by competition from unlicensed people who performed abortions resulted in the growth of abortion laws. This is why the bulk of the laws refer primarily to the person *performing* the abortion rather than the pregnant woman. The Supreme Court decision in *Roe v. Wade* upheld a physician's right to make a medical decision, not a woman's right to choose whether to give birth. The right was to privacy, that is, to the inappropriateness of state interference in the private sphere. *Roe v. Wade* did not grant women the right to an abortion. Eisenstein (1981) pointed out the additional class bias contained in the timing of these laws: they coincided with a decrease in the birthrate among middle-class women.

Referring to the economics of abortion, Eisenstein noted that under liberal rights to privacy:

Women . . . are *free from* the interference by the government in their decision to have an abortion. This does not require that government "interfere" by making public funds available to them. The *right to privacy* in the case of welfare women is just what they do not need. An abortion law based on this right actually denies women the state aid they require. . . . It is politically important to make clear to women that their right to control their bodies has not been accepted as a tenet of the state. (pp. 240-241, emphasis in original)

The Hyde Amendment (an amendment to FY1977 Medicaid appropriations) prohibited the use of Medicaid funds for elective abortion and effectively restricted the right to privacy between a woman and her doctor, thus selectively allowing for abortion along class lines.

Affirmative Action

Affirmative action is another controversy among liberal feminists. It violates the ideal of the meritocracy by supporting hiring based on other than meritorious grounds. Liberal feminists who lean toward welfare liberalism support affirmative action and believe in counteracting sexism by making the playing field more even. Liberal feminists who support classical liberalism object to the practice and argue that preferential treatment is unfair whether the preference is for or against women. Likewise, they believe that such policies subvert the standard argument concerning women's fundamental equality to men. They insist that affirmative action is counterproductive to the goal of making sex irrelevant in industry and in public policy.

Equal Opportunity

A third controversy, closely related to affirmative action, surrounds equal opportunity. According to classical liberal theory, inequality is a natural outcome of individual differences within a meritocracy. It is only when inequalities become extreme and do not reflect the distribution of resources one would expect to find that intervention becomes necessary (Nes and Iadicola, 1989). Welfare liberals see the argument that the opportunity to compete as an individual is equally available to all as quite unrealistic. Clearly, the meritocracy distributes resources unequally and unfairly, creating instability and ever increasing inequality. With the inheritance provided under liberal private property laws, succeeding generations will have neither equality of opportunity nor equality of outcome. The situation demands constant state intervention rather than increasing freedom from the state. Further, the meritocracy discounts people who lack the characteristics that the system rewards, for example, maleness and advanced education. This unequal distribution of resources denies women the possibility of genuine self-determination (Jaggar, 1983). When viewed from this perspective, classical liberal feminist support of a market-controlled meritocracy seems untenable, and the welfare liberal feminist arguments in favor of state intervention seem more desirable for women.

CRITIQUE

A major component of liberalism that liberal feminists fail to adequately address is the split between public and private issues (Jaggar, 1983). Eisenstein (1981) warned against the tendency of liberal feminists to argue for inclusion of women within the public sphere with little or no recognition of that strategy's tendency to shore up the split between public and private. "The right to privacy is actually an exclusionary right because you have to be self-sufficient and self-supporting before the right can actually protect you" (p. 240).

One of the most important criticisms of the exclusionary nature of liberal feminism, in practice as well as in theory, occurred in the 1800s when white liberal feminists in the suffrage movement abandoned black women, often going so far as to engage in racist rhetoric. This tradition of exclusion sometimes continued into the feminist activity in this century (Donovan, 1985). During both time periods, the needs of poor women and women of color tended to be ignored by white liberal feminists. A criticism levied particularly at 1970s liberal feminists (although certainly true earlier) was that they were inattentive to child care arrangements. The caricatures in this century and the last may have been of women abandoning their babies to participate in the movement (Faludi, 1991), but the reality was that many middle-class white women hired poor white women and women of color to provide child care (hooks, 1984). Poor women had fewer provisions by which to achieve their own free-dom from the responsibilities of motherhood and participate in feminist activity. Thus, poor women were effectively excluded from the movement, both by their own family responsibilities and by the added burden of caring for others' children while wealthier, primar-ily white women considered their child care problems, at least tem-porarily, solved.

This is not to say that all white feminists, or even most, hired other women to care for their children or that those who did, always hired women of color. Nor were white feminists unaware of the need for government attention to the lack of suitable child care arrangements. However, such arrangements happened regularly, and like their counterparts in the 1800s, twentieth-century white feminists often seem willing to postpone addressing the needs of poor women and women of color (hooks, 1984). Even today, NOW (National Organization for Women), the most widely known and influential liberal feminist organization, has yet to seriously address the issues of women's poverty or the concrete supports that poor women need most, such as publicly funded child care and an increase in the minimum wage.

In her pivotal book on liberal feminism, *The Feminine Mystique*, Betty Friedan virtually ignored the problems faced by poor white women and women of color. Advising women to leave the confines of housework to find fulfillment in the job market, Friedan evi-dently assumed that once employed, women would have escaped their miseries. The book—and for some time, the movement that the book helped to create—failed to address the issues of working- and middle-class white and black women who were already in the work-force. Because of such limited attention, hooks (1984) argued that much of the work of liberal feminists addresses the needs of a rather select group: white, middle-class, comparatively privileged women.

African-American women were not the only women of color to be ignored by mainstream liberal feminism. Chicanas were also left out although Pesquera and Segura (1993) described a theoretical stance developed by Chicanas that is quite similar to the liberal feminism described above. Chicana liberal feminism emphasizes access to social institutions and enhancement of the Chicano community. While similar to mainstream liberal feminist approaches, Chicana liberal feminism has a clearer emphasis on race and ethnicity.

The charge of racial exclusivity is not limited to liberal feminist theory. Rather, this criticism is extended to questioning the basic tenets of liberalism. Individual self-sufficiency and essential isolation, abstraction of the individual from her circumstances, commitment to rationality, along with the acceptance of the liberal split between public and private life and the inherent male bias of the tradition have been indicted for contributing to sexism and for ignoring larger social issues in favor of problem solving for individuals.

Eisenstein (1981) suggested that intertwining patriarchal and liberal ideologies contribute to the potential for liberal feminism to be co-opted. Rather than achieving genuine gains, women may only be witnessing attempts by classical liberal state and social structures to incorporate feminist terms into liberalism—without taking feminism seriously. For example, during the 1960s and 1970s, women started being described as "working mothers" without any substantial change in either their role as housekeeper/child rearer or their role in the sex-segregated job market. The sexual division of labor continued in public and in private. Eisenstein (1981) and Faludi (1991) argued that because of its potential for co-optation, liberal feminism is accepted, to some extent, by the state as the least threatening branch of feminism, and the state has encouraged presentation of that view as though it represented all of feminist thought.

The problems that stem from associating equality with abstract individualism become obvious when one examines the seemingly progressive notion that regardless of age, race, sex, or economic circumstances, individuals are entitled to equality (Jaggar, 1983). This is a problematic framing of the issue. Race and sex *matter*, and social policy cannot be blind to these distinctions. "Real human beings are not abstract individuals but people of a determinate race, sex or age, who have lived different histories, who participate in different systems of social relations, and who have different capacities and different needs" (Jaggar, 1983, p. 46-47).

Successes of Liberal Feminists

It is not unusual for critics of liberal feminism to continue to dismiss all current liberal feminist theory as a bourgeois, white movement (Tong, 1989). But liberal feminism's successes have not been limited only to white, middle-class and wealthy women, and the impact of liberal feminism has been extensive. Legal improvements have occurred and liberal feminists have contributed significantly to improving women's status in many areas. They have been quite successful at outlawing sex discrimination and at helping to define and contest sexual harassment. Liberal feminist efforts have helped secure and improve maternity leave, and they added women to affirmative action programs. They fought for women's legal right to abortion, and they succeeded in having rape in marriage outlawed (Jaggar, 1983). Liberal feminists have also been credited with educational reforms allowing more women to become professionals, although stability of gains has not been assured in these areas (Tong, 1989).

Liberal feminism's accomplishments, however, are not limited to the most recent wave of feminism. In more distant times, it was liberal feminists who achieved female suffrage. Later in the century, women gained property and economic rights within marriage and an improved legal position in child custody cases as well as more liberalized divorce laws through the efforts of liberal feminists (Donovan, 1985).

Eisenstein (1981) made a compelling argument for the potential of liberal feminism to radicalize women who become engaged in its struggles. Recognition of a sexual class identification among women is inherent in feminism. She posited that once women begin to see themselves as a class rather than as individuals, a more pervasive critique of social structures is inevitable. She went on to argue that the inherent conflict between the notion of liberal individualism and the reality of sex-class oppression would become self-evident, and liberal feminists would inevitably contrive a more radical political theory. The theory would be based on recognition of this contradiction and recognition of the instability of legal reform.

APPLICATIONS OF LIBERAL FEMINISM
TO SOCIAL WORK PRACTICE

In the following examples, liberal feminism is applied to each of the major methods of social work practice: policy, administration, community organizing, group work, case work, and research. The central argument of liberal feminism is that women are equal to men and should be treated as such in public spheres. Each of these applications focuses on seeking equal treatment for women.

Policy

"Equality of rights under the law shall not be denied or abridged by the United States or by any state on account of sex."

The quintessential struggle for liberal feminists engaged in policy work is the proposed Equal Rights Amendment (ERA) to the Constitution of the United States. The ERA is intended to integrate women into the mainstream of American life by eliminating discriminatory laws and traditions that prevent women from achieving full equality in the context of capitalism (Burnham and Louie, 1985). Although radical in the sense of far-reaching, since it would apply to half of the population, the ERA is ultimately a liberal proposal. It does not seek to fundamentally change the structure of society, but to include women in those structures, on equal footing with men.

In a somewhat more modest proposal, Betty Friedan (1963) called for a "GI bill" for women's education. She argued that, similar to men who were returning from war service, women needed financial assistance to promote their entry into the professions after having taken time out to raise a family. Interestingly, and as fits liberal feminism, she did not contest women's ongoing primary and individual responsibility for children by recommending equalization of child care between the sexes, or government- or community-provided child care. She discussed ways in which women's responsibility for child care could be incorporated into their education, for example, by providing summer camp while the women went to a six- or eight-week summer college program.

In the area of abortion rights, liberal feminists would argue that women, as autonomous individuals, must be allowed to exercise their right to control their bodies, free from interference by the state and that this right is essential to women's right to equality (Luker, 1984). They would support a woman's right to choose not only abortion, but also sterilization (Brandwein, 1986). Welfare liberals would also argue against restricting the use of Medicaid funding of abortions. On a micro policy level, a liberal feminist agency might have a policy in support of a client making choices for herself regarding reproductive autonomy (Kravetz and Jones, 1991) and lend support to activists who are attempting to secure a woman's right to abortion.

Administration

Liberal feminists might focus on training women for administrative positions traditionally held by males. They may also advocate that women workers and clients be taught assertiveness and confidence-building. The focus would be on overcoming women's socialization so that they could compete and advance in a male world. The goal would be to have more women in supervisory positions, thus achieving gender equality at the administrative level.

Lambert (1994) examined the disproportionate number of men in social work administrative positions. To counter this trend, she explored the ways in which women can be more readily trained in the skills most closely associated with organizational advancement. She suggested restructuring early job experiences to include women in more of the activities associated with administrative advancement: involvement in external management, consulting, facilitating, and training.[5]

Kathleen Ianello (1992) described The Business Women's Group, an organization whose focus, as indicated by its title, is to promote women's rights in business and the professions.[6] Although Ianello included a chapter describing this organization in her book, *Decisions Without Hierarchies*—a title suggesting a more radical

---

5. Lambert also suggested job rotation, an idea that fits more readily under radical feminism, due to its deemphasis on traditional hierarchies.

6. Its counterpart, BACW (Bay Area Career Women) is a lesbian organization in the San Francisco area, with quite similar goals—networking and the social and professional advancement of middle-class women, in this case lesbians.

feminist approach–she made the points that The Business Women's Group is a liberal feminist organization, that it maintains a hierarchical structure, and that its goals clearly fall within the liberal feminist tradition:

> To elevate the standards for women in business and the professions; to promote the interests of business and professional women; to bring about a spirit of cooperation among business and professional women of the United States; and to extend opportunities to business and professional women through education geared toward industrial, scientific and vocational activities. (p. 103)

The members seem split between older women who prefer that the group functions as a civic organization, providing support and encouragement for all women workers, and younger women who come to the organization to network and advance their careers, preferring to attract top level managers as members. The organization attempts, however, to maintain a middle-of-the-road approach to this split.

Community Organizing

Liberal feminists were active in the establishment of birth control clinics early in the twentieth century. Across the country, organizations such as the Women's Political Association of Harlem, the Booker T. Washington Community Center in San Francisco, and the Northwest Health Center in Baltimore organized in favor of birth control. In contrast to Marcus Garvey's well-founded fears of eugenics, many African-American women endorsed birth control while they fought against sterilization (Rodrique, 1990); Rodrique reported that a 1935 study conducted in Harlem revealed widespread family planning activities being practiced.

A more recently formed community organizing group, and one that has received considerable attention, is NOW (National Organization of Women). Founded in 1966, NOW's goal is equality in the areas of politics, economics, and social life. Although the organization adopted a birth control platform in its second year, its initial conservatism and plea for mainstream acceptance is evident in its refusal, due to concern about the controversy it would stir up, to work toward control over childbearing, in the forms of birth control and abortion information and access.

NOW's approach has been to organize women to work toward public policy change in such areas as passing the Equal Rights Amendment and including women among the protected groups overseen by the Equal Employment Opportunity Commission. NOW has also encouraged women to run for electoral office (Schneir, 1994). Historically, NOW has not been interested in challenging the institutional framework of society (Papachristou, 1976). Although four years after it began, NOW elected an African-American woman, Aileen Hernandez, as president and in the mid-1970s, adopted resolutions on poverty and support of minority people, the group continues to speak primarily for middle-class white women (Papachristou, 1976; Schneir, 1994).

Group Work

Liberal feminists have been active in the development of assertiveness training groups, which help women overcome their hesitancy to participate equally with men. Another application of liberal feminism has been support groups for working mothers who are trying to contend with the multiple responsibilities of child care, housekeeping, and paid employment.

Ann Abbott (1994) described a feminist group for women with substance use problems. Abbott contended that the primary deficit in current mainstream intervention was excluding women from diagnosis and treatment. After acknowledging the different physiological, social, and psychological contributions to women's problems in this area, she stated explicitly that an attack on male domination was not the focus of her recommendations; instead she stressed advocacy for women.

Janet Wolfe (1987) offered a cognitive behavioral therapy (CBT) group for women through which she assisted women in setting cognitive, emotional, and behavioral goals. A key component of many CBT groups is homework, that is, practice on what one has learned in the group. These assignments demonstrate most clearly what the facilitator has in mind for change. For example, in a six-session group, one woman participant practiced: (1) asking her lover to call her if he is going to be late; (2) being assertive with her lover, her boss, and gas station attendants; (3) crediting herself for her accomplishments in being assertive with her lover and her boss; (4) providing feedback to her lover about her wishes and feelings, and talking to interesting-looking people at parties; (5) attending an event without a male escort and "bragging" about her accomplishments; and (6) reading *Intelligent Woman's Guide to Dating and Mating* (Wolfe, 1987, pp. 170-171).

Jody Alyn and Lee Becker (1984) provided feminist therapy in a Women's Awareness Group to women in an adult day-treatment setting. Working with women who had been diagnosed as severely and chronically mentally ill, they provided a group that sought to increase participants' self-esteem, sexual knowledge, and familiarity with sex-related topics. The authors clarified that feminist therapy is not a political view or therapeutic technique, but rather a perspective they brought to their work, which, they believe, increased effective and productive adjustment on the part of the participants.

Casework

Social workers using a liberal feminist perspective might encourage women to study for the professions and to become more independent and self-sufficient. They may assist women in achieving access to services and resources available to men but denied to women; they may help lesbians to access services generally available only to heterosexual women. Janet Kenney and Donna Tash (1992) focused on the health care dilemmas of lesbian couples who choose to have children, and they discussed the social and emotional issues that the women might need to address. Social workers may need to assist in identifying health care providers who would allow equal access to services by lesbian couples wanting to conceive children: artificial insemination services, childbirth preparation classes, birthing centers. They may also need to assist the couple in determining whether and where to seek adoption by the nonchildbearing parent, as few courts allow such adoptions (Kenny and Tash, 1992).[7]

---

7. Currently, only Massachusetts, Vermont, and New York state law specifically allow for such adoptions.

If a lesbian couple chooses to adopt, the social worker may need to advocate for access and equal treatment of lesbians by adoption agencies and court systems. The couple may need support in negotiating a system that may not be particularly open to their needs, and the social worker may need to provide research evidence documenting that lesbianism does not negatively impact on a woman's capacity for child-rearing (see, for example, Lewin, 1993; Patterson, 1992).

Research

Reinhartz (1992) cited an historical example of feminist research that contested the notion that women who engaged in intellectual work would damage their reproductive organs. To demonstrate the liberal claim of women's ability to engage in rational enterprises without untoward effect, Marion Talbot canvassed the members of the Association of Collegiate Alumnae concerning their health.

A liberal feminist researcher would probably argue for inclusion of women in the design of research projects and encourage women practitioners to conduct research. They may also study specifically feminist topics, as Cynthia Berryman-Fink and Kathleen Verderber (1985) did when they designed a measurement of the term "feminist." Conceived of as a contribution to the struggle for equality between the sexes, they studied college students' attributions to the term. What they hoped to provide was a better understanding of the connotations associated with the term feminist and a way to measure changes in conceptualizations of people who label themselves as feminists. Words used to describe feminists included: logical, knowledgeable, realistic, intelligent, caring, comforting, aggressive, activist, working, ambitious, strong, nonconforming, and heterosexual.

Chapter 2

Radical Feminism

CONTRIBUTIONS AND CONTRIBUTORS

Radical feminism emerged from the political activism and analysis of the civil rights and social change movements of the 1950s and 1960s, and the women's movement of the 1960s and 1970s, but the ideas can be traced back to much earlier thinkers and activists including:

- Mary Wollstonecraft, (b. 1759; d. 1797) whose *Vindication of the Rights of Women* advocated economic independence for women, attacked prevailing notions of beauty, contested the "occupation of women by men" (1792/1967, p. 114), and discussed the ways women were oppressed as a group rather than as individuals.
- Maria Stewart, who, in the 1830s, was one of the first black feminists to advocate strengthening black women's relationships with one another. She encouraged women to build a community support system, and she argued in favor of black women's activism and self-determination. Stewart insisted that sexual and racial oppression were the fundamental causes of poverty among women (Collins, 1990).
- Elizabeth Cady Stanton, who, in the 1880s, argued against male sexual rights to women and attacked the religious justification of women's oppression. Stanton, like radical feminists a century later, learned her skills while working toward emancipation of blacks.

Many of the participants in mid-twentieth-century radical feminist activities and theory-building had participated in antiwar and civil rights organizations in the 1950s and 1960s (Donovan, 1985). White women met young black women who had organized as effectively as their male counterparts, and the encounters had a powerful impact on the white women's perceptions of femininity (Echols, 1989). These activists were also inspired by women revolutionaries in Vietnam, Cuba, and China (Echols, 1989), but initial theorizing was primarily a reaction against the antifeminism of both the left and the civil rights movements in the U.S.

Some radical feminists argued that focusing on gender as the primary source of oppression was necessary to counteract the trivialization of women's concerns by male members of the New Left[1] (Donovan, 1985; Echols, 1989). Others believed that sexism simply needed to be included in the list of oppressions attacked by political activists on the left. Still others maintained that while opposition to sexism was essential, the struggle against racism was important in its own right and should not be subsumed under feminism.

Ideas were borrowed from both the civil rights and New Left movements, including the New Left's concept that feelings of alienation and powerlessness had political origins and that personal transformation through radical action was a worthy goal (Echols, 1989). Radical feminists vehemently opposed the liberal feminist agenda of equal rights for women, and they contested the liberal strategy of incremental change (Echols, 1989).

Black women have been involved in radical feminist activity, but their presence was obscured by racism and elitism until the 1960s (Brewer, 1993; Combahee River Collective, 1983). For the most part, black women who explored the new radical feminist activities refused to participate for reasons similar to their withdrawal from liberal feminist activities. White women's analysis was at odds with that of black women, since the former consisted of: (1) defining gender as the primary oppression; (2) universalizing the mecha-

---

1. The New Left is the term applied to the radical activists who replaced earlier communist and socialist American activists in the 1950s and 1960s. Inspired by the Student Non-Violent Coordinating Committee (SNCC), a black civil rights organization active in the early 1960s, the Students for a Democratic Society (SDS) became the primary organizing force of the New Left, a movement known for anti-Vietnam war activism, university reform, and social change efforts (Isserman, 1995).

nisms of sexist oppression; and (3) seeking independence from men and developing the self sufficiency that many black women felt they already experienced. Ironically, the rise of black power, so important in fostering feminist consciousness among white women, had very different consequences for black women. Black power, as it was articulated by men, involved laying claim to masculine privileges denied them by a white supremacist society (Echols, 1989). Black women reported feeling either restrained and alienated as women by their male coworkers in civil rights and black power organizations, or recognized for their abilities but categorized as "something other than female" (Brewer, citing Echols, 1993, p. 15). They refused to accept yet another argument for male privilege and organized as black women with a radical analysis of both racism and sexism, but they did not always find a welcoming place in white women's radical organizations.

bell hooks took a cynical view of the women's movement, initially downplaying any perceived differences between liberal and radical feminists, identifying feminists as "Bourgeois white women . . . envious and angry at privileged white men for denying them an equal share in class privilege" (1984, p. 68). She did not share Echols's perception that radical feminists were genuinely concerned with class and race privilege. She doubted whether white women fully realized that all men did not benefit equally from sexism. Significantly, the texts to which Donovan (1985) attributed the earliest conceptualization of radical feminist thought were all written by white women: Kate Millett's *Sexual Politics* (1969); Shulamith Firestone's *The Dialectic of Sex: The Case for Feminist Revolution* (1970); Ti-Grace Atkinson's *Amazon Odyssey* (1974) and Mary Daly's *Gyn/Ecology: The Metaethics of Radical Feminism* (1978).

Asian-American feminists also criticized the limited understanding of white radical feminists, pointing out that racism was so often ignored by white feminists that the Asian women activists of the 1960s and 1970s tended to move into groups concerned with ethnic and racial identity rather than with feminism. This was not due to having chosen race/ethnicity as a primary loyalty. Rather, it evolved out of having been made to feel that a *choice* between racial/ethnic identity and gender issues was necessary (Yamada, 1983).

Native-American feminists tended to disagree with white feminists' critique of the nuclear family as the primary site of women's oppression. For one thing, tribal and community values did not pose the nuclear family as a model. Second, for some groups, Native women's oppression had far more to do with white attacks on tribal sovereignty than with male supremacy (Shanley, 1984/1988).

So radical feminism, initially at least, was not a broad-based movement, but it did provide a theory grounded in activism. In both the nineteenth and twentieth centuries, it emerged from, and was modeled after, activist responses to the oppression of blacks. While many radical feminists retained a commitment to opposing racism as well as sexism, many did not.

THE THEORY

Twentieth-century radical feminist theory is based on several fundamental ideas: (1) the personal is political; (2) women are an oppressed class and patriarchy is at the root of their oppression; (3) patriarchy is based in psychological and biological factors and enforced through violence against women; (4) women and men are fundamentally different; (5) society must be completely altered to eliminate male supremacy—incremental change is insufficient; and (6) all hierarchies must be eliminated.

The Personal Is Political

With the adoption of the slogan, "the personal is political," several areas formerly excluded from feminist analysis were incorporated into feminism (Tong, 1989). Radical feminists argue that individual women's experiences of injustice and the miseries that women think of as personal problems are actually political issues, grounded in sexist power imbalances. They insist that separating public from private issues masks the reality of male power, a system of domination that operates similarly in both spheres. Furthermore, they insist that the public and private systems of male control function in dynamic interaction. What happens "out there" in the bastions of male political arenas affects women as individuals on an extremely personal basis. So, for example, dismissing claims of sexual harassment by public figures devalues individual women's experiences of sexual harassment. Private-public divisions isolate and depoliticize women's oppression (Nes and Iadicola, 1989).

Attention to such personal aspects of male dominance became the hallmark of this branch of feminism. By describing the imbalance between women and men in the more obvious political arenas of law, politics, and employment and also in the personal areas—the home, the bedroom, and even people's self-perceptions (Jaggar, 1983)—radical feminism changed the feminist discussion and it changed the goal of feminism. Radical feminists complain of women's exploitation as housewives,[2] mothers, and sex partners, describing marriage as the formalization of women's persecution. Moreover, some radical feminists use the phrase *the personal is political* prescriptively to argue that a woman's personal life reflects her politics, the degree of her radicalism, and her commitment to feminism (Echols, 1989).

To promote the redefinition of personal problems as political issues, radical feminists engaged in consciousness raising, the specific activity for which radical feminists are best known. Ideas for consciousness raising were drawn from the struggles of the American civil rights movement, from Chinese revolutionary peasantry, and from Guatemalan guerrillas (Echols, 1989). Women would meet in small consciousness-raising (c-r) groups, which were popular in the 1970s, to discuss their personal experiences, and they made a conscious effort to draw connections between their daily lives and sociopolitical structures. Participants hoped to build a grass roots movement through c-r groups and, in the process, transform both themselves and their culture (Hartsock, 1979). Women sought to awaken a sense of class consciousness and sisterhood among participants. For this reason, similarities were stressed and differences overlooked (Echols, 1989). The model was hailed by many radical feminists as having a profound effect on their lives and on their politicization (Kravetz, 1986), but it was disparaged by others who felt that while the groups may have awakened women's consciousness of female oppressions, they did not lead to political activism often enough (Payne, 1973).

---

2. Pat Mainardi's (1976) widely read article, "The politics of housework," described day-to-day exploitation of women in the home.

Proponents of consciousness raising distinguish c-r from other groups, pointing out that the purpose of c-r is to analyze and dismantle male supremacy, rather than to seek personal solutions to women's oppression. At the same time, some radical feminists insist that c-r is therapeutic because it helps dissuade women form blaming themselves for their victimization (Echols, 1989).

Women: An Oppressed Class with Patriarchy at the Root

Radical feminists characterize society as patriarchal. By this they mean both that historically, families have been organized according to male lines of inheritance and dependence and also that society has been constructed in a way that accrues a disproportionate share of power to men. By characterizing contemporary society as patriarchal, radical feminists assume that the most significant and fundamental social division is gender (Jaggar, 1983). Male supremacy is thought to be the *oldest* political division and the basis upon which other systems of domination are modeled and justified (French, 1985). Thus, they argue that since the subjugation of women was the model, feminism will have to be the basis for any truly revolutionary change (Donovan, 1985).

Patriarchy is described as a cultural universal, with all institutions reinforcing that social order (Nes and Iadicola, 1989). The patriarchal structure consists of a system that privileges men through the complex political manipulation of individual identity, social interactions, and structural systems of power. It is not only legal systems that create and reinforce the sexual hierarchy, but all human interactions perpetuate and are permeated by male privilege (Eisenstein, 1981).

Women of color—notably black women—challenge this assumption of shared oppression based on gender, however, (hooks, 1990) and they criticize the notion of sex as the earliest or most significant division of power, pointing out that this perspective could only have been developed by women who did not experience or understand the equally fundamental oppressive structures of race and class. Critics are highly skeptical of the idea that systems of oppression could or should be ranked (Collins, 1990).

Patriarchy: Psychology, Biology, and Violence

Psychology. Radical feminists developed a psychological analysis of male supremacy (Echols, 1989) that has two main themes. Supporters charge that women are damaged psychologically by the internalization[3] of oppressive patriarchal messages (Echols, 1989), and they argue that psychological control of women is a significant component of patriarchal systems (Donovan, 1985).

Women's personalities and their sexuality are seen by radical feminists as having been constructed to meet men's needs, rather than women's (Tong, 1989). Furthermore, women are so limited in their roles and men so privileged in theirs that psychological problems are almost inevitable. Rigid sex-role prescriptions not only distort people, but they also lead to sex-based oppression. Supporters of this position recommend eliminating gender roles and striving toward androgyny (Jaggar, 1983). Initially, Millet (1969) suggested combining the most positive traits prescribed to each gender to create an androgynous person, and the ensuing discussion concerned which traits were positive and which were negative (Tong, 1989). But radical feminists soon dropped the idea of androgyny as they came to see that the ideal male and the ideal female were *both* distorted and that combining problematic traits would still not result in complete, healthy humans (Jaggar, 1983).

Radical feminists suggest that men become oppressors not by virtue of biology, but by rationalizing supremacy on the basis of biological difference (Koedt, 1973). Millett (1969) held that women are conditioned to serve men, and that it is because patriarchal ideology permeates the culture that women are assured of being confined to their castelike status. This psychology of sex role conditioning accounts for women's apparent complicity with patriarchy, evidenced in their subservient behavior (Echols, 1989). According to psychological accounts, women function in this mental state in all aspects of their lives, including personal relationships.

Some radical feminists found psychological accounts of patriarchy incomplete and insufficient to explain the pervasiveness of

---

3. Internalization, in this instance, is the psychological process by which women incorporate into their sense of self social and cultural messages that devalue women.

male supremacy and turned to biology for an explanation (Jaggar, 1983).

Biology. Shulamith Firestone's (1970) view of sex and biological reproduction best exemplifies this argument. She insisted that biological imperatives, overlaid by social institutions, reinforce male dominance and that the material base of social institutions in human biology determines destiny. Transcendence of biology, particularly reproduction, which sets up the dependence of woman on man and child on adult, is necessary to overcome the sexual division of labor and the sex distinctions (Jaggar, 1983). In other words, historically, men created social structures based on biology, with the intent of securing power over women. They then used biology as an explanation for the "naturalness" of the social order. Women, in freeing themselves from the biological (material as opposed to psychological) constraints of reproduction, could free themselves from the social structures that are based in biology. So to Firestone, the biological division of labor was the material basis for the political ideology of female subjugation.

Firestone (1970) postulated that nature produced the fundamental inequality and that this inequality is consolidated and institutionalized by men in their own interest. To Firestone, women's sacrifice of themselves to the natural division of labor is tragic and unnecessary. She recommended that humans abandon patriarchal forms of reproduction. She advocated a biological revolution on the part of women who, using technological advances, would free themselves from reproduction. Firestone argued for the elimination of marriage as it was then known, and she urged that women develop a variety of alternatives to current marital arrangements, including remaining single, participating in group households composed of unrelated people of various ages, living together as couples in informal arrangements in which society would have no legal interest, and living in limited contractual legal relationships (Firestone, 1970). Firestone was radical both in her belief that women should identify themselves as a subjugated class and join together to overthrow their male oppressors and in her insistence that women use test-tube fertilization and artificial placentas to eliminate the difference in relative contributions to the reproductive process.

Firestone's suggestions were criticized by other radical feminists who insisted that it was a mistake for women to give up biological reproduction, as it would consolidate rather than eliminate men's power over women. Women feared that technological reproduction would not equalize the natural reproductive power structure, but instead would invert it by appropriating women's reproductive power and handing it over to men who already controlled technology. Since it is not women's biology but men's control over it that oppresses women, lending further technological control to men would worsen women's situation (Tong, 1989).

Critiques of reproduction are not the only biological analyses in radical feminism. Some women argued that men dominate women because men are innately more aggressive due to hormonal differences (Jaggar, 1983). Susan Brownmiller (1975), in an influential book on rape, postulated that men rape simply because they can, because they have the structural capacity to rape and women have the structural vulnerability. The converse of this argument is the assumption that women's biology results in something totally different: a person who is likely to exhibit nurturance, warmth, and compassion; such a stance was developed by cultural feminists and will be discussed in Chapter 5.

Jaggar disagreed with the biological account of women's subordination, insisting that biology is as socially constituted as sex roles: "Biological determinism becomes not so much false as incorrect. We cannot say abstractly that biology determines society, because we cannot identify a clear, non-social sense of 'biology': nor a clear, non-biological sense of 'society.' The thesis of universal biological determination cannot be stated coherently" (p. 111). Moreover, Jaggar argued, whether applied to Susan Brownmiller's view of a male ideology of rape, as embedded in anatomy, or Firestone's depiction of reproduction-based culture, such biological determinism is incorrect and unnecessarily limiting. Eisenstein (1981) agreed, adding that the political structure of patriarchy is far more complex than can be explained biologically.

Violence and Pornography. Radical feminists studied the appalling prevalence of violence against women, particularly in the forms of physical and sexual assault, and they defined the violence as political in nature. They argued that violence against women is about domination and control, and it is men who are abusing women. Battering is woman abuse, and safe houses for battered women were created to help women move underground, away from men. Abortion policies that force women to obtain dangerous abortions illegally are also defined as violence against women, and in response to these policies, women started abortion clinics controlled by women (Jaggar, 1983).

Theorists criticized the frequent descriptions of sexual abuse in the writings of men such as D.H. Lawrence, Henry Miller, and Norman Mailer, describing these works as illustrations of ideological violence that depicted sexual politics with grotesque images of abuse (Millett, 1969). Arguing that rape and the fear of rape are used to control women socially and politically, Susan Brownmiller (1975) insisted that pornography and prostitution are both forms of violence against women because they promote an ideology that degrades and abuses the female body, thereby contributing to the phenomenon of rape. Regardless of whether women consent to participation in either sexual activity or pornography, degradation of women was seen as dangerous. "To degrade someone, even with that person's expressed consent, is to *endorse* the degradation of persons. It is to affirm that the abuse of persons is *acceptable*" (Audre Lorde as cited in Tong, 1989, p. 77).

Perhaps the most familiar advocate of a radical political definition of sexual violence against women is Andrea Dworkin, who is best known for her work on sexual assault and pornography. Dworkin (1988) remains one of the most outspoken activists in this area. She argues that patriarchal control is enforced, at least in part, through the use of pornography as propaganda and as violence. She studied the links between woman battering and pornography, describing the intersection—in hard core pornography—as the propaganda of sexual fascism and sexual terrorism. She pointed out the insidiousness of images of bound, bruised, and maimed women, calling the images "death threats to a female population in rebellion" (p. 201).

For Dworkin and many other radical feminists, rape is a political crime and a terrorist act (Donovan, 1985, quoting Pamela Kearon) and rapists are described as frontline shock troops and terrorist guerrillas (Brownmiller, 1975). Examining incest, sexual harassment, prostitution, and pornography, Dworkin determined that in all these instances, women's sexuality is captured by men to meet men's needs, but that the opposite—women exploiting men's sexuality to meet women's needs—could not occur in a patriarchal system. According to Dworkin, the hate that is often evident in violent pornography is a reflection of social reality. Women are presented as sex objects who enjoy humiliation and pain. Pornography, she said, "is a map of the real world" where there is patriarchal power (Dworkin, 1989, p. xxxiii). Because of this, she staunchly advocates the elimination of pornography.

She and Catherine MacKinnon have worked toward the passage of antipornography legislation. Not all radical feminists agree with this position. Many consider antipornography laws to be inappropriate censorship, and they are concerned about the implications of censorship for feminist writings. Robin Morgan, for example, argued that pornography, rather than being censored, "should just be helped not to exist—by any means necessary" (1993, p. 57).

Alisa Carse (1995) argued that although she believes pornography is damaging to women, legal tactics are doomed to failure. Instead, she suggested that education and protest are better suited to the fight against pornography. Pornography may indeed foster bigotry and contempt and contribute to the exclusion of women from equal participation in civic life, but the risk to legal safeguards afforded feminists[4] under constitutional law and the pernicious nature of pornography's influence argue against outlawing production, sale, and distribution of pornography. Pornography is difficult to define, difficult to prohibit, and its effects may be cumulative rather than specific in nature. That means that while we may believe, and even be able to demonstrate that a "pornographic view of women" is harmful, it is much harder to show that a particular piece of material, in and of itself, caused that harm. Additionally, pornographic views of women are found in many places (Carse cites MTV, advertisements, and women's romance novels) that would not be subject to antipornography statutes. Carse cited the history of the Dworkin and MacKinnon antipornography bill. When

---

4. For example, protection of lesbian erotica and sexually explicit feminist educational materials.

it was introduced in Indianapolis, it was supported by people who, in their hostility to feminism and to lesbians and gays, argued that pornography caused "sodomy" and destroyed families. These people hoped to eliminate several forms of sexually explicit material that feminists supported.

Carse (1995) argued that a broad-based, consciousness-raising campaign, coupled with the development of woman-positive, alternative erotica and the ongoing use of disruptive picket lines and other forms of aggressive education, would do more for the cause of feminism than legal battles over pornography.

The disagreement over whether pornography should be censored and whether women are, by definition, coerced into participation in it, continues. Some radical feminists believe that women are conditioned to an ideology of patriarchy and therefore consent to male power, making frequent violence generally unnecessary, although the threat of violence is needed as a backdrop to demonstrate what will happen to women should they resist patriarchal control. Dworkin (1993, 1995) continues to see violence more as foreground than background.

Women and Men Are Fundamentally Different

In contrast to liberal feminists' insistence on the similarity between women and men, radical feminists focus on differences between them. Women and men are thought to conceptualize power differently; for example, while men seek to dominate and control others, women are more interested in sharing power and in nurturing. A feminist belief in fundamental differences between women and men raise several interesting propositions.

Alice Echols (1989) cited Cell 16, a radical feminist group formed in the late 1960s, as the first organization to propose that women withdraw from men personally as well as politically. It was heterosexual separatism, not lesbianism, that was being advocated, but Echols argued the idea helped establish the theoretical foundation for lesbian separatism.

Most radical feminists agree that men benefit from sexism. There is a difference in opinion, however, as to exactly who benefits most and whether an institutional or individual analysis is more productive. bell hooks challenged the assumption of shared oppression based solely on gender is seemingly evident among many white radical feminists. Criticizing the notion that women are essentially similar to each other or essentially different from men, she warned black women to avoid accommodating themselves to white women's vision of radicalism (hooks, 1981). hooks insisted that radical feminism must acknowledge that all men do not benefit equally from patriarchal structures. She argued that while black women need to develop a radical analysis that is specifically feminist, adding black women's issues to already-existing formulations of white women's oppression is insufficient. Feminism needs to be entirely reformulated, starting with—not tacking on—considerations of racism.

Those who reject the more common radical feminist critique of patriarchy offer an analysis of *individual* benefit. They contend that all men oppress women and that it is individual men, not simply patriarchal structures, who benefit from, and therefore should be held responsible for, oppressing women. These women insist that an institutional analysis allows men to evade responsibility for their personal roles in maintaining male supremacy (Echols, 1989).

Whether the assessment is individual or institutional, assuming all men are a priori corrupt or were all corrupted by patriarchy has been criticized as politically dangerous and an analytic dead end (Tong, 1989).

Society Must Be Completely Altered

The radical feminist analysis of sexism is purposefully comprehensive. Radical feminists describe sexism as a social system consisting of "law, tradition, economics, education, organized religion, science, language, the mass media, sexual morality, child rearing, the domestic division of labor, and everyday social interaction," the purpose of which is to give men power over women (Willis, 1989, *x*). It is this pervasiveness of sexism that necessitates fundamental social change.

Radical feminists are sometimes impatient with the notion of reform, and they doubt the ability of a patriarchal state to legislate in the interests of women (Eisenstein, 1981). Instead of demanding equal pay, more women professors, legalization of abortion, and an increase in child care centers, radical feminists critique the basic structure of work systems, support a radical analysis of universities, insist that child care should be viewed as a social rather than individual responsibility, and maintain that the nuclear family is an unworkable social system (Evelyn Goldfield as cited by Echols, 1989). The most basic social institutions need fundamental change; therefore, the institution of marriage is rejected in theory and often in practice as well (Donovan, 1985).

Hierarchies Must Be Eliminated

Radical feminists react against the liberal feminists' seeming acceptance of a system that is stratified along gender and class lines. They are particularly unsettled by the liberals' refusal to acknowledge women's subordination in the family and the relationship of that subordination to other aspects of women's lives (Echols, 1989).

Radical feminists seek egalitarian functions within their organizations and institutions, and they try to eliminate all forms of hierarchy. Decisions tend to be made by consensus rather than by decree or by majority rule. Leadership is suspect, as it is thought to devalue the contributions of women who are not in leadership positions; decision making is diffused (Hartsock, 1979). More recently, radical feminists have extended their analysis beyond sexual hierarchies arguing that any hierarchy based on sex, class, race, sexual orientation, or some other characteristic, is inherently oppressive and should be eliminated.

CRITIQUE

Radical feminism expands the boundaries of feminist thinking, but it still leaves unanswered some fundamental questions about women's position in society. For example, it does not explain how the biology of sex becomes the social phenomenon of gender (Hartmann, 1981; Jaggar, 1983). Two unsavory possibilities, the inherent pleasure of oppression and biological determinism, have been suggested: (1) "rape, slavery and murder are . . . enjoyable or offer such benefits . . . that anyone would engage in these practices if the opportunity arose . . . women would be just as likely as men . . . if they . . . had the chance . . . and (2) for lack of a better answer, many radical feminists assume there is simply something wrong, biologically, with men that impels them to act in such cruel . . . ways" (Jaggar, 1983, pp. 289-290). According to Brownmiller (1975), rape is and will remain a constant, dependent solely on anatomical capacity and knowledge of that capacity. Her major hope seems to be that women will learn to be equally violent in fighting back and somehow men will willingly come to understand how wretched their actions are, and stop. Other writers have found this untoward view of the human condition immobilizing and ultimately damaging (Tong, 1989, citing Elshtain).

The knowledge of women's oppression did not generalize to the knowledge of social and sexual classes as readily as radical feminists seemed to expect; that is, women do not automatically understand one another's additional oppressions as lesbians, as women of color, as women with disabilities, or as impoverished women. "When lesbians and working-class women finally pierced the myth of women's commonality, the movement was temporarily paralyzed . . . proving to some that differences were inevitably crippling" (Echols, 1989, p. 11).

The fractured movement did continue, but it went off in multiple new directions–the cultural feminists who concentrate on similarities, the lesbian feminists who critique imposed heterosexuality and its implications for both lesbian and heterosexual society, and the womanists who best articulate the need for examining matrices of oppression that simultaneously examine race, gender, and class.

The most notable flaws of radical feminism, then, are its colorblindness, class blindness, and heterosexism. The declaration that "we will always take the side of women against their oppressors" ignores the reality of women's sometimes oppositional interests (Echols, 1989). Radical feminist commitment to universal sisterhood is intended to emphasize the unity of gender despite differences, but it has frequently been used to discount class, race, and other pertinent differences (Echols, 1989).

Although more recent theorizing has embraced diversity, the initial fear of differences damaged radical feminism as a movement and limited its adherents. Its antimale stance lost many women, particularly poor, working-class, and nonwhite women, who for a variety of reasons including economic and political viability, are not as willing to antagonize men. Many women do not define their best interests solely or primarily along sex/gender lines (hooks, 1984).

Many lesbians were lost to the radical feminist wing of the movement when a split developed between lesbians and heterosexual women. Although lesbians continued to work within radical feminist organizations, and in later years took a more prominent place within these organizations, some formed separatist organizations, developing activities and, as subsequent chapters will discuss, theories from a distinctly lesbian feminist perspective. African-American women also developed theories that reflected black women's perspectives.

Finally, radical feminism has been faulted for inadvertently contributing to a decrease in political activism by laying the foundation for cultural feminism, which is sometimes described as an apolitical and individualistic stance:

> The personal is political was one of those ideas whose rhetorical power seemed to . . . undermine its explication. It could . . . encourage a solipsistic[5] preoccupation with self-transformation . . . [and] lead to a search for personally satisfying modes of life while abandoning the possibility of helping others to change theirs. (Echols, 1989, p. 17)

Successes of Radical Feminism

As for its successes, radical feminists developed a more comprehensive view of sexism which includes sex, gender, and reproduction as central topics in political analysis. Some of radical feminists' early critiques of gender roles are now so well integrated into our culture that we may even forget they were once at issue, for example the phrase "man and wife," which juxtaposed a human and a role, now sounds ridiculous. Of course, some may question whether this is co-optation or genuine social change, but undeniably, we now seem less likely to define women in terms of their relationships to men.

Radical feminists exposed the ideology underlying pornography, sexual harassment, rape, woman battering, and prostitution. Despite

---

5. Political solipsism is the belief that the individual functions in opposition to and separate from the needs of others.

ongoing disagreements about the value of some of those critiques, they were instrumental in developing services that center on women's needs and do not focus on helping women adapt to sexist structures. By rejecting mainstream social organizations, rather than trying to include women in society's most problematic structures, radical feminists expose the co-optation and potential containment of liberal politics, and they demonstrate the possibility for women-focused social systems.

Radical feminists have responded to negative criticism regarding narrowness by working more diligently to identify and try to eliminate classism, racism, heterosexism, anti-Semitism, and other forms of discrimination from radical feminism and from society. For example, today's feminist events are far more accessible to a variety of women than they previously were, and there is a more concerted effort to ensure that many different opinions are heard (Jaggar, 1983).

APPLICATION OF RADICAL FEMINISM TO SOCIAL WORK PRACTICE

To qualify as an application of radical feminist theory, an activity would need to aim for some form of fundamental change that was considered, by women, to be in the interest of women.

Policy

Although many radical feminists disagree with her policy direction, Catherine MacKinnon insists that pornography is erroneously defined only as speech, that is, something which is protected by law. Arguing that what gets defined as protected speech is curious and needs to be reconsidered, MacKinnon provided multiple examples of the use of words that are not protected by law, for example, instructing an attack dog to "kill," agreeing to price fixing, posting a segregationist sign, or demanding sex in exchange for a promotion. Pornography, she and Andrea Dworkin argue, falls into the realm of activities (in its production, consumption, and after effects) that promote sexual violence. Using snuff films, in which women are actually murdered before a camera for men's sexual enjoyment, as the most extreme example, they define pornography as "graphic, sexually explicit materials that subordinate women through pictures or words"[6] (MacKinnon, 1993, p. 22). Dworkin and MacKinnon wrote an antipornography ordinance for the city of Minneapolis, MN. The bill was passed twice by the city council, but the mayor vetoed the measure on both occasions.

Administration

Kravetz and Jones (1991) reasoned that the organizational structure of a radical feminist agency tends toward the nonhierarchical or "flattened hierarchy." Women control such agencies, and education and policy work are integral components of a social worker's job. Organization members consider themselves primarily accountable to service users rather than to funders or administrators. Members of the organization frequently include former service users, for example, by hiring former residents to staff emergency shelters for battered women. Agency policy includes the expectation that social workers will be social activists and encourages service users to be the same. Personal *and* sociopolitical transformations are expected, and collective action on the part of both social workers and clients is supported (Kravetz and Jones, 1991).

Nancy Hooyman and Rosemary Cunningham (1986) supported a radical feminist perspective on administration when they argued that women administrators, rather than focusing on skills to promote advancement within traditional hierarchies, should reject the "individualistic, 'slice of the pie' approach" in favor of changing hierarchical institutions (p. 163). They contended that the training women typically receive, for example, how to overcome internal obstacles (lack of assertiveness or confidence) thought to keep them from moving into administrative positions, defines women as deviating from the preferred male mode of administration, holds women responsible for their workplace segregation, and ignores institutionalized sexism.

A feminist model of administration, they argued, eliminates false dichotomies, for example, the overblown distinctions among adminis-

---

6. For a more detailed discussion, see MacKinnon, 1993.

trators, staff, and clients. It reconceptualizes power as: (1) the ability to move others to action; (2) strength, and effectiveness distributed throughout an organization; and (3) the ability to help others fully develop their potential, as opposed to a finite form of energy used to control and dominate others. A radical feminist model incorporates a democratic structure, which acknowledges differential skills and contributions of people, shares rather than withholds information, and encourages people to expand their skills through such activities as job sharing, task rotation, and mutual sharing of accomplishments. Radical feminist administration values process, seeks fundamental structural change, and incorporates women's strengths instead of focusing on their "deficiencies."

Community Organizing

Community-organizing activities might take the form of protests against pornography, which argue that pornography promotes an atmosphere of violence and hostility toward women. Other activities might include education campaigns depicting rape and battering as forms of sexist oppression. It was not unusual in the 1970s to hear anecdotes of women who "patrolled" campuses near areas where women had been assaulted, often painting signs on sidewalks indicating "A woman was raped here" in an effort to raise the consciousness of academic communities concerning violence against women. "Take Back the Night" marches, which continue annually in some cities, began as a radical feminist attempt to change the social expectations as well as the safety of women who refused to be confined to their homes in the evening. These marches are often thought of as examples of women joining together to overthrow male oppressors. The campus escort services, which people can call to request an escort, if they need to cross campuses on foot after dark might be described as an outgrowth of radical feminist activism; however, some radical feminists argue that such services, typically staffed by men, are simply an extension of the "protection racket" in which women are not granted safety on their own, but only when they agree to be accompanied by and under the protection of males (Griffin, 1971).

A very different form of community organizing led to the development of New Economics for Women, an economic development organization of Latina activists that created an affordable housing complex designed to meet the needs of mothers who work outside the home. The residential complex includes "around-the-clock security; ample play spaces; an adult learning center; and a child care center that also houses boys and girls clubs and a teen leadership program" (The Many Faces of Feminism, 1994, p. 61). The organization is currently working on housing for single-parent families and for teenage mothers.

A long-standing example of radical feminist community organizing is the Boston Women's Health Book Collective. Credited with starting a revolution in women's health care, the Collective substantially changed the locus of control over women's health by providing women encouragement to take their health into their own hands and supplying the information necessary to do so. There have been innumerable self-help books published that were inspired by the Collective's. One example is *Our Bodies, Ourselves*, a book that has been updated repeatedly and translated into eleven languages (The Many Faces of Feminism, 1994).

Group Work

Although consciousness-raising is probably, to some extent, incorporated into nearly all feminist groups (Burden and Gottlieb, 1987), consciousness-raising groups are discussed under radical feminism as an acknowledgment of their origin within the radical feminist sector of the women's movement. Groups that incorporate consciousness raising (c-r) vary tremendously. The c-r component of a feminist group may be personally transformative; that is, it may provide an environment in which women have an opportunity to express anger and unfairness about sexist systems (Burden and Gottlieb, 1987); or it may be socially transformative, as it was more likely to be in the 1970s, when women worked on such activist projects as starting women's centers, creating women's newspapers, and developing directories of women's resources (Kirsh, 1987). Diane Kravetz (1987) reviewed the literature on c-r groups. Although she focused primarily on the personal rather than political outcomes, she did find that at least one goal of participants in some of the groups studied was to participate in a range of activities that were designed to change women's circumstances in their communities.

Groups for survivors of sexual assault often take a radical feminist perspective. Arguing that "incest is the training ground of the patriarchy," Patricia Groves and Connie Schondel (1994, p. 4) provided a couples' group for lesbian incest survivors. In it, they countered the social training by which women learn to tolerate sexual harassment and rape in their families, schools, and workplaces. Facilitators addressed personal issues, for example, the effects of incest and the effects of living in a misogynist culture on participants' current relationships. They also addressed the political: several of the couples attended a national lesbian and gay rights event that, the facilitators argued, empowered the participants to make the connections between their personal lives and the political arena and to recognize their individual strengths as well as their collective power.

Feminist Therapy Groups

Feminist therapy focuses on disordered power arrangements (Bepko, 1989). Women learn that their circumstances are not unique and that they are not alone in facing particular issues. Feminist therapy groups focus on respect, and they value other women for their intelligence, support, skills, and leadership. When women come to the groups, they often believe that their issues are unique to them and that men hold all power and should be depended on for problem solving and approval (Gottlieb et al., 1983). The goal of the groups is to examine these beliefs with an eye toward empowerment of the group members. The groups focus on the contribution of sexist structures to the problems women experience and how the women can understand themselves as having been shaped by the unnecessary narrowing of their roles. Feminist therapists try to demystify the therapeutic process, explaining techniques and sharing insights as part of a mutual problem-solving partnership with their clients (Sancier, 1981).

Casework

Interestingly, there is quite a bit of casework material on radical feminism. Although the theory addresses political aspects of life, its motto, "the personal is political," draws attention to the individual side of much of the theory–including the psychology of identification with the oppressor, whereby an oppressed person, in this case a woman, learns to denigrate her own goals, desires, etc., and comes to see the desires of male oppressors as originating from herself.

Goals of casework may include personal transformation through radical action; a focus on the political origins of feelings of alienation and powerlessness; worker and client activities as feminist social activists; or deprogramming of castelike status in an effort to end sex-role complicity.

Diane Kravetz (1986) provided an excellent overview of applications of feminist theory to clinical social work. She reviewed the pertinent literature on mental health, outlining principles of feminist practice. Virtually all of the examples and principles she cited fall within a radical feminist framework. Attention to sociopolitical awareness and to the impact of living in a sexist society are prominent themes, as is the development of new models of mental health and clinical interventions. Importantly, Kravetz argued, that "A feminist perspective [in clinical social work] defines the linkages between personal and social change and provides strategies and methods for empowering the oppressed to make meaningful changes in their lives" (p. 121).

Lisa Tieszen Gary (1991) described AWAKE (Advocacy for Women and Kids in Emergencies). It is a Boston area program for battered women in which the gender neutrality of terms such as family violence, spouse abuse, conjugal violence, and family dispute were put aside in favor of a more political view of the problem of *woman* battering. Advocates teach other staff about the victim-blaming inherent in the assumption that a woman who is being battered or whose children are being beaten "should just leave." They also help battered women understand and negotiate the patriarchal structure of court systems, hospitals, and social services. The program challenges the assumption of learned helplessness and demonstrates that women do indeed make multiple attempts to escape and that when systemic blockades are removed, they often protect themselves and their children.

For philosophical guidance, the program borrows from the work of Michele Bograd (1988), who focuses on both personal and social oppression of women, analyzing the institution of family and women's prescribed roles within it, and validating women's experience of the family as constricting. When workers become aware of child abuse, they are taught to not automatically assume it is the mother who is inflicting the abuse, or that it is within her power, without adequate assistance, to protect her children. Parenting classes are not seen as the solution for families in which a woman and her children are being beaten. Rather, AWAKE focuses on the development of a safety plan for the woman and children. The lens of individual pathology among battered women is discarded in favor of an analysis of and response to a hostile, patriarchal environment (Gary, 1991).

Workers are taught to understand their own feelings of coercion and powerlessness in the face of an unresponsive system of "helping" services and to challenge institutional responses that bolster patriarchy. Family preservation is not the goal; woman empowerment and child protection are (Gary, 1991).

Research

To be considered radical feminist research, a project would need to reexamine the questions being asked in research; for example, do the questions adequately address women's needs? To distinguish itself as radical feminist research, such activities would need to do more than "add women and stir." Radical feminist research would explore alternative ways to conduct research, and to assign research activities and authorship, for example.

Psychologist Terry Kramer (1983, as described in Reinhartz, 1992) devised a research method that falls within the radical feminist paradigm. Combining consciousness raising with group diaries she engaged sociology students in a computer-based anonymous group diary. The anonymity and collectivity of the diary were thought to contribute to students' willingness to express themselves. This approach used radical feminist consciousness raising, in that the women examined power dynamics, defined their personal experiences in political terms, and considered appropriate social action. Ultimately, the women participants hoped to analyze sexism within the department and influence the department to examine and change internal politics. They wanted the department to expand its approach to research methods, and they wanted to eliminate sexism within the department.

Chapter 3

Socialist Feminism

PHILOSOPHICAL CONTRIBUTIONS AND CONTRIBUTORS

According to Karl Marx (b. 1818; d. 1883), economic or material conditions are the root of culture and social organization. People's modes of living are a result of what they produce and how they produce it. Thus, all political and intellectual history can be understood by knowing the prevailing mode of economic production. Under capitalism, workers are ruled by the owning class who control the means of production[1] and the labor of the workers. Consciousness and the self change as material circumstances change; thus, Marx argued: "It is not consciousness that determines life, but life that determines consciousness" (Marx, 1932, p. 10).

Capitalism depends on the value of the products of labor exceeding the cost of production. The capitalist, when selling a product, gets back the cost and a surplus: capital. Three types of value were described by Marx: (1) use-value, or production of goods meant to satisfy immediate human needs, for example, a quilt made to be used by the person who made it; (2) exchange-value, or goods produced with the intent of even exchange for other needed goods, for example, vegetables bartered at a food cooperative, in exchange for grains; and (3) surplus value, or products intended to be sold for

---

1. Means of production refers to the organizational system by which goods are produced and the value of those goods distributed. In capitalist production systems, for example, factories are owned by private individuals who retain profits from the sale of goods. This is contrasted with state-owned or worker-owned businesses where any profit from labor is distributed among the laborers or to society as a whole.

more than they are worth in order to accumulate capital, for example, a vest that took $2.00 worth of materials and one hour of labor, for which the laborer was paid $4.50, is sold for $25.00. Even with an overhead of 100 percent of what it cost to produce the vest, there is still a $13.00 profit–which is the capital that goes to the capitalist, not the worker.

Capitalism is organized so that the ruling class comes to own the products of the proletariat's (members of the working class) labor, and so capitalism causes workers to feel cut off from their work and to lack a sense of meaning in their work lives. Since people tend to seek at least part of life's meaning in their work, this experience of being cut off causes a sense of alienation (Marx, 1977).

Frederick Engels (b. 1820; d. 1895) added to Marx's ideas an analysis of women's place in capitalism. Engels traced the origin of the traditional nuclear family, as we now have come to think of it, to the origin of private property.[2] Until people reached a stage when they were able to accumulate wealth, determine that it was owned by an individual or family, and decide that the wealth should be passed on, there was no reason to establish paternity, and thus, no reason for a stable reproductive pair (Engels, 1972). Engels maintained that women and men both had core roles in the maintenance of the nuclear family, but since women's traditional duties involved housekeeping and food preparation, and men's involved procuring food, owning and commanding slaves, and owning the tools necessary to their tasks, men accumulated more wealth than women did. Engels suggested that this wealth made men's position in the family more important than women's and that men had the impulse to exploit their position, overthrow women, and ensure the inheritance of their children (Engels, 1972, p. 119). Mother right,[3] which until that time had been the rule, needed to be overthrown so that men could control women's sexual behavior (thus, ensuring paternity) and pass wealth on to their offspring. "The control of mother right was the *world historical defeat of the female sex*" (Engels, 1972, p. 120, italics in original). Engels claimed no knowledge of how the

---

2. Engels (1972) placed this in the Ionic period of Greek history, which occurred toward the end of the second millennium B.C.

3. Matriarchy–descent and inheritance traced through the mother.

overthrow took place, but he surmised that "a simple decree sufficed" (p. 120). At the time of the overthrow, he argued, women were degraded and reduced to servitude within the confines of a patriarchal family.

Engels' primary concern was class, not women. He offered no explanation as to: (1) why men's accumulation of wealth came to be seen as more valuable than women's role in reproduction and household maintenance; (2) why women were assigned domestic tasks initially; (3) why wealth would be passed on to the children of the *father*; (4) why men would have an impulse for exploitation; or (5) why establishment of father right would require the degradation of women, when he presented no indication that mother right had included degradation of men. In any case, Engels' (1972) solution to the oppression of women by men was to eliminate private property. If there were no property to be passed on, there would be no reason to maintain an oppressive nuclear family structure.

Eli Zaretsky criticized Marx, Engels, and early radical feminists for failing to explain why women were assigned subordinate roles and tasks within the family although his own definition appeared to assume the very things he questioned: "By the 'family' I mean any grouping of parents or other relatives with children, *embodying a sexual division of labor*, and distinguishing itself as a unit by legal, economic and sexual rights and taboos" (Zaretsky, 1973/1986, p. 11, italics added). Zaretsky chronicled the ways in which the family has, at times, appeared to be in conflict with culture, freedom, and human ability to move beyond animal life. He argued that women's association with the family realm was a source of male supremacy and hatred of women: women's labor in the home was devalued because it was separated from the socialized production of surplus value. That is, women's labor in the home consisted of either use value or exchange value labor, and surplus value labor occurred outside of the home, away from women. He described the increasing separation of private life from work and posited that alienation from work encouraged people to define themselves more in terms of their private lives. He supported the call of radical feminists to attend to the personal, since that is where much of life now operates.

Zaretsky reviewed the changes in women's position subsequent to revolutions in China and Russia and concluded that the assumption that communism would automatically lead to women's liberation was erroneous. What was needed was a recognition of human interdependence and a clear focus on freedom for all members of a group, if freedom was to be achieved (Zaretsky, 1973/1986).

THE THEORY

According to Gayle Rubin, "There is no theory which accounts for the oppression of women–in its endless variety and monotonous similarity, cross-culturally and throughout history–with anything like the explanatory power of the Marxist theory of class oppression" (1974, p. 160). Nevertheless, many socialist feminists were dissatisfied with Marx's virtual neglect of women and Engels' insufficient analysis of women's oppression (Rubin, 1974).

Margaret Benston (1970) argued that women are typically excluded from, or insufficiently addressed in, analyses of class because of the erroneous view that women do not have a unique relationship to the means of production. She maintained that women's secondary status has an economic base, that personal and psychological factors stem from women's relationship to the means of production, and that a change in the means of production is a necessary but not sufficient condition for a change in the factors contributing to women's oppression. Benston (1970) defined women as a class, responsible for use-value activities found in the home. Since money determines value and women's work tends to produce use-value rather than exchange-value or surplus-value products, women have been defined as outside the system of production. Acknowledgment of the enormity of household labor, which women contribute to the economy, needs to be added to concepts of exchange-value and surplus-value commodities.

Two Italian feminists, Mariarosa Dalla Costa and Selma James, (1972) did just that. Their work is frequently cited by those whose solution is to pay women for the work they do in the home. Dalla Costa and James argued that the housewife and her work are essential to capitalism and the housewife is, therefore, *the* determinant of the condition of all other women. Their logic was: capitalism depends on the housewife's free labor to maintain its workers; if the housewife refused to continue to work without pay, capitalism could not function; pay her and you subvert the entire system of capitalist patriarchy by acknowledging the system's dependence on women's labor and by massively redistributing wealth.

Benston (1970) disagreed. Although women's unpaid labor in the home is vitally necessary to the maintenance of capitalist function, the wages-for-housework campaign, if successful, would only serve to keep women segregated in the home. The solution lies in converting private production of household work into public production. *Socialized*, industrialized housework would allow for more adequate production than the nuclear family household model. As it is, the family stabilizes capitalism by functioning not only as a mode of private production of use-value labor, but also as a system that is entirely dependent on a male laborer maintaining his ties with the means of surplus-value production. The need for a way to maintain women as a reserve army of labor, to be used during periods of need, and redirected home again when need decreased, (the most dramatic example occurring during World War II) also functions as a stabilizer for capital. Benston (1970) insisted that housework and childrearing are the responsibility of society, rather than of housewives and parents.[4]

Gayle Rubin (1974, p. 159) contributed an important analysis of the political economy of sexuality by describing the sex-gender system, the process by which society "transforms biological sexuality into products of human activity, and in which these transformed sexual needs are satisfied." Kinship arrangements are clear examples of sex-gender systems. Kinship depends on marriage ties. Individuals are "engendered" and heterosexuality is enforced to guarantee that they will marry: "the sexual division of labor . . . [creates] male and female . . . and it creates them heterosexual" (p. 180). Thus, lesbianism and other "inconvenient" forms of female sexuality are suppressed in service of the kinship system.

Rubin analyzed the exchange of women as commodities in marital arrangements in various cultures. This "traffic in women" forms

---

4. Certainly 1970s socialist feminists were not the first to suggest collective childrearing. In 1903, Gillman had proposed professionalization of housework and collectivization of childrearing and such household necessities as laundry. She argued against women's "24-hour wage-less oppression" and in favor of integration of women into the public world as a means of ending male domination (Donovan, 1985, p. 49).

the basis for women's oppression. "Production" in marital arrangements lies in the transformation of women into objects with
exchange value. Thus, sex–including gender identity, sexual desire,
and fantasy–is a social product, and gender is a socially imposed
division of the sexes.

Dual versus Unified Systems Theory

For some socialist feminist theorists, it is important to determine
whether capitalism and patriarchy are separate systems or a single
entity. These analyses can be divided into two branches: dual systems and unified systems models (Tong, 1989). Dual Systems theorists examine class oppression and sexual oppression separately, as
parallel but often interacting systems. Unified systems theorists
seek to explain oppression in terms of a single, overarching system
with multiple facets, such as sex, class, and race oppressions, with
the facets intersecting in various ways within the single system.

Dual systems theorists claim that women's oppression is quite different from that of other oppressed groups. For example, Juliet Mitchell (1973) noted the *interdependence* of capitalism and patriarchy. She
addressed four key structures, all of which would need to be transformed to eliminate women's oppression: production, reproduction,
sexuality and the socialization of children. Although they are interdependent, they are not the same; so each of these structures needs to be
analyzed separately. Mitchell contested the way that the sexual division
of labor is justified with claims of women's physical incapacity for
demanding labor. She reminded us that women *do* perform physically
demanding labor in and out of the paid labor force. She also pointed
out that the mode of reproduction does not necessarily change with
alterations in the mode of production or with technological advances.
For example, contraception should have made reproduction completely
voluntary for women, but it did not. Maternity, in terms of access to
birth control and medical manipulation of the birth process, remained
in the control of the state and has become a caricature of alienated
labor. Finally, Mitchell demanded that new knowledge regarding the
importance of the early years stop being used against women. The
psychology of childhood has become an instrument of women's
oppression, with the mother's continued presence described as essential for the child's mental health.

Heidi Hartmann (1981) also saw capitalism and patriarchy in collusion, but she countered the psychological explanations assumed by radical feminists. Offering a materialist analysis of patriarchy as a social and economic structure of society, Hartmann argued that capitalism and patriarchy are in partnership. She criticized: (1) early Marxists for expecting capitalism to draw all women into the labor force, thus eliminating the sexual division of labor; (2) contemporary Marxists for claiming that all aspects of women's lives reproduce capitalism; and (3) Marxist feminists for focusing on housework as production of surplus value, making housewives seem to be direct employees of capitalists (Hartmann, 1981).

Crediting Zaretsky for the observation, Hartmann (1981) pointed out that capitalism enhances sexism by separating wage work from home work and by requiring women to do the latter. Men's access to leisure time, personal services, and luxuries provides them with a higher standard of living than women; therefore, it is men as members of a patriarchal system, not just the capitalist economic mode, that benefit from women's labor. Men maintain control by excluding women from access to jobs that pay living wages and by reproducing women's subordinate position and caretaking role in the workplace. The relationship is codified in the family wage system.[5] Women's low wages and society's need for childrearing ensures the family will continue to exist as a necessary income-pooling unit (Hartmann, 1981).

Ann Ferguson and Nancy Folbre (1981) view patriarchy as being in conflict rather than in collusion with capitalism, arguing that men's control over women varied historically. Ferguson and Folbre's contribution to socialist feminist theory is the notion of women's "sex-affective production" defined as: childbearing, childrearing, and the provision of nurturance, affection, and sexual satisfaction. They contrasted Rubin's sex-gender system with sex-affective production, explaining that the latter emphasizes the importance of the *process* of women's labor. Increasingly, women's work is in the paid labor force, and there has been a corresponding "decrease in the

---

5. The family wage system assumes one adult in a family, generally a man, supports an entire family on a single salary while another adult, generally a woman, performs day-to-day survival functions for the entire family, thereby freeing wage earners to devote most of their time to waged work.

proportional amount of time women devote to sex-affective production (which benefits individual men) and an increase in the amount of time which they devote to extrafamilial production (which benefits the capitalist class)" (p. 326). Women now can "play their oppressors against each other—using individual employment as a means of backing up demands for more equality and more control over sex-affective production" (p. 326).

To unified systems theorists, all of the dual systems approaches are inadequate. Whether using the psychological theories or the material approach to explain patriarchy, neither method sufficiently encompasses both patriarchal and capitalist interests. According to Iris Young (1981), the psychological version of dual systems theory gives inadequate attention to history, overemphasizes childrearing, inappropriately universalizes women's experience, and fails to give the impact of patriarchy equal weight with the means of production. The materialist dual systems theorists' mistake is that despite the elimination of a focus on psychology, they continue to separate patriarchy from capitalism (Young, 1981). Materialist dualists describe patriarchy as a system of production that coexists with capitalism. However, this model of separate patriarchal and capitalist spheres distinguishes the family from the economy and accepts the gender-blind analysis of the relations of production (Young, 1981). Young noted that her analysis presupposes gender—a social division based on biology. Gender can best be understood in psychological terms, she argued, with neo-Freudian analyses used to explain how women become psychologically subordinated to men (Young, 1981). Young posited that privileging the category *division of labor* over the category *class* allows race, ethnicity, and gender to all be taken into account. Division of labor is a broader, more concrete categorical system and allows for the examination of the *activity* of labor. Young argued that the emergence of classes from changes in the gender division of labor explains the origin, maintenance, and changes in male domination.

Young asserted that it was unrealistic and inaccurate to expect equalization of the workforce under capitalism. "My thesis is that marginalization of women and therefore our functioning as a secondary labor force is an essential and fundamental characteristic of capitalism" (Young, 1981, p. 58). She maintained that capitalism is the first economic system that requires fluctuations in employment of the labor force and uses categories of race, ethnicity, and sex to determine employment status, with sex being the most obvious and most permanent category. Women's situation, never equal to man's, deteriorated under capitalism, by defining women as a secondary (inexpensive) labor force.[6] Exaggerating divisions between female and male laborers keeps wages low and provides privilege and status to men (Young, 1981).

Al-Hibri (1981) also described a unified system, declaring that capitalism is an advanced state of patriarchy. She located the quest for male supremacy in the male desire for immortality. The male, she argued, considers both reproduction and production to be paths to immortality. Historically, men were awed by woman's ability to bleed "suddenly and heavily without dying" (p. 171) and to reproduce. Man's negative experience of being unable to achieve immortality by reproduction is aggravated by knowledge of his former dependence on women for his existence. This leads to alienation and frustration, which in turn lead to jealousy and hostility toward women. Historically, patriarchy emerged in response (Al-Hibri, 1981).

The first thing early patriarchal men did was to "appropriate the gift of the female and her offspring." Justified by his subsequent discovery of his role in conception, he described the female as simply a container of his sperm and minimized women's role in reproduction. Women, meanwhile, were disinterested in male attempts at immortality because women's experiences were quite different. Women are very much a part of the cycle of life and therefore do not share men's exaggerated search for immortality. Understanding the potential of technology to control women and nature, men also deny women access to technological advancements. Using technology, men gain control of women and reproduction (Al-Hibri, 1981).

Whether capitalism and patriarchy are dual systems or a single, unified one, suggestions of socialist feminists for eliminating sex oppression generally include two key fronts: socialization of housework and child care, and increasing women's wages.

---

6. This, even though women were 30 percent of the paid industrial labor force as far back as the 1860s in France (Young, 1981).

CRITIQUE

Critics have noted that the characterization of men's work as production and women's as reproduction falsely suggests that men create society and women maintain it. Using theories that characterize women's work as production of people, focusing on the content versus the relations of women's labor, ignores the fact that women and men are both involved in producing things as well as people (Jaggar, 1983). The distinction between production and reproduction is false. It is a "relic of the public/private distinction socialist feminists have criticized in other contexts" (Jaggar, p. 157). Emphasis on women's domination outside the market can lead to neglect of women's domination within the market.

Although we have better *descriptions*, we are left with unsatisfactory *explanations* of the initial subjugation of women. If, as most socialist feminists agree, patriarchy preceded capitalism, how was it that men's labor came to be valued more highly than women's?

Although we tend to be more familiar with the writings of white socialist feminists, white women have not been the only critics of patriarchy and capitalism. Shanley (1984/1988) pointed out that Native Americans have long argued against the notions of private property and the nuclear family, and Pesquera and Segura (1993) described a concept of feminism held by some Chicanas in *Chicana Insurgent Feminism*. Women who hold this view contest racial, patriarchal, and class oppression. The perspective is akin to radical feminism, in its emphasis on oppressive relationships between women and men and it is similar to socialist feminism in its attention to class exploitation and opposition to the exploitation inherent in women's current relations to the means of production and reproduction.

Socialist feminism has also been criticized for failing to sufficiently address racism. Gloria Joseph (1981) insisted that it ignores the fact that the psychology and economics of black women and men are "qualitatively and culturally different from those of whites" (Joseph, 1981, p. 93). Some black women expressed a clear preference for leaving rather than redefining alienated work (hooks, 1984). Because the history of sexual inequality is quite different for blacks and whites, its current manifestation differs, as should the strategies for change (Joseph, 1981). Rather than attend the wedding of Marxism and feminism, Joseph hopes for "the impending marriage of Black revolutionary socialism and socialist feminism" (Joseph, 1981, p. 106).

Marxist-Leninists have criticized socialist feminism for its use of the concept *patriarchy*, claiming this departure from historical materialism[7] was such a bastardization of Marx's, Lenin's, and Engels' works as to be unworthy of using the classification, "socialist" (Burnham and Louie, 1985).

Beasley argued that feminist political economic theories are no more of a total picture of economic processes than traditional male economic theories, nor should they be. Different economic measures and analyses are needed for different purposes. Only a woman-centered study of economic forms would be adequate to the task of examining a "*sexual epistemology of economics*" (1994, p. 70). Beasley argued that such a theory must move beyond using "sex-blind/phallocratic" economic concepts, or what Alison Jaggar (1983) calls "sexual economyths." Instead, women's economic position and the power relations between the sexes need to be the central, rather than peripheral, focus of any theory that would accurately describe women's economic position.

Socialist feminists insist on a materialist analysis if not of *both* patriarchy *and* capitalism, then at least of women's relationship to capitalism. Thus, socialist feminism was more successful than liberal or radical feminism in centering the need for attention to political-economic systems and in calling for coalitions among economically oppressed groups.

APPLICATION OF SOCIALIST FEMINISM TO SOCIAL WORK PRACTICE

Policy

Figuera-McDonough (1994) argued against the ahistorical analysis of the family that is generally used to formulate policy. Failing to

---

7. Historical materialism is the theory of economic relations as the determinant force of social organization and development.

consider changes in family structure has the effect of undercutting rather than supporting families. She pointed out that policies tend to assume a need to support and maintain the nuclear family structure, as though it was the only desirable and the most long-standing one. The hierarchy and exploitation that appear to be inherent in the nuclear family structure and its traditional division of labor are not desirable for women. Rather than defining *variations* on the nuclear family as *deviations*, she argued for seeing them as normal adaptations to changing social conditions. Promoting solidarity among members of families, regardless of their composition, is the challenge of family policy.

Figuera-McDonough maintained, for example, that no-fault divorce does not acknowledge the differential contributions or responsibilities within current marriages. No-fault divorce assigns child support based on the discretion of a judge rather than on realistic costs for custodial parents, typically mothers. This often contributes substantially to economic hardship for women and children. At the same time, our divorce system also fails to encourage paternal responsibility through weak enforcement of child support laws.

Like other socialist feminists, Figuera-McDonough argued two things: (1) that family policy tended to ensure that the nuclear family, supported by a family wage, was the best model; and (2) that in a weakly regulated market economy, the family wage is simply not available to everyone (Figuera-McDonough, 1994, p. 46). This forced poorer women to work to maintain the family. Policies regulating marriage and divorce tend to help poor women least, since their husbands are also poor. Citing Mary Jo Bane's (1986) research, Figuera-McDonough contended that there is little economic incentive for poor women to marry, however, "separation and divorce do not cause poverty among mothers in the lower strata. Their economic situation before and after marriage breakup stays the same" (1994, p. 47).

Rather than assuming all families have similar needs, and basing family policy on meeting the needs of nuclear families only, we should be focusing on issues of: (1) access to work; (2) supporting families as they are currently structured; and (3) "making public institutions more attuned to families" with a particular focus on the most vulnerable, that is, the poorest families (Figuera-McDonough, p. 52).

Nancy Naples (1991) explored the sexism contained in the hidden gender assumptions of the Family Support Act (FSA) of 1988. Naples insisted that the state oppresses women and contributes to their impoverishment by using gender-neutral language, thereby masking gender-based intended outcomes. With the two exceptions of establishing paternity and exempting women in the third trimester of pregnancy from mandatory participation in workfare, gender-neutral terms–for example, parent versus mother or father–are used. Naples pointed out that although this may fit well with liberal gender blindness, the FSA applies to gendered people. She argued further that the FSA contains language that stigmatizes households, such as single mothers and their children, that differ from the male-headed two-parent household. Thus, the FSA supports a gendered division of labor. It also assumes that either a family wage is available to one of the parents, or that two parents, working in minimum wage jobs–which are presumed to be readily available and accessible to women and men, regardless of race–can pay for child care as well as the rest of a family's normal living expenses. The policy was devised to counter the lack of a work ethic–as opposed to a lack of work–assumed to be present among poor people.

Citing Pascall, Naples (1991) also criticized the FSA for attempting to control reproduction with measures such as those that allowed states to impose restrictions on teenage mothers, requiring them to live with their parents to receive Aid to Families with Dependent Children (AFDC), and restricting childbirth by creating opportunities for states to disqualify recipients who become pregnant while on Aid. Naples was particularly critical of the FSA for keeping women in caretaking roles that are devalued ideologically and often go unreimbursed economically. Naples also criticized policies that fragment social life with separate, often contradictory regulations covering such topics as minimum wage requirements, food stamp allotments, child care, health care, and employment. She advised that social workers document the inadequacies of the FSA program to ensure that accurate data would be available to help change the policy, thus providing poor women the opportunity to obtain jobs on which they can support their families.

Mimi Abramowitz took a more broad-based approach to improving women's economic position, arguing that in order to develop policy that would genuinely change women's circumstances, we need to stop limiting ourselves to viewing family policy in isolation from other social and economic policies. Abramowitz contended that the shift in income upwards from poor and middle-class people to wealthy individuals and corporations, which was particularly astonishing during the Reagan and Bush administrations, had the added effect of decreasing the political strength of women's, civil rights, and labor organizations (Abramowitz, 1988, p. 351).

One of the hardest hit programs was AFDC, the nation's largest income maintenance program for poor women and their children. Abramowitz (p. 353) argued that for a time AFDC had managed to reconcile the competing demands for women's home labor and market labor; that is, it regulated women's lives in two ways. The program helped those women who conformed to the family ethic, by staying home and caring for their children, by providing the financial resources for them to do so. At the same time, AFDC channeled other women into "the bottom rungs of the labor market." As time went on, AFDC came to be seen differently. In the 1980s the program became quite controversial, in large part because it helped women who violated both the rules of patriarchy and the rules of capital: "Despite its stigma and lack of generosity, the program simultaneously challenged the rules of male domination and, by allowing poor women to stay out of low level jobs, those of profitable accumulation of capital as well" (Abramowitz, 1988, p. 355).

Abramowitz pointed out that efforts to alter AFDC, under the rubric of welfare reform, were designed to change it from an income support to a mandatory work program. Abramowitz supported the provision of day care, health insurance, education, and training to poor women, noting the need for full implementation of such programs, to make work realistic. To be effective, she argued, welfare reform needs to have a broader view than the AFDC program as we know it. Instead, we need to examine the entire social welfare system along with our political economy, focusing on the broader issue of women's poverty rather than simply welfare dependency.

A labor market policy that assured employment . . . for all those able to work, that set the minimum wage to automatically keep pace with changes in the standard of living, and that tolerated neither unemployment as a means to check inflation nor discrimination of any kind would go far towards assuring that women would rely on jobs rather than AFDC. (Abramowitz, 1988, p. 367)

Abramowitz proposed supplementing full employment with an income support program that was not based on a particular form of family unit, and she argued in favor of setting a national benefit at the poverty line and tying the benefit to the Consumer Price Index.

Community Organizing

Analysis of sex and class have often come together in the history of labor union organizing (Balser, 1987). The list of issues addressed by women's trade organizations is long, but probably none is longer than that of the National Women's Trade Union League (NWTUL), founded in 1903 by working women, social reformers, and settlement house workers. It was not a separate union but an organization of women who were already members of unions, seeking to have their needs addressed.

NWTUL fought for an eight-hour work day, elimination of night work, protected machinery, sanitary workshops, separate toilet rooms for women, seats for women, prohibition of employment of pregnant women for two months before and two months after delivery, pensions for mothers during lying-in, protective legislation for women and children, factory inspection and an increased number of women inspectors, women physicians when physical examination of women was required, minimum wage created by an industry wage board, fire protection in factories along with fire drills, employer liability and compensation for accidents, banking laws to protect savings, weekly wage payment, control of employment agencies, advertisement during strike to acknowledge the strike, initiative, referendum and recall, and child labor laws. It had a suffrage department, and a training school for leadership roles for women.

A more recent example of feminist labor organizing occurred in the early 1970s when feminists formed several independent working women's organizations, primarily focusing on previously unorganized office workers. The most successful group, 9 to 5, began in Boston in 1973 and is now a national organization. The group did not limit itself to unionization. It also addressed equal opportunity for women, age discrimination, and banking and insurance companies' practices toward women workers (Milkman, 1985).

Administration

Ramsey and Parker (1992) explored the interrelationships of patriarchal and capitalist assumptions in bureaucracies. They proposed a new type of organizational structure they saw as more ideal, which they called neobureaucracy. One of the key elements of a neobureaucracy would be its resistance to remaining static. Importantly, it would incorporate a recognition of the potential social contribution of organized labor to increasing social benefits. A neobureaucracy would limit specialization while acknowledging expertise. It would discourage the assumption that only professionals should control certain organizational tasks. Teamwork and group achievement would supersede competition and individual "ownership of success" (Ramsey and Parker, 1992, p. 270).

Arguing that their model of a neobureaucracy had the potential to resist and change patriarchal and capitalist structures, Ramsey and Parker recommended that a central decision-making and coordinating entity be maintained within the organization. Participants in the organization would need to continuously renegotiate the membership and functions of such a center. Organizational rules would need to be flexible and take process as well as outcome into account. "A neo-bureaucratic organization would be one that depended on certain rules . . . but never acted as if these rules were other than guides to action . . . debate over the organization's means would be just as important as debate over the organization's ends" (Ramsey and Parker, p. 270).

Group Work

Suggesting that the rise in popularity of self-help groups may be more a reflection of "a growing, healthy skepticism of professionals and the welfare state bureaucracy" than "an extension of the self-absorption of the seventies," Ann Withorn (1994, p. 441) argued that self-help strategies can be combined with socialist feminist strategies. Withorn suggested that since it is grounded in the daily experience of working-class people's lives, self-help may have more potential than economic theory to contribute to progressive politics, in part because the solidarity typically found in self-help groups promotes concern with other group members.

Withorn did not argue that all self-help groups have progressive potential.

> At one end of the spectrum are the politically aware feminist self-help efforts . . . [where] self help is self-conscious, empowering democratic effort where women help each other and often provide an analysis . . . from which to criticize and make feminist demands on the system. At the other end are groups which focus on the specific problem only, like AA, other "anonymous" groups or disease victim groups, with self help used only as a means for coping with a problem, not an alternative model for society or even service delivery. (p. 442)

Withorn challenges us to determine how to (1) link self-help groups together in a broad social criticism; (2) assist such groups in becoming agents of social change; and (3) help them avoid shoring up "professional hegemony and the capitalist welfare state" (p. 447). Withorn cautions against dismissing the potential of self-help. "We cannot allow the all-too-real limitations of the current practice of self help to obscure the equally real opportunity" (p. 449).

Casework

Linda Canzoneri Klipfel (1994) argued that social workers who intervene with battered women need to maintain a clear focus on the political power of men within patriarchal structures. She urged that women should be counseled without their batterers since joint counseling assumes equal power in a relationship and implies equal responsibility for the battering. She argued for including a focus on oppression and the "struggles derived from the class-sexual division of labor and the issues . . . of production linked to jobs and wages . . . and the resultant male violence against women in all its forms" (p. 22). Canzoneri Klipfel did not separate direct service from indirect; she discussed social work responsibility at both levels simultaneously. She also did not argue for separatist organizing to affect change. She believes that some men have examined class and gender structures, and they are willing to work toward effective change. "Women working together *with* men will insure unity and strength in pressuring a patriarchal system of capitalist governmental relations to respond to the *real* needs of *real* people" (p. 24, emphasis in original).

Research

Arguing that "socially mediated interaction with nature in the process of production shapes both human beings and theories of knowledge," Nancy Hartsock (1987, p. 158) posited that women's position in society is profoundly different from men's; therefore, women's reality is different as well. Hartsock insisted on the need to take a feminist perspective or standpoint in conducting research on topics pertaining to women. Further, with her contention that "material life structures understanding" (p. 161), she argued that we cannot understand society or social structures until we take a feminist standpoint: "the ruling gender and class have material interests in deception. A standpoint, however, carries with it the contention that there are some perspectives on society from which, however well-intentioned one may be, the real relations of humans with each other and with the natural world are not visible" (Hartsock, p. 159). Hartsock urged that a feminist standpoint should be used in research to counter the control of both mental and physical production by hegemonic groups. Using the standpoint of women, who constitute an oppressed group, would promote both scientific analysis and political struggle. Hartsock insisted that such an analysis should begin with the sexual division of labor, in which women, although they participate in the paid labor force, are still defined as being responsible primarily for domestic labor.

Chris Beasley's (1994) work in economics contributed several important points to this argument. She accepted the feminist standpoint argued by Hartsock and said that we cannot understand women's relationship to economic structures without looking at women's roles in economic structures and examining economics from the point of view of women. She also said that one of the problems of sticking too closely to a Marxist analysis, with its inattention to sex, was that researchers assumed a continuity between the organization of women's unpaid and waged labor (Beasley, 1994). She insisted that household work studies tend to underestimate the character of women's labor, by ignoring the power dynamics of domestic work. Arguing that it is important to study *all* the work women perform, she pushed for a more accurate account of what it is that women do. She proposed that we alter our model for studying modern Western women's work to increase our understanding of women's economic position. Beasley suggested that we examine: sex differentiated, *waged* work; public unpaid labor, "service" labor, including travel, educational, and civic duties; all housework, including shopping, cooking, washing, house maintenance, gardening, etc.; what she termed "body work" including planning for nutritional needs and diets, exercise, and the effort that goes into maintaining current standards of beauty; pregnancy, childbirth, and childcare functions; health maintenance activities, including scheduling and attending medical appointments; sex; and emotional labor of caring for husband, children, friends, neighbors, and relatives. Both Beasley and Hartsock promote the use of a feminist standpoint to further not only improved *analysis* but also socialist feminist *outcomes*.

Chapter 4

Lesbian Feminist Theory

BACKGROUND

Lesbian feminist theory emerged in the 1970s, some say as an outgrowth of radical feminism. Some even argue that lesbian feminism is a central component of radical feminism (Kitzinger, 1987). For others, lesbian and radical feminism are distinct. Among the women who see a distinction are those who report that lesbian feminist thought and political activism emerged, in part, as a response to the inability of heterosexual feminists to adapt to, or to accommodate, either lesbian analysis or a lesbian presence in the women's movement.

The Response to Heterosexism Perspective

Lesbians grew tired of the invisibility or outright denial of lesbianism that occurred in the early years of radical feminism. Some women described fear, antagonism, and insensitivity between lesbians and straight women (Bunch, 1987). Heterosexual feminists sometimes seemed to capitulate to the "accusations" of lesbianism in the women's movement, accepting the moral/political valence of lesbianism as negative and denying that leaders were anything other than confirmed heterosexuals ("man lovers" rather than "man haters"). Meanwhile, lesbians argued that shrinking away from accusations of lesbianism was a betrayal of the essence of feminism. Eisenstein (1983) suggested that accepting such a discrediting of the women's movement was to succumb to "sexual McCarthyism."

Lesbians reacted to straight women's apparent fear of the "lavender menace" (a phrase attributed to Betty Friedan) with charges that heterosexual relationships involved "sleeping with the enemy." Heterosexuality was also charged with separating women from each other and encouraging women to compete with each other for male-identified heterosexual privilege (Bunch, 1993).

Once again declaring men the enemy, lesbians accused straight women of a failure of intellect, as well as politic, for their continued involvement with men: "Heterofeminists fail to reach theoretical clarity regarding male supremacy and the oppression of women, due to a cognitive dissonance about men . . . they cannot see the patriarchal forest for the individual male trees" (Cavin, 1985, p. 34). This "gay/straight split" in the women's movement was a painful, often bitter dispute in which lesbians and straight women engaged in angry divisiveness that took years to heal.

Antiheterosexuality was not condoned by all or even most lesbians, but lesbianism was thought to be mysterious to heterosexual people; likewise, heterosexual relationships were sometimes seen as curious to lesbians:

> What is *a topic* for (straight women), which some can and some cannot attend to fruitfully, is a condition of life for me. I avoid "alienating" them, but they constantly and (usually) unconsciously alienate me by their mostly uncritical and apparently unalterable, to me un-fathomable, commitment to heterosexuality. (Frye, 1992, p. 52)

It was not the individual participants who were problematic, but the institution of heterosexuality that needed to be dismantled, and that was because of politics, not personality. Charlotte Bunch (1987), for one, clarified that she did not doubt the sincerity and commitment of heterosexual feminists, but she distrusted heterosexuality, as it is institutionalized, defining men as intrinsically more important than women. Without lesbianism at least as a philosophical, if not actual, goal, feminism was said to be incomplete.

The "We're Not Female Homosexuals" Argument

Lesbian feminists did not find a political home in the emerging gay movement either. Although it may seem self-evident that lesbians experience both sexist and heterosexist oppression, this has not been easy to incorporate into theories of oppression. Gay scholarship tends to look only at oppression based on sexual orientation, ignoring gender (Kennedy and Davis, 1994). Gay men may be oppressed in some similar ways to lesbians, but they are still men. Gay men who seek equality with straight men do not necessarily oppose male privilege philosophically, nor do they work as political activists specifically for lesbian interests (Bunch, 1987; Frye, 1983; Kitzinger, 1987). Rich (1980) insisted that a lesbian feminist definition apart from gay male reality was essential, and that to simply include women as a female version of gay men was to erase women's reality and to deprive lesbians of a political existence.

The Radicalesbians' manifesto, "The woman-identified woman," was an early statement about lesbian feminism. Published in several formats in the 1970s, it is still cited today as one of the most cogent initial statements of the position of lesbian feminists. The paper downplayed distinctions between the interests of lesbian and heterosexual feminists, and highlighted differences between gay men and lesbians. It argued that while verbal harassment (what today we call "hate words,") may criticize both lesbians and gay men for refusing to participate in sexually assigned roles, the "grudging admiration" accorded the tomboy and the "queasiness felt around a sissy boy" indicated the contempt with which the proscribed female role was held (Radicalesbians, 1994, p. 163). The paper described the lesbian as being attracted to women, rather than repelled by men. To many lesbians, particularly women of color, the distinction was critically important: "When I say I am a Black Lesbian, I mean I am a woman whose primary focus of loving, physical as well as emotional, is directed to women. It does not mean I hate men" (Lorde, 1990, p. 322).

The arguments in support of the need for heterosexual women to openly welcome lesbians and lesbian issues into the women's liberation movement were simple:

Argument one. It was essential for the women's liberation movement to deal with lesbianism openly. To do otherwise would subject the movement and individual women to the threat of "exposure" of lesbianism. If labeling and similar threats could be used to frighten and de-politicize women, then women could be effectively separated from their sisters. Furthermore, women could be prevented from directing their attention away from men, and thus, continue to be controlled by male culture. As long as women refused to consider the possibility of a primary commitment with a woman, they were reserving a particular kind of value and love for men, thus affirming male primacy. Radicalesbians insisted that as long as women sought, above all, to be acceptable to men, the term lesbian could be effectively used against individual women and the movement as a whole.

Argument two. Energies needed to be directed toward women rather than back toward male oppressors. Ignoring the heterosexual structure that bound women in one-to-one relationships with their oppressors would continue to drain women as they labored to create nonsexist men. It was a delusion to think that the new, nonsexist men would then "allow" women to be liberated. That tactic would simply reinforce male power (Radicalesbians, 1994).

The Outgrowth of Radical Feminism Perspective

In the meantime, some lesbians started to question their place as a despised minority or a troublesome public relations problem. They began to think of themselves as the backbone of the women's movement (Abbott and Love, 1977). They combined their wariness of a heterosexually defined feminism with their radical feminist analysis of male-female relationships and insisted that whether or not men were actual perpetrators of rape and battering, by virtue of the social hierarchy, they all had the potential for dominance and exploitation. Additionally, men were described as fundamentally different, if not as a result of biology, then as a result of rearing and choice. Exceptions were acknowledged, but, lesbians argued, since men generally got more than their fair share of attention, it was not reasonable to expend energy seeking out, establishing relationships with, and nurturing the exceptions (Trebilcot, 1994).

The lesbian was called "woman prime" (Johnston, 1973) and described as the embodiment of feminism (Abbott and Love, 1977). It was not only the practice of lesbianism, but the theoretical stance, that was seen as valuable since lesbian feminism provided a theoretical direction from which to counter male supremacy (Bunch, 1987).

In sum, early lesbian feminist thought was a combination of the thinking of: (1) lesbians who felt denied, silenced, or even expelled from the women's movement by heterosexual feminists; (2) lesbians who were dismayed by the inability of the gay movement to incorporate lesbian perspectives; and (3) radical feminists whose analysis of sexism extended to an analysis of heterosexism.

THE THEORY

Defining Lesbianism

One of the first things that lesbian feminists attempted was to define themselves–not as simple at it sounds. One definition held that lesbian feminists were women who defined themselves independently from men (Johnston, 1973). Arguably, this was lesbian feminists' first claim of power. "The slave who excludes the master from her hut thereby declares herself *not* a *slave*. And *definition* is another face of power" (Frye, 1983, p. 105). Like radical feminists, lesbian theorists look to each other, rather than to men for an understanding of who they are (Radicalesbians, 1994). They argue that lesbianism is a political perspective critical of heterosexual institutions (Farwell, 1993, citing Barbara Smith) and a political commitment rather than a sexual preference (Eisenstein, 1983). Women insist that lesbian feminism and, more important, lesbianism are not reducible to considerations of genital sexual activity. Lesbianism may be something a woman was born to, or something she chose. Trebilcot insisted on each woman's right to define whether her lesbianism is something she discovered, created, some of each, or something else entirely. What matters most is that the woman herself gets to decide (Trebilcot, 1994).

Lesbian feminists describe themselves as different. They are different from heterosexual women in forming their primary attachments with women and having experienced certain oppressive circumstances *as lesbians* that shaped their sense of themselves (Penelope, 1990). They are different from other feminists in naming heterosexism as a key oppressive system rather than a variation on the theme of patriarchy. They are different from men in their biology, rearing, and access to power and privilege. They are different from gays in the need to analyze sexism and remain conscious of themselves as women. They are different from other marginalized groups in their ability to "pass" (Goffman, 1963) and in not having been raised (for the most part) by people who share their orientation and its related status. Most especially, although understood only recently, they are different from each other. Shane Phelan argued, in fact, that the most striking thing about lesbians is not the ways in which they differ from heterosexuals or the distinctions between lesbian and heterosexual cultures, but the diversity among lesbians, the ways they differ from each other (Phelan, 1994).

Initially, lesbianism was described by lesbian feminist theorists as an application of feminism. Ti-Grace Atkinson is often credited as having said, "Feminism is the theory and lesbianism the practice." Another account credits Jill Johnson with: "Feminism is the complaint; lesbianism is the solution" (Hoagland, 1988). By whichever version, lesbianism was conceived of as a political choice as opposed to a private sexual activity. The point is crucial:

> Male society defines lesbianism as a sexual act, which reflects men's limited view of women: they think of us only in terms of sex. They also say lesbians are not real women, so a real woman is one who [has sexual intercourse with] men. We say that a lesbian is a woman whose sense of self and energies, including sexual energies, center around women–she is woman-identified. (Bunch, 1987, pp. 161-162)

A lesbian feminist then, is defined by some theorists (though certainly not all) as someone who has a particular political outlook and devotes her energies to women. Some women argue, "all women are lesbians," meaning that all women have the capacity to love women (Faderman, 1981).

Joyce Trebilcot spelled out four arguments in support of the potential lesbianism in every woman: (1) because most people's first relationship is with a woman–their mother–lesbianism may be more "natural" for women, and heterosexuality more "natural" for men; (2) as long as women and men exist within the confines of a patriarchal society, equality can not occur in a heterosexual relationship. Even though individual men may renounce male privilege, those privileges are still accrued to men by society; (3) feminism needs all of a woman's energy; and (4) women need to take responsibility for their own sexuality, apart from male definitions (1994, p. 98).

Whether lesbianism entails a political analysis is, of course, open to debate. For some, the political analysis is only coincidentally related to lesbianism:

> A *lesbian* is a woman whose sexual/affectional preference is for women, and who has thereby rejected the female role on some level, but she may or may not embrace a lesbian-feminist political analysis. A *woman-identified woman* is a feminist who adopts a lesbian-feminism ideology and enacts that understanding in her life, whether she is a lesbian sexually or not. (Bunch, 1987, p. 198)

Early lesbian feminist theorists saw themselves as the vanguard of the women's movement (Cavin, 1985), speaking from the conversion point of the women's liberation and gay liberation movements, pushing the "boundaries of permissibility" for themselves and for women in general (Kennedy and Davis, 1994, p. 375), and envisioning the end not only to patriarchy, but to hierarchies based on race, class, age, and sexuality (Radicalesbians, 1994). Lesbian feminists argue for the necessity of a lesbian analysis of women's status, insisting that no women will ever be free to choose to be anything until all women are free to choose to be lesbians. Bunch called the domination of heterosexuality a "mainstay of male supremacy" (Bunch, 1987, p. 198). The stance outside of the center is seen by some as a valuable position from which to critique society (Bunch, 1987), but it is seen by others as a relatively powerless margin to be avoided (Calhoun, 1994).

Heterosexuality and Lesbian Invisibility

Clearly, a description of the institutionalization of heterosexuality was necessary. The first step was to identify heterosexuality as a political as well as personal institution, in which some members of society–heterosexuals and most often males–are given more power than others (Bunch, 1987). Step two was to review, in light of lesbianism, the radical feminist analysis of the sociopolitical nature of gender assignments. Step three was to analyze the effort involved in ensuring that the majority of people are heterosexual. The final step was to question the necessity for heterosexuality as a basis upon which to organize society. The implications go well beyond the place of lesbians in society. Once gender identities are exposed as socially rather than naturally created, the rationale for lesbian subordination is lost. Thus, the arbitrariness of exclusive organization of sexuality, romance, love, and marriage around the heterosexual imperative is also exposed (Calhoun, 1994).

A political theory of heterosexuality is essential, and lesbian feminism provided a vantage point from which to create a new analysis. First, lesbians and heterosexuals need to be examined as members of different sexuality classes. Then, heterosexuality can be seen as a political structure that is separable from patriarchy, at least in theory. Otherwise, lesbian oppression would be understood simply as a special case of patriarchal oppression, blinding us to the "irreducibly lesbian nature of lesbian lives" (Calhoun, 1994, p. 559). A critique of the institution of heterosexuality is particularly poignant for women who are already multiply oppressed on other grounds. Cheryl Clarke insisted that black women have enough brutality, racism, male supremacism, and imperialism in their history already. They do not need to endure the "psychic mutilation of heterosexual superiority" as well (Clarke, 1983, p. 130).

Protecting the idea of heterosexuality as the only option requires lesbianism to be kept hidden. Lesbian feminists insist that it is vital to acknowledge not only that heterosexuality is accorded *greater* standing than lesbianism, but that lesbians are given no standing at all (Calhoun, 1994). Although many lies about women's limitations had already been exposed by feminist theorists, destruction of these connections among women seemed especially onerous. Adrienne Rich accused heterosexuality, as an institution, of drowning in silence the erotic feelings between women (Rich, 1979b).

Opposing the view of heterosexuality as natural, Marilyn Frye (1992) reasoned that a key mechanism of male domination is near-universal female heterosexuality, a component of which is compulsory sexual availability to men. She argued that the seemingly benign heterosexual systems of romance, heterosexual intercourse, and marriage, as well as the more obviously dangerous systems of incest and other forms of sexual assault, serve as the primary heterosexual training sites of "subordination and servitude to men." The secondary training sites consist of the ritual preparations for female subordination, where girls and women are habituated to proper deportment, attire, decoration, and bodily restriction and distortion. Through these practices, girls and women are shaped into a particular form of bonding to dominant males.

Women began to question why such measures needed to be brought to bear on the development of women's romantic and sexual loyalty to men if heterosexuality was, indeed, so natural and inevitable. It also seemed evident to lesbian theorists that compulsory heterosexuality served the interest of very unsavory social structures from the pimp to the incest perpetrator, and that only with honest presentation of social and economic alternatives would women be able to break free (Rich, 1980).

> Female heterosexuality is not a biological drive or an individual woman's erotic attraction . . . to another human animal which happens to be male. Female heterosexuality is a set of social institutions and practices defined and regulated by patriarchal kinship systems, by both civil and religious law, and by strenuously enforced mores and deeply entrenched values and taboos. Those definitions, regulations, values, and taboos are about male fraternity and the oppression and exploitation of women. They are not about love, human warmth, solace, fun, pleasure, or deep knowledge between people. If any of the latter arise within the boundaries of these institutions and practices, it is because fun, solace, pleasure and acknowledgment grow like dandelions and are hard to eradicate, not because heterosexuality is natural or is naturally a site of such benefits. (Frye, 1992 p. 132)

The path out of subordination seemed clear. If female heterosexuality is the path to replication of the patriarchy, then women need to abandon that institution as part of the dismantling of patriarchal structures (Frye, 1992).

Not only are *social institutions* designed around heterosexual men's dependence on women, *individual men* depend on women as well. Some view such dependence less than kindly and urge women to abandon the caretaking of men (Frye, 1983). Given such a critique of social arrangements and the call for the dismantling of such basic social institutions as marriage and heterosexuality, it is not difficult to understand why lesbian feminism and lesbianism are seen as such threats to the social order. They were. They are.

Lesbian feminist theorists argue that the threat of lesbianism is not known only to lesbians themselves. It had been clear throughout patriarchal history the damage that could be caused by knowledge of lesbianism. Lesbian feminist theory notes men's apparent fear of lesbianism and acknowledges that there is much of which to be fearful:

> Lesbianism is a threat to the ideological, political, personal, and economic basis of male superiority. The lesbian threatens the ideology of male supremacy by destroying the lie about female inferiority, weakness, passivity, and by denying women's "innate" need for men. Lesbians literally do not need men. (Bunch, 1987, p. 164)

But not all lesbians threaten social structures similarly. For example, black women, who are less likely to succumb to the ideal of the nuclear family with the man at the helm and the stay-at-home mother, do not necessarily see lesbianism as a threat to black family structures. Audre Lorde (1990) insisted that black lesbians are not a threat to the black family, pointing out that many black lesbians have families of their own. This is not to say that lesbianism is generally welcomed and supported in black communities, but it does point out two things: (1) black family structure may not be threatened by lesbianism in quite the same ways as white family structures, and (2) a lesbian family is only a threat to family structures if "family" is defined quite narrowly.

Still, the threat to the established order is undeniable (Trujillo, 1993). Cheryl Clarke described the threat of lesbianism as a dangerous rebellion against patriarchy and against women's assignment to concubinage in the form of male dependence. She contended that for a woman in "male-supremacist, capitalist, misogynist, racist, homophobic, imperialist . . . North America" to be a lesbian is inherently an act of resistance regardless of whether she is closeted or open about her lesbianism (1983, p. 128).

Adrienne Rich called lesbians disloyal to civilization because such connections among women hold enormous potential for social transformation (Rich, 1979). In response to this threat to the status of heterosexuals and heterosexuality, love between women has been erased (Trujillo, 1993).

> Whatever is unnamed, undepicted in images, whatever is omitted from biography, censored in collections of letters, whatever is misnamed as something else, made difficult-to-come-by, whatever is buried in the memory by the collapse of meaning under an inadequate or lying language–this will become, not merely unspoken, but *unspeakable.* (Rich, 1979, p. 190, emphasis in original)

Separatism

If the radical feminist analysis of male violence against women was insufficient to ignite a separatist movement, being ignored or marginalized as lesbians by both feminists and gay liberationists could not help but contribute to talk of separatism, an ongoing point of dissension common in many political movements. Lesbian separatism is defined in myriad ways, but all definitions come down to some level of female withdrawal of support from men and/or male institutions. Separatism can include distancing oneself from men and male-identified institutions, rejection of male-defined roles and activities, ending or avoiding close relationships with men, refusing to work with men, refusing to socialize with men, avoiding male-identified media, or withholding support or commitment from men. Or it can mean simply ceasing to be loyal to men (Frye, 1983).

Bev Jo pointed out that separatism does not entail an absence of contact with all patriarchal structures. Women who define themselves as separatists continue to hold jobs and to interact with civic and business officials, grocery clerks, and landlords, most of whom are men. Rather, for some women, separatism means avoiding relating to men when it is not necessary to do so (Jo, 1981).

Separatism can also manifest as the desire for a woman-only space where women can be with each other, free from male harassment or influence (Jo, 1981). Once an integral component of many feminist functions, woman-only space has now gone out of favor. With the advent of feminist backlash, organizers have succumbed to accusations of male bashing and in the wake of coalition building with gay men, specifically lesbian functions have fallen by the wayside. Women-only events are becoming rare (Jo, 1981).

Practically speaking, however, separatism has always had its limits. Criticized by some women for being a privileged white woman's position, separatism has often come under attack from within lesbian feminist circles as well. In its extreme forms, separatism has been seen as a political mistake. Shane Phelan argued that lesbians are central to society regardless of how much society denigrates them. She pointed out that there is no place lesbians can escape to and be accepted as who they are, and she urged lesbians to avoid the temptation of imagining that they belong somewhere else. The only way to belong is to eliminate the obstacles to belonging, to recognize and retain our place in the dominant culture, and to claim that place as a space from which to engage in political intervention (Phelan, 1994).

ARGUMENTS WITHIN THE THEORY

Sexual Activity

Some lesbian feminists believe that sex is political and therefore relevant to debating and theorizing (Calhoun, 1994). One of several disagreements in lesbian feminist thought concerns specific sexual activities. Quite different sexual mores have coexisted among various groups of lesbians at least since the 1940s, according to Kennedy and Davis (1994), and these differences have often been contested theoretically. The most vocal disagreements have, on one side, those who believe that any activity between consenting adults is appropriate to the expression of lesbian sexuality and that constrictions of any kind support marginalization of lesbians and contribute to sociopolitical repression of sex. (See, for example, Samois, 1981/1987.) Antilesbianism, sodomy laws, etc., are given as examples of such repression. On the other side are those who oppose sadomasochistic (SM) sex and other forms of purposefully introducing power discrepancies into sexual activity. These women argue that such activities replicate sexist and oppressive power dynamics and perpetuate the male images of sexuality that radical feminists and lesbian feminists have fought so hard to eliminate (Calhoun, 1994).

Choice of Orientation

Also debated is whether sexual orientation is a freely chosen political/relational/sexual preference, an inborn characteristic, a social construction that is culturally determined, or some combination (Rich, 1980). Lesbian feminists debate the etiology of lesbianism, the validity of searching for etiologic explanations,[1] and the potential use and abuse of differing explanations. Some argue that biological explanations, aside from failing to reflect the experience of many people, can be used against lesbians in the same way racist theories of genetic differences among racial groups have been used against people of color. Alternatively, social and political explanations do not account for those who displayed a same-sex orientation quite early in life. The notion of preference also involves political risk, however. Liz Kennedy and Madeline Davis argued that the concept of preference is simplistic and dangerous in a heterosexist society. Preference can be used as justification for punishing lesbians for engaging in "capricious and immoral behavior" (Kennedy and Davis, 1994, p. 385).[2]

Do You Have To Be a Lesbian To Be a Feminist?

A third debate centers around the need to be lesbian in order to be a radical feminist, with one side insisting that women need not make that progression personally to validate the choice for women (Faderman, 1981). On the other hand, Marilyn Frye, while agreeing that lesbianism may not be a necessary prerequisite to the project of radical feminism, argued that we would have to fundamentally alter our conceptualization of heterosexual women to accommodate radical feminism within heterosexual lives. A woman does not need to be a lesbian to embody radical feminism, but she cannot follow any patriarchal standard of

---

1. The standard questions are: "Do we inquire about the etiology of heterosexuality?" "What does it mean that we search for explanations of one and not the other?"

2. For more on the biology versus preference debate, see Bunch, 1993; Faderman, 1991; Rich, 1980; and Trebilcot, 1994.

heterosexuality. "You have to be a heretic, a deviant, and undomesticated female. . . . You have to be a Virgin"[3] (Frye, 1992, p. 136).

The Phobias

A more recent debate concerns the lesbian feminist use of such concepts as homophobia and lesbophobia. At first the disagreement centered around the accuracy of the common use of the term homophobia, an irrational fear and hatred of lesbians and gay men, when what was often being referred to was heterosexism, the assumption of heterosexuality, the belief that heterosexuality is superior and the enforcement of heterosexuality as the only viable option for intimate human relationships. More recently, Kitzinger and Perkins (1993) have pointed out that homophobia and lesbophobia are terms invented by psychologists who, however well-intentioned, explain the world in terms of individual pathology rather than social and political phenomena. Use of psychological terms allows the focus to be on sick individuals rather than on political structures. If the disorder is defined as psychological, regardless of who has the disorder, the solution for the problem will still be a psychological one. Furthermore, the term has failed in its attempt to shift attention from *lesbians* as sick to *those who hate lesbians* as sick since now, many lesbians are being diagnosed as having "internalized their homophobia." Kitzinger and Perkins argued that accepting such terms implies acceptance of the psychological paradigm.

> Before psychology invented "homophobia" we wrote about "lesbian oppression," "lesbian hatred," "anti-lesbianism," or "heterosexism." . . . The word "homophobia" defines fear of lesbians as *irrational*. There are, according to the psychological definitions of "homophobia," no rational, sensible, logical rea-

---

3. An explanation of Frye's meaning of virgin is informative: "The word 'virgin' did not originally mean a woman whose vagina was untouched by any penis, but a free woman, one not betrothed, not married, not bound to, not possessed by any man. It meant a female who is sexually and hence socially her own person. In any universe of patriarchy, there are no virgins in this sense. . . . Hence Virgins must be unspeakable, thinkable only as negations. . . . Radically feminist lesbians have claimed positive virginity and have been inventing ways of living it out, in creative defiance of patriarchal definition of the real, the meaningful" (Frye, 1992, p. 133).

sons for fearing lesbianism. This is completely at odds with radical lesbian politics. We cannot think of lesbianism as a challenge to heteropatriarchal structures and values and simultaneously claim that fear of lesbianism is irrational. If lesbianism is a blow against the patriarchy, the bonding of women against male supremacy, then it is entirely *rational* for men to fear it. (Kitzinger and Perkins, 1993, pp. 58-59)

Kitzinger and Perkins pointed out that a liberal psychological understanding of lesbianism holds that lesbians are just like heterosexual women with the relatively minor difference of sexual preference or lifestyle choice and that lesbianism does not threaten the nuclear family or the social order. While this may arguably be true of liberal lesbians, it is not true of lesbian feminist theory, which *does* aspire to a radical reconstitution of the social order. Kitzinger and Perkins pointed out the dangers of using the "we are just like you" strategy: (1) heterosexuals are not that dumb. They already know lesbians are a threat; (2) lesbians may come to believe their own rhetoric about harmlessness (aspiring to powerlessness?); (3) it is not true; (4) while "lying to the enemy" may sometimes be politically expedient, such lies have to be carefully chosen with full knowledge of "the extent to which our politics are defined by those lies" (1993, p. 62).

To Marry or Not to Marry

Related to the phobia debate is the argument concerning marriage and other assimilation versus retention of "outlaw" status. Arguing that lesbians should fight for recognition of the female-female unit as a primary social unit, Calhoun insisted that heterosexual privilege rests on the right of access to sexual, romantic, marital, and familial relationships and that lesbians should fight to open the institution of marriage to nonheterosexuals (Calhoun, 1994, p. 581). Countering that this was simply a liberal demand for access to systems as they are, not a call for radical restructuring, Bunch (1987) argued that not only are lesbians different, but that society needs those differences.

Phelan (1994) insisted that seeking a share of heterosexual privilege by claiming to be the equals of heterosexuals was a losing battle. Inherent in the argument that "we are just like you" was a denigration of lesbianism and lesbian difference. Additionally, that approach fails to challenge heterosexism. Phelan insisted that rejecting a liberal framework of equality did not require (as others have argued) that lesbians forego claims to civil rights, even though civil rights claims have tended to be made from a liberal perspective of inclusion rather than a radical perspective of fundamental change.

Insisting that rights are a form of power, Phelan (1994) argued that newly acquired rights shift the differential of power in favor of those with the new rights. She argued that obtaining rights is one step in a more radical process and civil rights arguments make more sense when seen as one component of oppositional politics rather than when they are thought of as the primary goal. Speaking of her own vulnerability as an academic without lesbian civil rights, she pointed out that lesbians who are out of the closet are forced to depend on the decency of colleagues. Although many universities now have sexual orientation clauses in their nondiscrimination statements, there are few places where there is legislation in place to *enforce* nondiscrimination clauses. Thus, lesbians rely on benevolence, rather than rights: "This is not the position of citizens–it is that of well-treated subjects" (Phelan, 1994, p. 126).

Dual versus Unified Systems Revisited

In arguments similar to those of socialist feminists, some lesbian feminists considered whether heterosexual patriarchy was a single or dual system. Calhoun pointed out many feminist theorists including Bunch, Rubin, Rich, Wittig, and Millett theorized that heterosexism functions as both a product and an essential support of patriarchy and that both lesbians and heterosexual women live with the demand for women to be dependent on and accessible to men (Calhoun, 1994). Calhoun argued that in responding to the charge of undermining the credibility of feminism, lesbians in the 1970s had fashioned a form of assimilationist politics in which they professed their loyalty to feminism, deemphasizing difference. This occurred because it was not yet time to examine heterosexuality as a political system from which heterosexual men *and women* benefited, with heterosexual feminists participating willingly in a powerful class alliance with heterosexual men.

Because of this history, Calhoun (1994) thinks lesbian feminists have difficulty with the notion of dual-systems theory, that is, heterosexuality and patriarchy as two theoretically separate systems. Calhoun acknowledged the discomfort lesbians may feel in comparing heterosexism to gender, race, and class oppression and she noted that claiming lesbianism as an "irreducible dimension of one's political identity" may be a difficult stretch for lesbian feminists. Yet, she insisted that sexuality politics must be separated from gender politics to allow for the development of a specifically lesbian feminist theory and to avoid having to stretch other feminist theories to accommodate lesbianism. It is important to be cognizant of this. Otherwise, feminists may assume that because they are historically intertwined, the collapse of one oppressive system will necessarily bring about the collapse of the other. Calhoun posited that challenging heterosexual society is not the same as challenging patriarchy. The two struggles (lesbian feminist and radical feminist) are not only different, they may even be oppositional. She claims that the focus on patriarchal power relations distracts lesbians from effectively challenging heterosexism. Likewise, the lesbian challenge to enforced heterosexism precludes an effective focus on patriarchy (Calhoun, 1994).

Calhoun pointed out the logic of a dual system, arguing that like capitalism and patriarchy, heterosexuality and patriarchy are analytically distinct. Even with the overthrow of one, the other can still survive. She reminded us that the requirements of the heterosexual system are that men display masculinity and desire for women, and that women, in turn, display femininity and desire for men. The heterosexual system does not necessarily depend on the hierarchy of male over female, but it does privilege heterosexuality over lesbianism. Calhoun used matriarchies as examples of heterosexual systems that may not require female subordination, illustrating the possibility of heterosexism without patriarchy. To illustrate the opposite, she discussed butch and femme roles between lesbians. Calhoun sees such roles as patriarchal despite the lack of heterosexuality.[4]

---

4. The characterization of butch and femme roles as patriarchal is another heavily debated topic. See, for discussion of the butch and femme roles, Faderman, 1992; Kennedy and Davis, 1993; and Nestle, 1981.

CRITIQUE

Lesbian feminism is a critique of heterosexism and sexism in our culture. It does not question whether heterosexuality should exist or whether heterosexuality should be the most common mode of coupling. It protests the devaluing of alternatives to heterosexuality, and it argues against the imposition of any one form of sexual or affectional orientation. Above all, lesbian feminist theory is a critique of a hierarchy–that system that allows for some people to be held as intrinsically more valuable based on the sex of their partner. But it is unlikely to be seen that way.

Just as critiques of racism are thought of as helping only, or at least primarily, people of color, lesbian feminism is likely to be thought of as a theory for *lesbians,* with limited application outside that relatively small population. And so, functionally, if not theoretically, its application is limited.

Queer Theory and Lesbian Feminism

With the advent of the gay and lesbian movement, two perhaps unanticipated things have occurred. First, some radical women are finding more of a theoretical home in "queer theory."[5] Second, some lesbian feminists have determined that heterosexism may be a more salient oppression for them than sexism. With the new movement as an option, and in part as a result of disagreements within feminism, some lesbians are choosing queer theory over feminism, to the consternation of some lesbian feminists who remain concerned that, like their gay movement counterparts before them, queer theorists may forget about women's oppression (Kennedy and Davis, 1994). Instead of the radical feminism that seemed to permeate emerging lesbian communities twenty years ago, women who come to lesbianism in the 1990s encounter the queer movement, which is all too likely to be dominated by men who ignore or trivialize feminism (Trebilcot, 1994).

On the other hand, ignoring the gay movement, as lesbian feminists tended to do, can mean loss of some lesbian history, a history

---

5. Queer theory seeks to examine the experiences of people who are marginalized based on sexual orientation. "Queer studies" examines lesbians, gays, bisexuals, transgendered, and other similarly disparaged people.

that is often best retained in gay communities. It is important to know about the 1950s butches and femmes who showed enormous courage in the face of massive oppression, yet these stories are usually missing from feminist accounts of women's past (Calhoun, 1994). Shane Phelan (1994) insisted that there are some clearly overlapping political interests between gay men and lesbians, even if such interests result from social oppression rather than from self-definition: as long as lesbians are oppressed as "homosexuals," there is a common struggle with gay men. The challenge lies in insisting that gay men join lesbians in challenging hegemonic interpretations of women.

The rhetoric of lesbian feminism seems to have softened with the rise in conservatism. Take, for example, the use of the term heterosexism. Now, in the 1990s, when the term is used, often it means the assumption (possibly benign) of heterosexuality, that is, the unconscious failure to consider alternatives. In the 1970s, heterosexism referred to the heterosexual imperative, that is, the sinister and often oppressive enforcement of a particular sexuality, social organization, and worldview. The increase in cultural and political conservatism appears to be having a closeting effect, too, and may be contributing to a slowing down in lesbian feminist theorizing:

> Many of us have slipped into an uneasy silence or slammed shut the doors of the closets behind us for a second or third time. We need to keep reminding each other that, *as far as we know, nothing like us has ever happened before. As far as we know,* there has never been a Lesbian Move-ment, and we are *global* in our connectedness. Too many lesbians have learned, again, to think of themselves as "small," "tiny," insignificant. We've heard so much about "broader issues" and "the big picture" that some may think that the Lesbian Perspective is a tiny "narrow" one, restricted to an "insignificant" minority. (Penelope, 1990, p. 100, emphasis in original)

Contributions of Lesbian Feminism

Atkinson argued that even if we do not believe in Amazon legends, we seem to need to create them, to have some historical sense of women's resistance to men's oppression (Atkinson, 1974). Lesbian feminism *did* force us to rethink heterosexuality and recognize the heterosexual imperative. In reexamining the effort that goes into maintaining an image of heterosexuality as the only option, we come to appreciate how forced the categories of sexual orientation, family membership, and gender actually are. With the recent combinations of radical lesbian and queer theories, theorists have pointed out that ending patriarchy will not necessarily end heterosexism. Once again, feminists are alerted to the complexities of oppression and the pitfalls of single-issue campaigns: eliminating sexism could still leave many forms of oppression intact.

APPLICATIONS OF LESBIAN FEMINIST THEORY TO SOCIAL WORK PRACTICE

Policy

As noted above, lesbian marriages are seen by some as assimilationist and, therefore, in the realm of liberal feminism. They are seen by others as transformative, fundamentally in opposition to the heterosexual imperative, and therefore supportive of lesbian feminism. Carol Tully (1994) argued for a cross between the two perspectives including a redefinition of the family and inclusion of lesbian (and gay male) families among groups who have access to the social resources and sanctions accorded to heterosexual married couples.

Closely related to the arguments for change in marriage policy is a call for change in policy regarding lesbian and gay parenting. Again, these are, by some definitions, liberal civil rights issues. From another perspective, these changes have the potential to profoundly alter sex and gender constructions. Charlotte Patterson (1994) lists policies that need to be changed including: recognition of lesbian and gay marriages, second-parent adoptions so that both women can be legal parents for their children, and changes in insurance regulations to allow the nonbiological mother to be able to provide family insurance.

Administration

The administrative examples listed here are clearly more issues of access for lesbians than applications of specifically lesbian feminist theory. Although some might argue that providing access to lesbians entails a fundamental redefinition of employee families, it may be difficult to counter the argument that these examples are applications of liberal equality to lesbians.

Lesbians and gay men have long sought domestic partnership coverage to provide benefits to their partners and their partner's children. The University at Buffalo, SUNY, like a growing number of universities and private businesses, provides such benefits to its employees. Coverage includes health, prescription, dental, and vision programs. These benefits were negotiated through the unions representing SUNY employees. Other benefits that lesbian workers sometimes seek include bereavement leave and educational benefits for their families.

Community Organizing and the Need for Lesbian Community

Community organizing is a complicated notion when applied to lesbian communities. For one thing, the term lesbian community has a multitude of meanings. It is used to refer to geographical units, as in the Northampton lesbian community, or to friendship or socializing networks, for example, to refer to lesbian bar-goers or lesbian athletes in a given locality. The term can refer to all U. S. lesbians who have a particular political orientation, for example, the lesbian *feminist* community. To speak of organizing the lesbian community, one would need to clarify which of these or many other meanings one had for the term. There is increasing agreement that it is inaccurate to speak of the lesbian community as though there is a single entity to which most lesbians in America feel belonging. Certainly, a broad-based self-awareness seems to have emerged in the second half of the twentieth century, and in that sense, there is a single lesbian community. In other contexts, it would be more accurate to acknowledge multiple subcommunities, each of which has developed its own culture (Kennedy and Davis, 1994).

On the other hand, the need for common organizing is no less urgent for lesbians than for other marginalized groups, however difficult the definition may be. Marilyn Frye argued for the necessity for an ongoing sense of community, providing the needed support for creative invention of new social systems and to help lesbians retain their insights. "Without a community of sense, an individual cannot keep hold of her radical insights; she becomes confused, she forgets what she knew" (Frye, 1992, p. 8). Rich (1979a) pointed out that it is important to avoid the essentialism of the earlier attempts at building lesbian community when, as radical feminists, the search was for similarity rather than for an appreciation of diversity among lesbians, because without acknowledgment of differences of race and class, as well as other differences among lesbians, not only will the effort fail but lesbians will fail to learn who they really are.

One example of a temporary creation of a temporal/geographical lesbian community is the Michigan Women's Music Festival. For twenty years, thousands of women, predominantly lesbians, have gathered in "women's space," that is, an area that is open only to women for several days in August. In addition to the enormous variety of activities devoted to the creation of women's culture (best addressed under cultural feminist theory), "Michigan" served as a model for regional, national and international women's gatherings. These gatherings function as a means of organizing women while providing entertainment, education, and brief periods of separation from interaction with men and the demands of patriarchal hetero-sexual society.

Group Work

Group work seems like a particularly useful method of intervention for lesbian and gay youth, and a number of authors have commented on the benefits of providing social support and information groups to these populations. (See, for example, Remafedi, 1990; Uribe, 1994.) Lesbian and gay social support groups offer young people an opportunity to find friends, develop social skills, observe positive role models, overcome isolation and rejection, and have fun in safe environments (Remafedi, 1990). It would be helpful to determine whether the adult lesbian and/or gay community could function as a resource providing recreation or support as an adjunct to social group-work interventions (Robinson, 1991).

Social workers might also consider offering support and information groups to family members, or at least encouraging them to contact organizations that provide such services. Remafedi (1990, p. 1175) maintains that few parents can be expected to know how to provide the needed support and guidance for lesbian and gay children. Most parents are lacking in information about lesbians and gays. In response to this, P-FLAG (Parents and Friends of Lesbians and Gays) an international advocacy organization, emerged to provide such services.[6]

One of the most successful and widely emulated programs for lesbian and gay youth is Project 10. The program has four primary purposes: education, reduction in verbal and physical abuse, suicide prevention, and dissemination of accurate AIDS information (Uribe, 1994).

In order for any of these groups to be thought of as applications of lesbian feminist, rather than "queer theory," it would be necessary to examine the specific needs of the girls and women and to help them understand how these might differ from the issues faced by gay boys and men. In some cases, it would be more beneficial for girls to have their own groups so that the combination of sexism and heterosexism could be a primary focus and could be examined from the perspective of the socially subordinated gender. Ideally, girls would be offered the option of joining with boys or gathering on their own. The same caveats apply to the policy example above and the case work example below.

Casework

In her work with lesbian and gay youth in rural areas, Pat Gunther focused on several needs, including redefinition of lesbian and gay lives as positive and acceptable alternatives to heterosexuality. In this way, she attacked the compulsory nature of heterosexuality. Gunther resolved to improve the psychological and social well-being of youth while using herself as a social-change agent.

Gunther advocated to libraries and schools to update materials on lesbians and gays, and to teachers, medical professionals, and ministers to provide affirmative and sensitive services to lesbian and gay youth. Gunther also arranged for role models in a fashion similar to Big Brothers and Big Sisters. She described her openness about her own lesbianism as both a personal lifestyle and a profes-

---

6. Federation of Parents and Friends of Lesbians and Gays, Inc., P.O. Box 27605, Washington, DC 20038-7605. There are over 200 chapters in the U.S. and Canada.

sional practice serving to integrate the personal, professional, and political components of her life.

The social worker can help lesbians address the dilemma and frustration of the common, mutually exclusive demand for closeting *and* being out: if they are closeted, they are accused of being ashamed of who they are; if they are out they are accused of being "in-your-face." As with radical feminism, applying this theory to casework would necessarily involve attention to both personal and social change, but in this case, the worker and clients would have an interest not only in combating sexism, but also in subverting the heterosexual imperative.

Research

The research example is a study of lesbian issues more than an example of how lesbian feminist theory could be used to formulate a new approach to conducting research, that is, the topic rather than the method are lesbian feminist. Judith Bradford and Caitlin Ryan, members of the National Lesbian and Gay Health Foundation conducted a survey of lesbians because they believed that lesbian health care concerns were ignored by mainstream medicine. They wanted to end invisibility, discrimination, and lack of health care services for lesbians, and they wanted to ensure that lesbian health care needs were defined by lesbians.

They set out with the clear intention of producing social action research, that is, research that not only examines a topic, but also, in the process and outcome of the research, promotes social justice. A specifically lesbian feminist component of the project was that the researchers defined obstetric and gynecological issues and care as potentially being completely unrelated to reproductive health even though the women seeking such care might be sexually active.

Any social work that uses lesbian feminist theory to guide intervention would need to include some attempt to destroy the heterosexual imperative. Lesbian feminist social work would not simply seek inclusion of lesbians in the fight for women's liberation and group empowerment. It would redefine basic social units, such as family constellations, and restructure society so that multiple forms of human connections, and the social structures on which they are built, are valued for their contributions.

Chapter 5

Cultural and Ecofeminist Theories

CONTRIBUTIONS AND CONTRIBUTORS

Distinctions are made here between radical and cultural feminism although some theorists argue that they are actually variations on the same theme. One of the overlapping tenets, carried over from the earlier stages of radical feminism, is that gender stands as the fundamental division among humans, privileged over class, race, and other sources of inequality. Another important similarity is the call for a radical restructuring of society. A definitive distinction is that radical feminists seek to eliminate sex roles whereas cultural feminists premise a profound and pervasive difference between women and men and glorify those aspects ascribed to womanhood that they consider superior to, or more valuable than, opposing aspects in men. For example, women are said to be nurturing and caregiving, and these aspects are privileged over the competitiveness ascribed to men.

Alice Echols (1989) differentiated between the implementation of radical and cultural feminist theories by describing radical feminism as a political movement that was dedicated to *eliminating* the sex-class system. She described cultural feminism as a countercultural movement that was aimed at *reversing* the ways that women and men were valued in our culture. Differences between cultural feminism and ecofeminism, on the other hand, are not so easily articulated. The departure seems to be more one of emphasis than theory, with ecofeminists carving out issues of peace, ecology, and spirituality. For that reason, ecofeminist ideas are included here.

The origins of cultural feminism go back at least to the mid-1800s when Margaret Fuller published *Woman in the Nineteenth Century* (1843). Fuller countered the mechanistic view of the Enlightenment rationalists with a romanticist's focus on knowledge gained through emotion and intuition.[1] Her ideas foreshadowed twentieth-century cultural feminists' call for separatism as a means of developing the self, as well as their initial concern for developing a sense of community among women, and for connectedness in relationships (Donovan, 1985). Nineteenth-century cultural feminists posited the existence of an ancient matriarchal religion. Infused with female attributes of pacifism, cooperation, nonviolent settlement of differences, altruism, and other positive characteristics emanating from the experience of motherhood, the Matriarchate was contrasted with men's violent tendencies, traceable to their prehistoric hunting and fishing roles in which death, rather than life, was celebrated (Donovan, 1985). Women were said to be needed in the public sphere, not only to ensure their own development, but also to reform a social and political world corrupted by the wars and tyranny of men. In the 1890s Anna Julia Cooper argued that women had a special humanizing attribute with which they would change the public sphere; however, Frances E. W. Harper, in a critique that would be repeated over a century later, questioned whether any group, including women, had a "monopoly on purity" (Donovan, 1985, p. 24).

Social workers who practiced in the late nineteenth and early twentieth century are often connected with this branch of feminist thought, as the following passage from Josephine Donovan's work suggests:

> They believed that women were different and that they had a separate cultural and ethical heritage, described by Fuller, Gilman et al., as maternal, cooperative, altruistic and life-affirmative. This vision provided a fundamental motivation for the

---

1. In America this romanticism was called transcendentalism. Countering the liberal posture that government was needed to "shield . . . the individual from . . . tyrannizing forces," transcendentalists held that people were inherently capable of unfolding and developing in a positive direction when unimpeded by interference from society or government (Donovan, 1985, p. 32).

social reform-pacifist feminists of the turn-of-the-century—women like Jane Addams, Emily Greene Balch, Crystal Eastman, Lillian Wald, Sophonisba Breckenridge, and Florence Kelley. (1985, p. 54)

Late twentieth-century cultural feminism borrowed from and built on early radical and cultural feminist theories and from contemporary radical feminists as well. Firestone's (1970) work called for a "feminist revolution" that would include a fundamental reconceptualization of the family, traditional sex roles, and child-rearing practices and an end to motherhood.[2] Although generally taken as a radical feminist critique leading to socialist feminist analysis, Firestone's *The Dialectic of Sex*, by basing arguments about the origin of sexist oppression in biology, actually renewed feminist interest in the key concept of cultural feminism: women as profoundly different from men (Donovan, 1985).

Ecofeminism, as noted, is often indistinguishable from cultural feminism. Introduced in the 1970s by Françoise d'Eaubonne, the term "eco-féminisme" referred to feminists whose primary concerns were overpopulation and destruction of natural resources. Ecofeminists saw these problems as having arisen secondary to a male-identified approach to living in the world (d'Eaubonne, 1974). More recently, the term ecofeminism has come to refer to a cluster of feminist theories that explore similarities, overlaps, and intersections between the oppression of women and exploitation of the environment (Braidotti et al., 1994; Lahar, 1991). From both ecofeminist and the broader cultural feminist formulations came the idea of the need for women to rebuild or create a new woman's culture.

THE THEORY

Women are characterized by cultural feminists as quite different from men, but there is disagreement as to whether the differences

---

2. Recall that Firestone advocated a biological revolution: women would use technological advances to free themselves from reproduction. This, in turn, would free them from the unnecessary division of labor that had been based on natural reproduction.

are innate or environmentally induced. Some attribute female character and culture to colonization[3] by men. Others offer a biological explanation (cf., Jane Alpert, "Mother Right," 1973). The proponents of biology describe gender differences as immutable and incontrovertible (Echols, 1989), but rather than present women's biology as problematic, as had Firestone, these theorists present it as the solution to women's problems (Jaggar, 1983). Male violence–from war to rape–is blamed on male anatomy (Brownmiller, 1975) while women's biological capacity to give birth, whether employed or not, is believed to ensure the presence of nurturance, warmth, connectedness, and the common sense necessary for the continuation of the species (Gilligan, 1982).

For environmentalists like psychologist Carol Gilligan, women's nature is seen as socially constructed.[4] The outcome of socialization is that girls and women tend toward relational connections and boys and men adhere to rational, logical rules of justice. Aggression is thought to result from a failure to connect with other humans and from viewing *individuals* rather than the *relationships* among people as paramount (Gilligan, 1982). Environmentalists argue that women's voices and perspectives are needed to correct the imbalances that have been perpetrated by a culture that was built on male "voices."

> The voice that set the dominant key in psychology, in political theory, in law and in ethics, was keyed to separation: the separate self, the individual acting alone, the possessor of natural rights, the autonomous moral agent. . . . Speaking of connection, of responsiveness and responsibility in relationships, women heard themselves sounding either selfish or selfless, because the opposition of self and other was so pervasive and so powerfully voiced in the public discourse. (Gilligan, 1995, p. 121)

---

3. Colonization is the process of claiming the right to control over another's life and the benefits of that person's labor. It can also be understood as the process of usurping another group's land and its resources; for example, when Europeans claimed ownership of Native American lands, they enacted the process of colonization.

4. Gilligan (1982) still sees women's nature as integrally related to childrearing responsibilities.

Regardless of etiological theories, both environmentalists like Gilligan and naturalists like Alpert agree on two things: motherhood matters, and women's nature is superior to men's.

The Place of Spirituality

Cultural feminists often stress the spiritual potential of the women's movement. Feminist spirituality can be divided into three general strands.[5] The first includes critiques of traditional male-centered religions, particularly criticisms of Judeo-Christian religions,[6] exemplified by theologians such as Mary Daly (1968/1985), Renita Weems (1988), and Judith Plaskow (1979, 1990), but this strand also includes critiques from outside of the Judeo-Christian tradition, for example, the work of Paula Gunn Allen (1991) and Fatima Mernissi (1987).

Mary Daly called the women's movement of the 1970s a spiritual movement that "has the potential to awaken a new and post-patriarchal spiritual consciousness" (Echols, 1989, p. 253, quoting Daly). In the process of creating a new system of thought and language by which women could free their minds from patriarchal chains, Daly (1978) revived the romantic tradition of depending on intuition to uncover the "patriarchal reversals" of language that obscure meaning.

The second strand of feminist spirituality includes various goddess religions, discussed both by those who examine ancient histories of woman-centered spirituality, such as Riane Eisler (1987), Marija Gimbutas (1982), and Merlin Stone (1976), and by those who are involved in creating new visions of goddess worship, for example, Z. Budapest (1986). The third strand is ecofeminist spirituality, which attends to the connections between the natural world and feminist spirituality, as described by Paula Gunn Allen (1990),

---

5. I am indebted to Patty Kaiser for pointing out this way of grouping the different directions of feminist spirituality.

6. This was reminiscent of Matilda Joslyn Gage's *Woman, Church and State* (1893), which documented the damage done to women in the name of religion, and Elizabeth Cady Stanton's *The Woman's Bible* (1895 and 1898), which was a reworking of the male-focused Christian bible. In thinking that, as we have seen, surfaced again in twentieth-century radical and cultural feminist theory, Gage had charged that the church "trained men to believe that woman was but created as a plaything for their passions" (Donovan, 1985, p. 41, quoting Gage).

for example. The distinction between goddess religions and ecofeminist spirituality is not always clear-cut, since ecofeminists,
although focusing primarily on communing with and healing the
earth, often draw on goddess worship, as in the work of Irene Javors
(1990) and Starhawk (1990).

The Importance of the Feminine

Cultural feminists celebrate women for the qualities men denigrate and fear (Jaggar, 1983). Essentialist[7] arguments concerning
women's goodness challenge dominant assumptions and foretell a
revolution resulting in "a proud gynocratic world that runs on the
power of women" (Echols, 1989, p. 256, quoting Morgan, 1978).
Similar to nineteenth-century predictions, this change would be
accomplished by integrating the feminine into the public world and
ending all violence.

Cultural feminists want to coalesce the women's movement and
eliminate the splits among women. To accomplish these goals, they use
claims of universalism and downplay differences, including very
important differences. In this regard, African-American women pointed out the tokenism and marginalization of their concerns at conferences and other functions (Echols, 1989). In a frequently cited work,
Audre Lorde (1984) criticized Daly's *Gyn/Ecology* for maintaining a
Western European, Judeo-Christian frame of reference in its cata-
loguing of worldwide atrocities against women. Lorde pointed out
that the work supported only negative images of the cultures of
women of color, and while it offered instruction on ancient goddess
religions, it ignored non-European goddess images.

Although there is often mention of a prehistoric time when the
world was women-centered (Daly, 1978; Griffin, 1979), white cultural feminists speak, for the most part, of creating a *new* women's
culture: "I invent, dis-cover and re-member" (Daly, 1978, p. 24).
African-American women writers, on the other hand, turn to more
recent history of black civilizations, preserved by their mothers,
whom they call revolutionary in their conservation and recreation of

---

7. Essentialism is the assumption that all members of a group, in this case
women, share certain characteristics and that while individuals and subgroups may
vary, they are the same in important or essential ways.

an Afrocentric worldview and culture, (Collins, 1990). Collins called black women "cultural workers" whose tasks were "to make culture, transmit folkways, norms, customs . . . build shared ways of seeing the world that insured . . . survival . . . . This culture was a culture of resistance, essential to struggle for group survival" (p. 147). De Lauretis (1990) noted the attention to cultural identity in works by Cherrie Moraga, Alice Walker, and Audre Lorde. More and more women of color seek to maintain the cultures of their mothers, arguing for the retention of their mothers' moral vision as the foundation of feminism (Donovan, 1985).

Supporters of cultural separatism contend that feminists should learn from previous movements that, despite men's capacity to learn and regardless of disavowal of biological explanations for male behavior, women need to come together to formulate theory and strategy–as women, without men (Sloan-Hunter, 1988). This is quite similar to the separatism described by lesbian feminist theorists. The Sloan-Hunter reference notwithstanding, in this application, the focus tends to be less on political analysis and more on building culture. Women focus on developing women's enterprises and services that are owned by and serve women. Sometimes these enterprises have an expressly political agenda, as in women's centers that offer their space to women's political groups. At other times, the separatist organizations are intended more for retreat and entertainment as in women's music festivals.[8]

Cultural feminists who emphasize environmental influences on human psychology and behavior are not without hope for men, however. Women's culture holds promise for all people; men are considered trainable. Donovan argued that contemporary cultural feminists are more likely than their nineteenth-century predecessors

---

8. Physically building a separatist women's cultural community, which actively discouraged membership by men, is not a concept new to this century: Kisner (1972, p. 47) quoted the following report from *Woodhull and Claflin's Weekly* of October 23, 1873: "The establishment of a women's community within the limits of the town of Woburn, about twelve miles from Boston, was begun yesterday by the formal raising of the frame of the first building. In this community all the land is to be owned by women, and so far as the management of the affairs of the village is concerned, woman suffrage is to be realized to the extent of the utter political disqualification of (men)."

to systematize cultural feminist ideology and to teach it. Women's and men's natures are now seen as more changeable, whereas prior cultural feminists had often insisted on the immutability of women's and men's natures (Donovan, 1985). Still, differences between women and men are thought to remain significant, and contemporary cultural feminists often speak of women as being more closely connected to natural forces, thus seeming to accept as positive the association of men with culture and women with nature. This is especially evident in ecofeminist writing.

Ecofeminist Theory

Ecofeminists often argue that women are closer to nature, but they contest the ways that the association between women and nature has been used to disempower women (Roach, 1991). Proponents of the idea of a positive association between women and nature include Mary Daly (1978), Susan Griffin (1978), Vandana Shiva (1990), and Starhawk (1990). Although they accept the association, they insist that patriarchy devalues traits such as compassion and nonviolence, which are traditionally associated with women. They argue that infusing these "feminine values" into ecological theory will improve our interactions with the natural environment (Davion, 1994). All these authors have discussed the woman/nature connection in spiritual terms, thus continuing the association of spiritual feminism with the position of "nature ecofeminists" (King, 1990) and cultural feminism.

Ecofeminism and Other Ecological Traditions

Ecofeminists often turn to a branch of ecological work called Deep Ecology to examine the links between ecology and feminism while continuing to distinguish ecofeminist views from those of other ecologists who are less concerned with women's issues and perspectives.[9] The term "deep ecology" refers generally to approaches opposed to

---

9. Deep ecologists, in turn, distinguish their work from "shallow ecology," or that segment of the ecological movement which focuses on pollution and depletion of natural resources, and focuses primarily on the ecological problems of developed countries (Cuomo, 1994).

anthropocentrism (the centrality of humans) or, more specifically, to supporters of the "Gaia hypothesis." This hypothesis, named for the goddess of earth in Greek mythology (Mariechild, 1981), was developed by Lynn Margulis and James Lovelock. It holds that the earth and all its systems function as an organic whole, complete with self-regulatory properties (Braidotti et al., 1994).

> The major tenet of the Gaia hypothesis is the assumption that Gaia is a total self-organizing and self-reproducing, organic, spatio-temporal and teleological system with the goal of maintaining itself . . . by diversification, co-operation, and mutualism. Gaia and its sub-systems are organized hierarchically with mutualism between the different levels of hierarchies. . . . Man's (sic) development of the technosphere is viewed as a threat to the survival of Gaia. Therefore adherents to the Gaia hypothesis present a total critique of techno-bureaucratic development, because it fundamentally alters essential ecological regulatory mechanisms. (p. 153)

Deep ecologists criticize the anthropocentrism inherent in the domination of nature by humans. Domination, it is argued, alienates people from the environment, destroys nature in the process, and leads to the destruction of humans—since we depend on the environment for our survival (Braidotti et al., 1994).

Although deep ecologists examine exploitation of the *environment* and recognize the contribution of social factors, they tend to downplay the importance of exploitation of *humans* and the multiplicity of social oppressions (Cuomo, 1994; Slicer, 1994). Ecofeminists argue that deep ecologists misunderstand the daily survival needs of women because the ecology movement tends to be composed of white, male, middle-class professionals who are out of touch with the labor involved in the daily maintenance functions for which women tend to be held responsible (Salleh, 1993).

Val Plumwood maintained that respect, compassion, and responsibility serve as the best guides to proper relationships between humans and nature (1991). Rather than characterizing nature and humans as a single connected whole, an idea popularized by the Gaia hypothesis—which Plumwood refers to as the indistinguishability account—she repeats Grimshaw's (1986) point that one can only care for others if one can distinguish them from oneself and distinguish others' needs from one's own. "Respect for the other results neither from the containment of self nor from a transcendence of self, but is an expression of self in relationship, not egoistic self as merged with the other, but self as embedded in a network of essential relationships with distinct others" (Plumwood, 1991, pp. 20-21).

CRITIQUE

It is important to place changes in feminism within their historical contexts. The activism of the 1960s and 1970s declined in the 1980s and 1990s as the country's political mood shifted toward the conservative. The dismantling of social welfare services accompanied by rhetoric about individual culpability for social ills was the 1980s backdrop for the ascendancy of cultural feminism. Cocks (1984) argued that ironically, instead of recreating the world, cultural feminists unwittingly joined with "phallocentrists," by highlighting women's inherent difference from men, whereby "the dominant culture and the counterculture engage in a curious collusion, in which . . . a rebellious feminism takes up its assigned position at the negative pole" (1984, p. 113). Echols (1989) called cultural feminists' celebration of femininity a "recycling of stereotypes" about women. It is not difficult for conservatives to support the cultural feminist position while interpreting difference as inferior or incapable (Donovan, 1985). Calling cultural feminism reactionary, Elshtain argued that the idea of women as intrinsically morally superior was problematic on three counts: in attributing female superiority to physiology, in assuming rationality was a flawed male trait, and in portraying women as passive and powerless victims of male violence (Eisenstein, 1983).

Twentieth-century cultural feminists moved away from biological determinism (Donovan, 1985), but even when women's nature is credited to powerlessness, the trap is similar. If moral superiority is attributed to powerlessness, it will disappear as soon as women have power and begin to take on the characteristics of powerful people (Echols, 1989).

Similarly, Elshtain (1982) argued that if women are indeed more moral, compassionate, and caring–resulting from their roles in the birth and childrearing process–changing women's and men's roles might be a mistake. Rather, if morality and responsibility emerge from women's spheres, those spheres should be preserved and perhaps extended to men. However, the loss of the private sphere accompanied by significant alteration of current male-female intimate arrangements might preclude the development of those positive characteristics that cultural feminists associate with women.

Cultural revolution, portrayed as a fundamental prerequisite for feminist progress, was neither achievable nor sufficient in its aims. The tendency of feminist culture-building to focus on separatism and individual healing processes became nonrevolutionary. Instead of sustaining a radical feminism as intended, women's culture often encourages withdrawal from the struggle (Echols, 1989) and shelter-seeking rather than disruption of patriarchal structures (Hess, Langford, and Ross, 1988).

The organizations, especially the financial arrangements of ones that sought to build women's institutions, have also come under attack. The intent was to provide economic security for less privileged women by hiring disenfranchised women, for example, lesbians, working-class, and Third World women, and by allowing workers time for outside political activities. Unfortunately, the reality of "spare time" for politics did not always materialize, and it soon became evident that functioning in a capitalist system favored people with resources–however "alternative" a cultural feminist venture might have been conceptually (Echols, 1989). In some cases, for example, the Feminist Economic Network and the economically successful Olivia Cruises, there were no attempts to evade, analyze, or dismantle capitalism, but simply to join it, in these cases, as businesses catering to women (Echols, 1989).

In other ways, however, cultural feminism succeeded in that it achieved ascendance and contributed to building a positive view of women's culture (Echols, 1989). Development of women's businesses and other institutions was certainly not wholly without merit. Women's publishing houses, distributing companies, and bookstores have provided literature about ongoing developments in feminist thought and activity. The feminist writings of women of color (see the bibliographies at the end of the book) are now more widely available and are more often acknowledged by a broad range of feminists as central, rather than peripheral, to feminism. "Woman-space" *does* offer a respite from male supremacy and from psychological–and sometimes physical–assaults by men (Jaggar, 1983) as well as a chance to experience women's support and participate in a celebration of women (Echols, 1989).

APPLICATION OF CULTURAL FEMINISM TO SOCIAL WORK PRACTICE

Policy

Some goals of cultural feminist social work on a policy level might be to eliminate the Judeo-Christian model as the base of policy and to incorporate the feminine into the public world by focusing on the positive attributes traditionally ascribed to women, for example, compassion and attention to human relationships. Arguing that law and social policy should pay more attention to relationships between people, Minow (1990) insisted that focusing on relationships provides a new model for dealing with problems of difference. This same approach could be used to design workplace policies regarding childbirth and child care, for example.

Administration/Organization

Smith (1986) advocated for permanent autonomous institutions for black feminists, including political, social service, and artistic organizations, all of which would contribute to the quality of life of men, women, and children. She included in her information for social workers, documentation of the flourishing literature and music that contribute to black feminist cultural work. Social workers employed in service agencies could, by participating in such efforts, contribute to the development of black feminist culture.

Community Organizing

In the early 1980s a lesbian land-collective in eastern Kentucky advertised that it was expanding its group and searching for women committed to developing and using a cooperative living arrangement and implementing a consensus decision-making process. Members of the collective wanted to construct a new community that was owned, built, governed, and shared by women (Jaggar, 1983). The idea of creating a separate culture was infused with some older radical feminist concerns for community and interdependence.

A similar cooperative, Oregon Women's Land, operates in the Northwest. It consists of a core of women who live there but welcome those who come for a short or lengthy respite. Social work involvement in such enterprises might be as minimal as keeping up-to-date on these activities and informing women who might be interested in such an all-encompassing commitment to build a woman's culture. Alternatively, a social worker might assist residents in identifying resources that might be available to them or assist in the process of obtaining 501-c-3 (nonprofit) status for the purpose of receiving tax-free donations.

Another example of community organizing comes from ecofeminism. Since "minority" communities often bear the brunt of pollution, it is not surprising that women of color, especially those who live in poverty, have organized, not to save forests, but to save their neighborhoods from environmental destruction. In 1986, the City Council of Los Angeles made plans to build a thirteen-acre incinerator that would burn 2,000 tons of waste a day. The plan called for the incinerator to be placed in a poor, residential community populated by people of color. The women in the community organized against the planned threat to their homes and their health (Hamilton, 1990). The women were outraged by statements that congenital deformities and cancers associated with such projects were "acceptable risks." Called "irrational, uninformed, and disruptive," by supporters of the incinerator, (p. 220) the women nevertheless were successful in defending their community against the project.

Group Work

Using Gilligan's and Belenky's work as guiding theoretical approaches, Elizabeth Rubin (1992) designed a group for adolescent girls. A primary goal was to help the girls find and validate their inner voices. Rubin also sought to help the girls learn to live in a culture that is still controlled by men and to guide the girls toward valuing "relatedness, community, ecology, consensus, and healing" (p. 77). Her group was conducted at a high school, but she advocated incorporating the model into earlier grade levels, prior to the onset of adolescence, at which time girls are said to "lose their voice."

Casework

A social worker using cultural feminism as a guide for casework intervention might encourage the development of women's spirituality from a feminist perspective or support an increasing cultural identity of women clients, particularly awareness of and greater identification with their mothers' cultures. Such work might also focus on individual healing from the androcentric corruption of society.

Drake (1992) described a process by which a woman may engage, with the assistance of a social worker or other counselor, in a personal transformation through undertaking a metaphorical journey. Drake used mythology to structure her work, encouraging women to find meaning for themselves and to follow the path to an authentic life by using "embedded personal narrative in the framework offered by the hero story" (p. 52). She discussed the use of the "journey" metaphor as a four-step problem-solving process: (1) *hearing the call*, in which a woman may choose or be forced into some important change in her life; (2) *envisioning the rebirth*, wherein a woman must formulate a dream, relying on her inner strength, while maintaining her integrity and authenticity as a woman in a male-dominated world; (3) *forecasting the journey ahead*, in which a woman envisions a psychospiritual death, struggle, rebirth, and return to the place from which her journey began; and finally, (4) *taking the journey*, in which a woman acts out the process envisioned in the forecast. The worker's role is to assist the woman in finding the resources and inner strength to undertake the journey "with courage and dignity" (Drake, 1992, p. 64).

Using feminist spirituality, Russell (1990) advocated an approach that could be used to apply ecofeminism to casework. Arguing that "the patriarchal psychology of Freud is being superseded by a more nurturing and holistic view of the human personality" (p. 226), Russell suggested meditating to increase a sense of bonding with the earth and to try to bring oneself into harmony with natural cycles. By such action, "we align ourselves with the regenerative powers of the Earth" (p. 229). This, she believed, would transform both the self and the world.

It should be noted here that the much esteemed psychodynamic psychological work of the theorists and clinicians at the Stone Center at Wellesley College (Jordan et al., 1991) is based largely on Carol Gilligan's work, and so fits into the model of cultural feminist practice.

Research

Susan Griffin's (1978) book, *Woman and nature: The roaring inside her,* is an excellent example of cultural feminist thought applied to research. The research topic is, as the title of the book indicates, woman's relationship to, and oneness with, nature. The method, Griffin pointed out, is quite unconventional. By use of insight and by interweaving cognitive with emotional processes, Griffin explored male and female "voices," and thus, the male and female parts of the self. Griffin argued powerfully for the use of such a feminist synthesis of thought and feeling as an alternative to patriarchal thought (Reinhartz, 1992).

Chapter 6

Womanism: African-American Women's Feminist Thought

BACKGROUND

African-American women have contributed significantly to the development of all of the divisions of feminist theory examined in this book. Liberal, radical, cultural, lesbian, socialist, postmodern, and global feminism have been heavily influenced by African-American feminist theorists. In addition, black women writers and theorists developed a new branch of feminist theory. Although some women of color who are not African-Americans have written about womanism, and some of that work is included here, the writers whose work is discussed in this chapter are, by and large, black women theorists and activists.

Not all the writers included in this section call their theory by the same name. Some prefer the term womanist over feminist, believing that the former more accurately reflects the work of black women (Brown, 1990; Ogunyemi, 1985; Walker, 1984). Some describe themselves simply as feminists, (hooks, 1990); others say they are black feminists (Collins, 1990) or Africana Womanists (Hudson-Weems, 1993). The term womanist continues to be widely used among black feminist theologians, but writers in other disciplines are now more likely to describe their work as black feminism or African-American feminism. This chapter retains the name womanism because the term was used by the African-American writers who first developed this branch of theory and because it highlights the unique contributions of black theorists and activists.

Historically, the projects that black women have undertaken constitute both an assessment of the problems women face within oppressive structures and a statement of what should be done to solve those problems. The description of one such project is used here as an introduction to womanist thought since starting with a history of abstract, theoretical concepts would understate the centrality of activism to womanist theory. Theorizing accompanied the work, but *doing* social change was more important. This is evident in the nineteenth century black women's organization, The Independent Order of Saint Luke, to which Elsa Barkley Brown (1990) retrospectively applied the term womanist.

Founded in Baltimore in 1867 by Mary Prout, The Independent Order of Saint Luke began as a women's sickness and death mutual benefit organization. In 1895, under the direction of Maggie Lenna Walker, the Order organized a juvenile branch that, among other things, offered an educational loan fund for young people. Just as other societies of the time, it combined insurance and banking functions with social and political activities. The Order ran a department store, which provided a number of job opportunities to black women as this work was considered significantly better than more commonly available jobs, for example, tobacco labor or service in private homes.

The Order organized a Penny Savings Bank in recognition of the limited economic resources of black women who, despite meager earnings, were deeply committed to the development and maintenance of a mutual assistance network among black women (Brown, 1990). The Order also published a weekly newspaper, *St. Luke Herald*, devoted to expanding economic opportunities–particularly for women–within the black community. The *St. Luke Herald* addressed such issues as segregation, lynching, and the lack of educational opportunities for black children.

The motto of the Independent Order of Saint Luke, was *The Hand That Rocks the Cradle Rules the World* (Brown, 1990). Black women did not assume a contradiction between domesticity and political action (Giddings, 1988). They used the motto to indicate that it was not necessary to abandon the role of mother to achieve economic and political goals. They saw these goals as supporting rather than conflicting with, attention to their families and communities (Brown, 1990).

During her leadership of The Order, Maggie Lenna Walker contended that the expansion of women's economic and political roles was essential, and that without women's progress the entire race would fail to achieve its full potential. She argued in favor of supporting black-owned businesses and demanded that black businesses provide jobs to black rather than white women since black women experienced high unemployment rates. She also saw black employment in black businesses as a way to stem the continuous loss of skills, resources, and finances to white communities. Her plan was to build a self-sufficient community independent of economic reliance on whites (Brown, 1990).

The Place of Theory Building

Barbara Christian (1988) argued that for people of color, theorizing is more often dynamic than static. She maintained that the dynamism is more reflective of life and is a necessary balance to static hegemonic prescriptions of what thinking, writing, and theorizing ought to be. Her position was that black women's activism was often at the heart of the work, with theory sometimes emerging later. Christian (1988) expressed concern about the separation between theory and activism that sometimes occurs as theory increases in complexity. She insisted that without activism informing the theory, positive social change will not occur.

Christian (1989) also expressed concern over the co-optation of marginal viewpoints in theory building, notably in academic circles. She cautioned against generalizations concerning culture, language, and gender, and she argued that activism is sometimes sacrificed to the development of obscure theories, with theory building then described as *being* rather than *supporting* activism. Over valuing abstract philosophical ideas, she warned, can easily tend toward dismissal of other writings as unsophisticated.

> [Black women's writing] is called "political," "social protest," or "minority" literature, which in this ironic country has a pejorative sound, meaning that it lacks craft and has not transcended the limitations of racial, sex, or class boundaries--

that it does not do what "good" literature does: express our universal humanity. (Christian, 1985, p. 160)

Yamada (1983) agreed that the political writings of women of color are often discounted, pointing out that feminist activism by virtually any "out group" of women is mistaken for a personal as opposed to an ideological perspective, and the two are seen as contradictory.

In Defense of Feminism

Despite the lengthy history of black feminist organizing (Higginbotham, 1993), uniform support among black women and men for feminist movement or for womanism has not existed (Joseph and Lewis, 1981). Some men and nonfeminist women members of black communities see black women's interest in feminism as an imitation of white women. Smith and Smith (1983) contended that there was a concerted and relatively successful effort in the 1970s to dissuade black communities from supporting feminism. Smith and Smith argued that black men and the white power structure were threatened enough with the political potential inherent in a cross-racial bonding among women that black women's involvement in feminist activism was disparaged, discounted, and denied. Nor has knowledge of the historical role of black women in women's rights efforts been generally available since then (hooks, 1990). Even today, too few people know that black women have *long* been involved in examining and attacking racism and sexism, and that they have often attacked both systems simultaneously.[1]

According to Joseph and Lewis (1981), black women's attitudes changed considerably in the early 1980s, and although most black women do not feel they are part of *the* women's movement, they do support feminist ideals. In fact, it has often been reported that black women are more supportive of feminist organizations and activism than white women, and most black women believe that race and gender issues should be given *equal* priority (Wilcox, 1990).

---

1. Witness abolitionist Sojourner Truth; and writer, editor, and antislavery lecturer Frances E. W. Harper; and Anna Julia Cooper, who argued that it was not only white racism but also black male sexism that kept black women out of college in the late 1800s (Flexner, 1959/1971).

Although many womanists concentrate on activist efforts, others have clearly been more theoretical in their approach. For example, Elizabeth Higginbotham (1992) described the complexities of race in America by arguing that race functions as a metalanguage.[2] That is, the notion of race, which is a social construction like gender or class, serves as a lens through which people are viewed. It also serves as a rationale for the construction of social relationships. Because the notion grew out of a master/slave relationship, class is also a component of race, despite the presence of a black middle-class and a small black-upper-class.

Race is an all-encompassing and powerful determinant of people's lives. Race and gender are experienced, however, quite differently by black and white women because gendered identity is constructed and is often represented in polarized and antagonistic ways for black and white women (Higginbotham, 1992). White women, for example, are often unaware of their own experience of race or the privileges accorded to them as members of the dominant group; thus, it is sometimes difficult for white women to understand the importance that many black women put on race, or the relative constancy of the effects of social perceptions of racial differences.

But race cannot be separated from gender since both are experienced simultaneously. Because of this, black women who work toward feminist goals tend to focus their efforts at the intersection of sex and race, and usually, as with the women of The Independent Order of Saint Luke, on class struggles as well.

THE THEORY

Paula Giddings (1985) documented the history of African-American women, and Patricia Hill Collins (1990) detailed current black feminist thought. Both works illuminate the specific point of view that can only emerge from the dynamic interaction between black

---

2. According to the *Merriam Webster's Collegiate Dictionary*, 10th edition: a metalanguage is a language used to explain another language. In the metalanguage of race, we discuss race and racial differences with a language in which race hierarchies are so intrinsic that even in a discussion of racial issues, the racism in our terms is often invisible.

women and the multiple systems of oppression, historical and current, against which they have struggled.

Defining Black Womanism

> Womanist. From *womanish*. . . . A black feminist or feminist of color. From the black folk expression of mother to female children, "You acting womanish," i.e., like a woman. Usually referring to outrageous, audacious, courageous or *willful* behavior. . . . Responsible. In charge. *Serious.*
> *Also:* A woman who loves other women, sexually and/or nonsexually. Appreciates and prefers women's culture, women's emotional flexibility . . . and women's strength. Sometimes loves individual men, sexually and/or nonsexually. Committed to survival and wholeness of entire people, male **and** female. Not a separatist, except periodically, for health. Traditionally universalist. . . . Traditionally capable. . . . Womanist is to feminist as purple is to lavender. (Walker, 1983, p. xi)

Womanism is a philosophy and a consciousness that concurrently addresses racism while it attends to sexism in the black community and in the culture at large. It focuses on racial, cultural, sexual, economic, and political matters (Brown, 1990). Womanism uses racial consciousness to underscore the positive aspects of African-American life (Ogunyemi, 1985). But womanism does not focus solely on a social agenda. Self-healing is among the goals (Brown, 1990). Alice Walker (1983) and bell hooks (1993) have argued that a belief in the capacity for both personal and social change is essential for black women and necessary in a culture that so often seems bent on the destruction of black women.

To survive, despite racist and sexist valuations, black women need to define themselves quite differently from the way they are viewed by those in power. It is necessary to claim all aspects of personhood so that neither race, nor sex, nor class are hidden or discounted (Christian, 1985). All aspects of the self are acknowledged; both action and articulation are emphasized in womanist theory (Lorde, 1984).

As noted, womanism combines rather than dichotomizes theory and action. Other dichotomies that womanism dispels include the either/or characterizations of race and sex, which women often felt within black male and white female organizations. Womanists argue instead that such characterizations contribute to hostility and fail to sufficiently allow for overlapping categories. Because of categorical thinking, it becomes more difficult, if not impossible, to conceive of race, sex, and class as a single consciousness with a single struggle needed to overcome them (Brown, 1990).

African-American feminists and womanists have argued that additive models of oppression–in which oppressive systems are seen as parallel and only occasionally intersecting–hide from view, and therefore from change, interlocking systems. That means we cannot consider one system of domination, then move on to consider others successively, without exploring the intersections. It also means we need to revamp theories of oppression as we learn more. When we expand our understanding of racism, we need to reexamine our understanding of sexism and classism, in light of what we now know about how racism operates.

Besides failing to account for the mutual dependencies of systems of oppression, additive models do not account for people of mixed racial and ethnic identity (Collins, 1990). When our categories become blurred, for example with biracial or multiracial people, we often see how limiting the study of a single category of dominance can be. Instead, womanism proposes a "both/and" worldview (Brown, 1990). Instead of posing race and gender as contradictory opposites where a woman is expected to identify either as black or as a woman,[3] womanism allows for a unified whole (Brown, 1990; Ogunyemi, 1985). Working from an assumption of interlocking systems is a paradigmatic shift away from focusing on separate, interacting systems. It is a move toward an inclusive view of mutually dependent oppressive systems (Collins, 1990). This is more than an extension of the unified system of socialist feminism, which tends to privilege class over race. Womanism starts with the perspective of black women rather than white men and centers on a *complex matrix* of oppressions.

---

3. Note the title of a widely read anthology: *All the women are white, all the blacks are men, but some of us are brave.* Gloria T. Hull, Patricia Bell Scott, and Barbara Smith, (Eds.), (1982). New York: The Feminist Press at the City University of New York.

Collins (1990) described oppressive systems as woven together into an overarching structure of domination, however distinctive the strands of oppression based on such single characteristics as sexual orientation, race, class, and ability may appear. This matrix of domination is structured on multiple levels: (1) personal, (2) group or community, and (3) the systemic level of social institutions. Other groups, such as white lesbians, women with disabilities, or Jewish women, experience the matrix in different ways, but overall, the experiences are of *systems* of domination (Collins, 1990).

Using poverty as an example of the differences in experiences of oppression, black feminists have pointed out that it is important to recognize that the current concept of the "feminization of poverty" applies primarily to the "nouveau poor" (Davis, 1990), that is, middle-class white women whose poverty is a function of separation and divorce. It does not address the growing number of poor white women who find themselves unable to escape poverty. Importantly, discussions of the feminization of poverty often completely ignore black women's poverty, which tends to be more closely related to their long standing social class position. The feminization of poverty analysis all too often neglects the disproportionate impact–particularly on poor women of color–of large-scale economic transformations and the dismantling of the welfare state (Collins, 1990). The analysis often fails to examine the differential effects of policy changes on women of various ethnicities and races.

Thus, it becomes clear that separating class and gender issues from race presents a skewed picture. Not only is the impression inaccurate, but the lives of the women under discussion are not lived in separate strands. It is vital, therefore, to define and describe the whole system of oppressions (Smith and Smith, 1983).

Separatism versus Coalitions

Inclusion and exclusion of groups takes on a new dimension when one considers how a single, multifaceted oppressive structure works. There are several ways in which black women could have divided antioppression work, for example, when considering the places of black men, white women, black lesbians, or women of color who are not African-American.

Black Men. Theorizing about the place of men in feminist movements tends to be different for black than for white women. Because racism, a system that affects both women and men, is so central to the analysis, black women's philosophies tend to avoid exclusion of men (Joseph and Lewis, 1981). With an analysis of oppressive systems as interlocking, black men do not need to be excluded from the womanist struggle. Christian argued, for example, that acknowledging the ways black men are fetishized as sex objects is possible without denying sexism within black communities and without having to focus on gender instead of on women's issues (Christian, 1989).[4]

Audre Lorde explained how easy it is to take advantage of black women's quarrels against black men. Because of this, black women need to distinguish carefully between the goals held by supporters of oppressive power structures and the goals black women have for resolution of their conflicts with black men. Such friction has the potential to be used to the detriment of all blacks. Lorde contrasted this position with that of white women, who have the potential to be seduced into joining in oppressive conditions with the promise of shared racial power. This path, however undesirable it may appear to many white women, is simply not open to black women (Lorde, 1984).

Other Women of Color and White Women. Although some feminists support black separatism from white women as a strategy (for example, Barbara Smith argued in favor of forming Black Women's Studies Institutes), many black feminist writers promote a coalition-building strategy that includes other women of color and often includes white women as well.

Among black women with feminist consciousness, few advocate separatist strategies (Wilcox, 1990). Audre Lorde insisted that it is only in coalition that women can learn to value difference for its potential to strengthen women's efforts for change. But we need to develop new patterns of experiencing and working with difference as *equals* rather than as dominants and subordinates (Lorde, 1984).

Lorde explained that difference, in and of itself, does not separate people: refusal to recognize difference does. Instead of examining differences, energy tends to be devoted either to ignoring them or to

---

4. This is not to say that black women's political organizations do not exist. There are many such organizations, as a few minutes on the Internet will demonstrate.

claiming that difference is an insurmountable barrier. This is not to deny that barriers exist. They do, and not only between white and black women. Women of color have learned negative stereotypes about each other too, but a desire to dismantle the dividers, instead of contributing to them, does exist (Lim, 1983; Cameron, 1983). Coalition building does not rest on a belief that it is necessary or possible for women to truly understand each other across race and class lines. However, recognizing the systems of domination as political tools that are functional to the established hierarchies can lead to coalition work (Joseph and Lewis, 1981). Reagon (1983) provided a moving description of the pain and the potential for danger in coalitions. But, she argued, coalitions are inevitable: "There is nowhere you can go and only be with people like you. It's over. Give it up" (Reagon, 1983, p. 357).

Townes assumed that womanism already includes a multiracial focus, but that such inclusiveness sometimes contributes to strain among women. Diverse women sharing authority is inevitably stressful, she said, but she believes that a commitment to justice can keep multiracial womanists working together (Townes, 1993).

Clenora Hudson-Weems disagreed. She distinguished Africana Womanism both from feminism and from Alice Walker's definition of womanism. She prefers to develop theory and activism from an Afrocentric perspective that she calls Africana Womanism. Because it is grounded in African culture, she argued, it focuses on the unique experiences and needs of Africana women (Hudson-Weems, 1993). For Hudson-Weems, feminism is hopelessly white. She refers to black women who embrace any version of it as "mere assimilationists" or "sellouts" who lack true commitment to their culture and people. She argued that the legitimate complaints that Africana women have against Africana men should be addressed in the context of African culture rather than in the context of feminism. Hudson-Weems believes in a hierarchy of oppressions that should be addressed in the following order: racism, classism, and then sexism (Hudson-Weems, 1993). Other black feminists who use an Afrocentric perspective, while centering the needs of African-American women, are less willing to rank order the oppressions they experience (Brewer, 1993).

Women of color who are not African-Americans have used a womanist theoretical approach–although not necessarily the term, womanist–to describe a variety of sociopolitical positions. For example, Pesquera and Segura (1993) discussed multiple axes of class, race-ethnicity and gender oppression that they referred to as *Chicana cross-positioning.* They described Chicana Cultural Nationalist Feminism as an analytical system that incorporates the idea of *Chicana cross-positioning* and is advocated by some Chicanas. It is similar to womanism in its emphasis on multiple axes of oppression, but like Africana Womanism, as described by Hudson-Weems, the approach tends to acknowledge but deemphasizes sexism and focuses on the unique needs of one ethnic group: Chicanas. Chicana Cultural Nationalist Feminists subscribe to a cultural nationalist ideology[5] and the ideology of *la familia.* Pesquera and Segura (1993) expressed concern that Chicana Cultural Nationalist Feminism overlooks the possibility that cultural traditions often support patriarchy.

Alma Garcia, on the other hand, disagrees with that conceptualization, arguing that Chicana feminism has moved in directions similar to womanism as described by Walker, Ogunyemi, and Brown. That is, it examines the intersections of the multiple systems of oppression experienced by women of color *without* discounting the impact of sexism (1990).

Lesbians. Recall that Alice Walker's definition of womanism reads, in part, "A woman who loves other women, sexually and/or nonsexually." Audre Lorde's widely read novel, *Zami,* focused on the image of black women working together as friends and lovers and argued that the potential for lesbianism is clearly present in womanism (Christian, 1985). But with increased visibility, black lesbians suffered more criticism and questioning of their commitment to black communities (Lorde, 1984). Lesbian baiting[6] is as present in black communities as in white, and lesbianism is often presented as a white women's "problem." Lorde insisted, however,

---

5. Cultural nationalism is a commitment to a sense of national consciousness, with an emphasis on preservation of culture.

6. Lesbian baiting: taking an active antilesbian stance, for example, attributing negative characteristics to lesbians and then using accusations of lesbianism as a way of pressuring women into heterosexuality.

that failing to consider lesbianism, or to advocate only for tolerance, weakens any political discussion of difference and abandons the creativity of, and the necessity for, difference (1979).

Black lesbians have presented a serious challenge to black feminists theorists. Pointing to the link between sexual orientation and power, they insist that black feminist theorists fully incorporate the axis of sexual orientation into the womanist understanding of matrices of oppression. Black lesbians refuted the notion of lesbian oppression as inconsequential, and they exposed how heterosexist oppression affects black lesbians as intensely as race, class, and gender oppressions do (Collins, 1990). Collins drew parallels between white feminists who understand sexism but not racism and black men and women who oppose racism but continue to rely on heterosexual privilege to the detriment of black lesbians.

In sum, womanism is a unified system analysis. It assumes that each oppressive system needs the others to function. According to Collins (1990), this creates a distinct theoretical stance which, in turn, contributes to a reexamination of basic social science concepts.

CRITIQUE

Womanism's support of a return to "our mothers gardens" resembles white cultural feminism in its valuation of the past and its apparent belief in black women's inherent goodness. Attention is sometimes focused on preserving history. Halting of cultural obliteration is indispensable to self-definition, but the quest for the moral vision of the mothers sounds similar to Gilligan's essentialist claims of women as inherently more moral than men. It is simplistic to think black culture is always supportive; Gloria Joseph and Jill Lewis (1981) sound familiar arguments to such essentialism, insisting that replacing insensitive white male leaders with black women will not necessarily improve things. Rather, change will be dependent on the political analysis, vision, and commitment of leaders, not on their skin color or sex. As the theory has developed, however, womanists have focused more on the complexity of oppression. Although Walker's definition was the jumping-off point, it is unlikely that today's womanists would argue that simply replacing white men with black women would solve the problems inherent in the matrix of domination.

A more serious criticism has come from women of color who sometimes see womanism as akin to Hudson-Weems' definition of Africana Womanism, a view that consciously excludes other women of color in favor of an Afrocentric perspective. Initially, a single matrix was discussed that used the African-American women's experience as the nearly exclusive racial "outgroup," and there seemed to be some hesitance to incorporate the axis of sexual orientation. Later writings, however, allow for multiple matrices, and these matrices are known to vary. For example, Native American women have different experiences depending on nation, band, geographic residence, etc. The matrices experienced by indigenous women will differ, in turn, from each other depending, for example, on whether a woman is a member of a band or tribe; and these experiences will differ, in turn, from other women of color whose ancestors were not native to this area (Weaver, in press).

African-American feminists have been consistent critics both from within and from outside of what has often been described as a primarily white women's movement. Black women were builders of, and participants in, various forms of feminist activism, but racism within the movement, its often single-issue focus, and the tendency to catalogue hierarchies of oppression have discouraged many African-American feminists from participation in an integrated women's movement.

Womanists expanded and recreated a radical understanding of feminism to account for the realities of black women's history and experience. Black women generally refused to choose between giving their attention to battling racism *or* sexism *or* classism. A focus on multiple systems of oppression is found in more recent socialist feminist work and in some radical feminist theory as well. But nowhere is the case argued so strongly or so well as it is in womanism. Whereas some socialist feminists argued that patriarchy and capitalism are mutually reinforcing, black feminists make the case for analysis of *many* varied oppressive systems, all of which function in mutual support.

Until womanism, there was no clearly delineated branch of feminist theory that encompassed an equal commitment to furthering women as well as blacks. Womanists' and black feminists' most profound contribution to feminist movement has been the insistence that all systems of oppression be attacked with equal force at precisely the same time. Black women *must* deal with more than one issue at a time (Reagon, 1983) and so must everyone else who is oppressed by multiple systems of domination. Replacing an additive analysis– race + class + gender–with an embedded multiplicative analysis– race × class × gender–womanists have focused on "the simultaneity of oppression" instead of trying to address one or two axes as though they functioned or were experienced independently (Brewer, 1993, p. 16). Rather than weakening social change efforts, as both white feminists and black men have sometimes feared, using a multifocus strengthens and extends both analysis and action (Christian, 1989).

Finally, the coalition work recommended by many womanists is, by nature, difficult. Moving beyond coalition to the formation of alliances among women who are different from each other is even more challenging (Molina, 1990). Womanism provides a theoretical guide for negotiating these often troublesome connections.

APPLICATION OF WOMANIST THEORY TO SOCIAL WORK PRACTICE

Policy

Using womanist theory at a policy level, social workers might fight against the use of such coercive birth control measures as mandated use of Norplant or other long-lasting contraceptives for drug using women who, in many–though certainly not all–instances, are poor women of color (Leiberman and Davis, 1992). A womanist or practitioner of black feminist social work would take a multi-issue approach and focus on the coerciveness involved, the likelihood that the target population was women of color, and the economic access of such women to legal recourse and alternative methods of birth control (Smith, 1986). This focus might also include a critique of the use of Norplant as a substitute for access to the adequate food, nutrition, and prenatal care that contribute to healthy pregnancies and as a substitute for effective and accessible drug and alcohol treatment programs for pregnant women.

Administration/Organization

Spelman College is the oldest traditionally black women's college in the world. Although Spelman started offering women's studies courses in the 1970s, it did not have a program with a black feminist perspective until 1981. Because it was a women's college, many people thought it was not necessary to have an explicitly women-centered program (Guy-Sheftall, 1993). A number of faculty and students disagreed. Careful to avoid alienating the relatively conservative college administration or those who are hostile to the term, organizers avoided the word "feminist" in descriptions of their plans for a center. But feminist it is.

The organization is now a women's research, women's studies, and women's resource center (NWSA, 1990). It has sponsored a community enrichment program for Third World women, the 1983 National Black Women's Health Project conference, and a 1990 conference on the state of the art in black women's studies. The Director of the Center, Patricia Bell Scott, collaborated in founding *SAGE: A Scholarly Journal on Black Women*, which began publishing in April, 1983 and has published biannually since.

In another vein, Valli Kanuha (1994) described the inadequacy of services for battered women of color. For example, women of color have reported that they find service providers insensitive to racial and cultural contexts. Given this, it is unlikely that, when they are battered, African-American women would see such services as a viable option (Kanuha, 1994, citing Ashbury, 1987; Richie, 1985).

There are other factors to consider when designing services to be used by battered women. A woman of color who reports battering to the police is more likely to have her partner mistreated while in custody. Although this should *not* preclude her from seeking and obtaining police protection, service providers need to be aware that the consequences may be different for men of color than for white men, and that the battered woman may need to address this. Takagi (1991, as cited in Kanuha, 1994) reported that African-American and Native American women who report battering are more likely than white women to lose custody of their children. It is vital for service providers to incorporate into agencies for battered women advocacy against such additional victimization.

Developing cultural competence is only one of the strategies suggested by Kanuha (1994). Hiring staff who reflect the racial, ethnic, and class composition of the community, providing outreach to women of color, and providing non-English speaking services are a good beginning. The next step is to ensure that African-American, Asian/Pacific Islander, Latina, and Native American women from a variety of classes contribute to the design, development, and implementation strategies of the agency. Otherwise, the strengths and particular challenges of women from one or more of the communities may be misunderstood, and well-intentioned services may simply force diverse women into a model best suited for middle-class women and/or white women.

Community Organizing

Patricia Zavella (1993) described a campaign to organize Chicana cannery workers in Northern California. Two approaches were used to organize the women. One was based on an ethnic/nationalist and class perspective and was led by men. The other, the "women's committee," used a "multilayered analysis" in order to analyze race/ethnicity, class, and gender simultaneously. The women did not organize simply as rank-and-file workers within the union. They also ruled out organizing solely on the basis of gender, in which women would be considered in terms of their socially assigned domestic obligations outside of work, or the gender stratification on the job, for example. Nor did the women's committee advocate organizing the women solely on the basis of their commitment to Chicano cultural values, by simply including women's interests within a Chicano perspective. Instead, they centered the issues of women at the juncture of ethnicity, sex, and class.

Zavella (1993) reported that the women's committee was more responsive to gender issues than the companion organization coordinated by Chicano men. She advocated taking the concept a step further in future actions by better incorporating women's practical concerns–such as child care–into the workers' demands.

Group Work

As part of my dissertation research on marginalized women (Saulnier, 1994), my colleagues and I provided an intervention group for black women who, although abstinent when they started the group, all had histories of problems with drugs and/or alcohol that they wanted to discuss. The facilitator, an African-American social worker, had expressed an interest in participating in the research project, had helped design the group, and then facilitated it. The intervention focused on the need for both personal and social change. We had identified a number of topics for discussion including racism; sexuality; body image; relationships; heterosexism and homophobia; disability discrimination; the desirability of abstinence from alcohol and drugs; environmental pressures to drink; stress related to marginalization; coping with unfair discrimination by drinking; problems inherent in powerlessness models of alcohol and drug treatment; and individual, family, cultural/ethnic, social, economic, and political factors contributing to the development of alcohol and drug problems.

The women addressed all of those topics and more. They expressed a clear need to talk about alcohol and drug issues in the context of racism and sexism. They had a strong preference for working with other black women, saying they felt better able to make the connections among different aspects of alcohol and drug problems when all the group members were black women. They felt strongly about wanting to develop better ways to help black women, and they talked about bell hooks' work, particularly *Sisters of the Yam*, in that context (Saulnier, 1996). They did not discuss their lives, goals, or problems in terms of separate fragments or mutually exclusive categories, but as interwoven wholes, consisting of many aspects, including race, sex, class, and sexual orientation (Saulnier, 1994).

Casework

Lillian Comas-Diaz approached psychotherapy with women of color by combining information about participants' multiple-group membership, into an approach she called "psychotherapeutic decolonization" (1994, p. 287). Comas-Diaz argued that the metaphor of colonization (versus oppression) more accurately reflects the obligation of people of color in the United States to adapt to the dominant culture. She incorporated the following processes into her work: (1) recognition of the social context of colonization; (2) correction of cognitive errors that reinforce colonized mentality; (3) reaffirmation of an integrated racial and gender identity; (4) increased self-mastery and dignity; and (5) transformation of both the self and the colonized condition (p. 291).

Comas-Diaz (citing Kleinman, 1989) discussed the concept of *empathic witnessing*, whereby a clinician who is dissimilar from the client and perhaps unfamiliar with the client's culture affirms the client's reality while acknowledging the limits of the clinician's own familiarity with the client's ethnocultural history and experience. Comas-Diaz (1994) argued that affirmation of a complex racial, ethnocultural, and gender identity facilitates resolution of conflicted identity issues, and that incorporation of culturally based spiritual healing is conducive to the repair of any spiritual imbalance that may be experienced by women who are attuned to spiritual issues.

Research

John Stanfield II (1994) described an approach to qualitative research that he called ethnic modeling. It is similar to feminist standpoint research in that it centers the *cognitive maps* of the people who are studied. In this case, it would be women of color. By incorporating Higginbotham's notion of a metalanguage of race into the analysis, that is, by assuming that cultural and personal experience are filtered though socially imposed concepts of race, a researcher could criticize and revise both research strategies and the social problems under study. Stanfield called for new methods of distribution of research findings. By extension, it would be necessary, in the conduct of womanist or black feminist research, to ensure that information is provided where it is needed most–to those who make policy and to women of color for their personal and political use–rather than focusing solely or even primarily on scholarly publications available to few people.

Chapter 7

Postmodern Feminist Theory

CONTRIBUTIONS AND CONTRIBUTORS

Postmodernism is an epistemology, that is, a theory of knowledge and understanding, defined initially by French philosophers. It questions essentialism in all its forms, starting with the notion of general, all-encompassing principles meant to explain either natural or social realities (Nicholson, 1990). Among the many Enlightenment beliefs criticized by postmodernists are the following:

1. The notion of a stable, coherent self.
2. The belief that reason provides an objective, reliable and universal basis for knowledge.
3. The certainty that knowledge acquired from reason will be "true."
4. The belief that reason and knowledge exist independent of the knower.
5. The tenet that truth subjected to reason provides rules which are right for all rational beings.
6. The notion that truth, in the service of power will not be distorted and that freedom and progress can be assured.
7. The canon that science, which is neutral in its methods and contents but socially beneficial in its results, is the paradigm for all true knowledge.
8. The principle that language is transparent and provides a correspondence between word and thing; objects are not linguistically (or socially) constructed; they are simply designated by naming. (Flax, 1990)

Several key concepts in postmodern theory are language, discourse, difference, deconstruction, and positionality. *Language*, in postmodern terms, is a system that not only constructs meaning, but also organizes cultural practices. Words, whether spoken or written, lack fixed and intrinsic meanings, so that one must always know the context, speaker and the social processes that contributed to the use of words in order to understand their meaning (Scott, 1990). Current and historical documents are not assumed to be understandable or truthful; nor is the reconstitution of the past, attempted by the study of historical documents, likely to be successful as one could never know whether the author was intentionally misleading, for example (Foucault, 1972).

A *discourse* is a structure of statements, terms, categories, and beliefs that may be expressed in organizations and institutions. "Discursive fields overlap, influence and compete with each other; they appeal to one another's 'truths' . . . [and are] . . . assigned the status of objective knowledge" (Scott, 1990, pp. 135-137). To understand a discourse, one must first know who is speaking, who has the "right" or is considered qualified to use that particular discourse (Foucault, 1972). The function of a discourse varies, with accepted and excluded discourses interacting in various strategies. It is in discourse that power and knowledge are joined (Foucault, 1980).

In *difference*, meaning is created by means of contrast, with a positive definition dependent upon the negation of something else that has been presented as its opposite. Difference assumes such binary oppositions as unity/diversity, universality/specificity (Scott, 1990). The concept of difference, according to Wittig, determines that subordinates are different and therefore "other." Since it is dominants who are used as the standard, "men are not different. Whites are not different, nor are the masters. But blacks, as well as slaves are" (Wittig, 1988a, p. 436).

Deconstruction consists of "exposing a concept as ideological or culturally construed rather than as natural or a simple reflection of reality" (Collins, 1990, p. 14). Deconstruction entails analyzing the ways in which difference operates, thereby revealing the ways in which seemingly dichotomous terms are interdependent (Scott, 1990). According to Flax (1990, p. 41), postmodern discourses are all deconstructive in their attempt to question concepts usually taken for granted, particularly notions about truth, knowledge, power, and language.

Positionality refers to the situation of the speaker, the speaker's level of power, institutional context (Foucault, 1980), and the site from which a discourse is made (Foucault, 1972). But power, according to Michel Foucault, does not lie in institutions. Rather it is found everywhere, in complex, strategical situations in society "exercised from innumerable points, in the interplay of nonegalitarian and mobile relationships" (1980, p. 94). Resistance always accompanies power because power exists only in relationship. Therefore, despite, or perhaps because of the multiplicity of positions from which one can argue, there are multiple sites, or a plurality of resistances (Foucault, 1980) to oppressive power.

Postmodernism has been especially critical of science, on multiple counts, including the claim of science to transcend the perspective of any individual person or group (Nicholson, 1990). Postmodern theorists refute scientists' claim that although their choice of questions may be influenced by values or culture, the truth of the answers the scientist finds is not refutable since the criteria of truth are independent of the scientist's perspective (Nicholson, 1990). Objectivity, postmodernists argue, fails to account for the "situatedness" of those who claim to legitimize knowledge (Nicholson, 1990). Objectivity reduces multiple principles to a basic few by ignoring or discounting variation.

Scientists' claims of transcendence and objectivity are said to mask the ideological power relationships between scientists and those whom they study. "The role of ideology does not diminish as rigor increases and error is dissipated . . . . To tackle the ideological functioning of a science . . . is to . . . treat it as one practice among others" (Foucault, 1972, p. 186). In other words, once we acknowledge that scientific methods function within a particular ideology, we see that science is only one of many approaches to knowledge acquisition.

THE THEORY

There is a dynamic process involved in the development of postmodern feminism so that it is hard to say whether to start with postmodernists having been influenced by feminists or vice versa.

> However, what appear to be new and exciting insights . . . that culture is composed of seriously contested codes of meaning,

that language and politics are inseparable, and that construct-
ing the "other" entails relations of domination–are insights
that have received repeated and rich exploration in feminist
theory for the past forty years. (Mascia-Lees, Sharpe, and
Cohen, 1989, p. 11)

The difference between feminism and postmoderism, according
to Weedon (1987), is that the starting point of feminists is the
patriarchal structure of society. According to Flax (1990, p. 55), the
tasks of postmodern feminist theorists are: (1) to articulate feminist
viewpoints of society; (2) to analyze how women are affected by
the social world; (3) to examine the role of power and knowledge
relationships in shaping the ways women think about the social
world; and (4) to imagine ways in which the social world can be
transformed. Both feminist theorists and postmodernists seek new
paradigms of social criticism outside the bounds of traditional philosophy (Fraser and Nicholson, 1990). There are four ways to view
the relationship between these sets of theories: (1) in terms of their
complementarity; (2) in terms of postmodernism's lessons for feminism; (3) in terms of feminism's lessons for postmodernism; and
(4) in terms of their oppositionality.

Complementarity. Feminist theory has been described as a type
of postmodern philosophy (Flax, 1990) although for feminists,
social criticism supersedes interest in philosophy (Fraser and
Nicholson, 1990). Each contributes to the other: "Postmodernists
offer sophisticated and persuasive criticism of foundationalism[1] and
essentialism, but their conceptions of social criticism tend to be
anemic. Feminists offer robust conceptions of social criticism but
they tend, at times, to lapse into foundationalism and essentialism"
(Fraser and Nicholson, 1990, p. 20).

Lessons of postmodernism. Postmodernists find feminism guilty of
essentialism so that even when history is taken into account, as by
socialist feminists, for example, there is still a tendency to imbue all
women and men in a given era, with categories specific to their gender
(Fraser and Nicholson, 1990). Postmodernists point out that feminists

---

1. Foundationalism is the Enlightenment practice of trying to ground claims of
truth and value in reason or logic (Larsen, 1990).

often have sought a single cause to explain women's oppression cross-culturally. According to Fraser and Nicholson (1990), feminist theories falsely universalize the theorist's own era, society, culture, class, sexual orientation, and ethnic or racial group. Such analyses of gender and sexual difference need to be replaced with a plurality of difference. The goal, according to Alcoff (1988), should be for gender to lose its position of significance in society.

Lessons of feminism. Some feminist theorists object to what they see as the reduction of oppression and suffering to language (Marks and de Courtivron, 1980). Regarding research, feminists insist that there is a profound difference between postmodern and feminist research approaches. Postmodern anthropologists, for example, write from the position of the dominant speaking for the "other," while feminists speak from the position of the "other" (Mascia-Lees, Sharpe and Cohen, 1989), putting themselves into the text (Cixous, 1981). But postmodernism has been criticized for failing to address gender subordination and patriarchal constructs (Fraser and Nicholson, 1990). Mascia-Lees, Sharpe, and Cohen (1989) argue that feminist theorists, functioning as political activists, need to ensure that postmodern practice advances the recognition of the need to balance the masculine perspective with the feminine since, without a clear recognition of political structures of postmodern research and theorizing, there is a serious danger of hidden agendas.

Oppositionality. Describing postmodernism's use of positionality as "interpretationism," Sandra Harding expressed alarm at the potential of such a stance for discounting the knowledge claims of feminists. The danger lies in postmodernists claiming that while feminists have a right to interpretations, for example, of the reasons for rape and the function of family forms, feminist interpretations are simply a matter of opinion (Harding, 1990). The notion that it is impossible to decide truth has been called a new version of an antifeminist argument that feminists' perceptions are skewed and limited, and that what feminists describe as misogynist acts actually are activities which help women (Alcoff, 1988).

Treating all interpretations as equal, with each voice contributing its unique story, denies a hierarchy of discourse, masks power differentials and exploitation, and eliminates the rationale for fighting oppression (Mascia-Lees, Sharpe, and Cohen, 1989). It returns gender to its invisible position in modern discourse (Alcoff, 1988). Feminist consciousness may be less likely than right-wing consciousness to fall victim to normative social discourse, but Alcoff maintains that postmodern nominalist[2] subjectivity does not offer feminism the grounds on which to argue that point. She asks, "How can we ground a feminist politics that deconstructs the female subject?" (Alcoff, 1988, p. 419).

Deconstructionist arguments are said to discount as essentialist the "differing and sometimes multiple identities painstakingly *constructed* in the very recent past, by lesbians, older women, women of colour, disabled women, and working-class women" (Stanley, 1990, p. 153). If all generalizations, including *woman*, are socially constructed, we are left with "a nominalist ontology"[3] and a return to individualist politics (Nicholson, 1990). If categories such as "women" do not exist, neither does oppression of women. With the loss of generalized categories, we lose the basis of demands for rights and services for women (Alcoff, 1988) and the basis of our challenge to systematically unequal distributions of resources between women and men (Lovibond, 1989).

Some feminist scholars have noted that it may not be coincidence that just at the time when women and non-Western men have begun to successfully challenge the Western male as the proper subject of study, a theory has been proposed by those who are losing the privilege to define truth, that questions whether truth *can* be defined. "Postmodern theorizing can be understood as . . . a metaphor for the sense of the dominant that the ground has begun to shift under their feet" (Mascia-Lees, Sharpe, and Cohen, 1989, p. 16).

Postmodern Feminism and the Meaning of Woman

Although several Americans are included here, it is often French theorists to which we must turn to describe postmodern feminism. Helene Cixous, Julia Kristeva, Luce Irigaray, and Monique Wittig are probably the best-known French postmodern feminist theorists (Jaggar, 1983). The bibliography on psychoanalytic feminist theory

---

2. Nominalism is the notion that all abstract terms are simply convenient tools of language or thought, existing as names only, without corresponding realities.
3. Ontology is the description of the nature of being and reality.

lists the work of each of these theorists. Here, their attention to postmodernism is addressed. Postmodern feminists examine the network of power inherent in language as it acts upon social reality (Wittig, 1988a). The most obvious place to begin is with the disagreement as to the utility of the concept "woman."

"A woman cannot 'be,' " insisted Kristeva (1981, p. 137). The word "woman" is a social rather than natural construct, and neither can, nor should be, defined. By taking woman as our starting point, given the term's existence only in oppositional *difference* to the notion of man, feminist practice based on the notion of "woman" could only be negative, formed in reaction to the concept of "woman" (Kristeva, 1981). " '(W)oman' does not exist for us," echoed Wittig. It is only an imaginary formation" (1985, p. 137). The plural, "women," however, is a different matter. The notion of "women" evolved from an understanding of a social relationship–a political and ideological relationship of exploitation (Wittig, 1985).

The distinction is not taken up by all feminists. For example, Alcoff used the singular "woman," which, she maintained, was defined in terms of positionality, rather than by naturally inherent internal characteristics. "The external situation determines (her) relative position . . . safe or dangerous, powerful or weak, according to . . . relations to other(s)" (Alcoff, 1988, p. 433). Alcoff went on to say that it is by identifying women's position in networks of relations that a feminist theory, accounting for shifting contexts, can be grounded; activism is then related to addressing the positional lack of power and the need for radical change to ameliorate that lack.

Self-definition is a component of this same disagreement, with some declaring we should describe women but *feminists alone* can do this. Others challenge the wisdom of retaining *any* categorical definitions including women. The former argue that men, who have a different view and often different interests, have distorted and devalued feminine characteristics (Alcoff, 1988) and so feminists should redefine women, in accordance with actual experiences. Patricia Hill Collins (1990) provided an historical example: rather than accepting existing assumptions about what a woman was, Sojourner Truth engaged in a deconstructionist argument by challenging the standards of femininity. This approach does not challenge whether women *should* be defined, but only whether the definition typically assigned is *accurate* (Alcoff, 1988).

The other side of the self-definition argument is supported by Kristeva:

> As long as any libertarian movement, feminism included, does not analyze its own relationship to power and does not renounce belief in its own identity, it remains capable of being coopted both by power and an overtly religious or lay spiritualism. (Kristeva, 1981, p. 141)

Wittig is also critical of attempts to define women as a distinct category: Self-definition of women requires an assumption of difference from men and "(t)he function of difference is to mask at every level the conflicts of interest including ideological ones" (Wittig, 1988a, p. 436).

Some see a nominalist argument as helpful here. Following de Beauvoir's contention that women are made, not born (de Beauvoir, 1981), de Lauretis argued that the concept "woman" has some utility and that some people who have been labeled essentialist may in fact be describing a sociocultural construction, not an innate feature; thus, they may well be attacking patriarchy as an historical construct in need of revision (de Lauretis, 1990). Ironically, Wittig used the same de Beauvoir quote to establish her argument concerning the uselessness of the word woman: "No biological, psychological, or economic fate determines the figure that the human female presents in society; it is civilization as a whole that produces this creature, intermediate between male and eunuch, which is described as feminine" (Wittig, 1988b, p. 440).

Continuing the disagreement leads to a discussion of the analysis of gender. If gender analysis is a fundamental goal of feminist theory, as Flax (1990) contended, then feminists must be able to examine the structure and experience of gender relations. It is Alcoff who came to the rescue of postmodern feminists:

> If we combine the concept of identity politics with a conception of the subject as positionality, we can conceive of the subject as nonessentialized and emergent from a historical

experience and yet retain our political ability to take gender as an important point of departure. Thus we can say at one and the same time, that gender is not natural, biological, universal, ahistorical, or essential and yet still claim that gender is relevant because we are taking gender as a position from which to act politically. (Alcoff, 1988, p. 433)

When conceptualizing "women" as an historical construction, varying across and within societies and time (Fraser and Nicholson, 1990), the diversity allowed for contradicts universalizing and replaces unitary notions of woman "with plural and complexly constructed conceptions of social identity, treating gender as one relevant strand among others, attending also to class, race, ethnicity, age, [and] sexual orientation" (Fraser and Nicholson, 1990, pp. 34-35). Feminist postmodernism insists on retaining the activism of the earlier feminist movement to be effective (Flax, 1990), seeking not only description, but also social change (Alcoff, 1988).

Postmodern Feminism and Science

Postmodern feminists have criticized science from a specifically feminist perspective. Wittig pointed out the tendency to dismiss feminist work by judging it as insufficiently sophisticated in level of analysis, wrought with confusion between discourse and reality, and stemming from a misunderstanding of science (Wittig, 1988a). Feminists challenged the notion of objectivity and scientists' claim to be uninfluenced by essentialized conceptions of gender, proposing that the only way to avoid narrowness was through inclusion of many points of view (Nicholson, 1990). Nicholson was careful to point out, however, that wariness of scientific methods is not unique to postmodern feminists. "Feminist scholars have not been alone in launching a criticism of the alleged neutrality of the academy . . . Marxism . . . and the movements of black and gay liberation have also questioned the supposed 'God's eye view' of the academy" (1990, p. 3).

In line with Alcoff's conception of women as not comprising an essential category, yet constituting a political position, Sandra Harding (1990) defended a feminist standpoint within a postmodern framework. She described two major strands of feminist analysis of science: feminist empiricists and feminist standpoint theorists. The empiricists tend to focus on the elimination of male bias in scientific research, assuming that a stricter adherence to scientific method would better represent women. They claim an accumulation of empirical support for feminist notions; they argue for acceptance of feminist research by mainstream researchers, despite its political grounding, since it has empirical support; they produce data which conflicts with sexist claims (Harding, 1990). According to Harding (1990), their conservatism, in failing to challenge *the methods themselves*, sometimes leads to acceptance of feminist criticism by scientists and may pave the way for antiracist and anticlassist political movements to have their work accepted as well. Cixous is somewhat less optimistic when she insists that such work responds to the "deaf male ear, which hears in language only that which speaks in the masculine" (Cixous, 1981, p. 251).

Feminist standpoint theorists, on the other hand, argue that although knowledge is meant to be grounded in experience, it is actually tested in limited and distorted ways by science. Allegiance to the scientific method is not required since standpoint theorists deny the method's claim to lack of bias, purporting instead that seeking knowledge from women's standpoint can overcome androcentric, Western bias. Feminist standpoint theorists are less likely than empiricists to support the essential nature of women, and they are more likely than empiricists to support the centrality of political activism (Harding, 1990).

Importantly, standpoint theorists point to the potential of social liberation movements to advance knowledge. They point out the many periods during which liberation struggles led to new understandings of classism, racism, and other social problems. Women's similarities and differences are accounted for within feminist standpoint research, without necessitating essentialist arguments. Rather, this approach "*analyzes* the essentialism that androcentrism assigns to women, locates its historical conditions and proposes ways to counter it" (Harding, 1990, p. 99).

CRITIQUE

It is neither possible nor necessary, as Wittig (1988b) has pointed out, to ignore differences among women or to reduce women to their oppression in order to address the needs of women as a class or group. Essentialist arguments concerning the *nature* of woman are contingent upon her identity as a subjugated person, and therefore, cannot provide an escape from sexism (Alcoff, 1988). Although disagreement persists as to whether the singular "woman" or the plural "women" is the more pertinent usage, there does seem to be agreement that the focus should be on women's position in society, rather than on any "inborn" characteristics.

As to the question of whether gender is basic, DiStefano (1990) believes that a conception of gender as basic in the sense of inescapable or overdetermined is warranted, given the pervasiveness of cultural and social gender structuring. But this does not mean we must declare gender differences inherent and fixed. To do so is to "naturalize" and excuse historic and present oppression (Wittig, 1988b). Yet, even in these convictions we need to remain flexible: "We cannot simultaneously claim (1) that the mind, the self and knowledge are socially constituted and that what we can know depends upon our social practices and contexts and (2) that feminist theory can uncover the truth once and for all" (Flax, 1990, p. 48).

According to Nicholson (1990), we need not lose concepts of gender nor search for relevant theory to accommodate postmodernism as long as we attend to historical changes and avoid false generalizations. Feminists can retain the capacity to analyze macro-structures and the embeddedness of sexism in contemporary societies (Fraser and Nicholson, 1990).

Caution is needed. Feminists must choose a theoretical approach that does not deny the categories that provide women the springboard from which to advocate social change (Flax, 1990). A political theory is useful only in so far as it explains how social power is exercised and how oppressive relations of gender, class, and race can be transformed (Weedon, 1987). Harding (1990) called for a "principled ambivalence" toward postmodern theory, reflecting the contradictions women encounter in the world.

In some sense, we come full circle with postmodern feminism. Enlightenment notions may have been regressive, but we still need some of them: "critics of the feminist epistemologies join those they criticize in believing in the desirability and the possibility of social progress, and that improved theories about ourselves and the world around us will contribute to that progress" (Harding, 1990, p. 99).

Several writers caution against the search for one true feminist theory or language. Flax (1990) points out that such a pursuit reveals how embedded feminist theory is in the processes it is trying to critique. hooks described feminism as multiply located in language and experiences, and she insisted that analysis of race and class converging with gender requires a new language (Childers and hooks, 1990). Finally, Collins cautions us (1) to not overestimate the power of "dominants," as the ideology may not be as cohesive or uniform as we imagine; and (2) to persist: "Persistence is a fundamental requirement of this journey from silence to language to action"[4] (Collins, 1990, p. 112).

APPLICATION OF POSTMODERN FEMINISM TO SOCIAL WORK PRACTICE

Social workers can assist in the "insurrection" of subjugated meanings and help get them into the agency, school, hospital, commission, institution, community, and profession through externalization. Such an approach to practice helps clients edge into the larger and often oppressive world, strengthens the self, and emboldens the folklore of the group. (Saleebey, 1994, p. 351)

Policy

A postmodern feminist approach to policy would examine the possibilities for transformation of power/knowledge relationships. Kathleen Nuccio and Roberta Sands (1992) examined poverty policy, particularly some of the proposed solutions to "feminization of poverty." What they found was a tendency to describe men according to their employment status and women according to their marital status. They were alarmed that some proposals were based on essentialized notions of women and men, and seemed to be aimed at preserving and creating good-paying jobs for men while

---

4. This pathway was described by Audre Lorde in 1978. See Lorde, A. (1984). *Sister Outsider*. Freedom, CA: The Crossing Press.

encouraging marriage as a poverty response for women. Using a deconstructionist analysis, they criticized the notion of a *culture of poverty* because it blames women for creating their own poverty by linking poverty to women's attempts to avoid dependence on men.

Nuccio and Sands also found a return to rhetoric about a "family wage," but rather than reflecting the current reality of female-headed households, they found that the rhetoric assumed a household would consist of a male head, with only a peripheral financial contribution from women. Instead of agreeing that femaleness and single parenthood cause poverty, Nuccio and Sands proposed that we seek solutions that incorporate a feminist perspective. "The impoverished state of women and children is supported by an economic structure in which there is a gap between wages of women and men, an inadequate welfare system, and an unreliable system of child support" (Nuccio and Sands, 1992, p. 37).

Lack of adequate child care has been taken up by many feminists. Alcoff (1988) examined the problem and suggested an approach to policy that avoids the equation of femaleness with motherhood and child care. Citing Riley (1988), Alcoff described child care policy in a way that allowed women to demand child care without essentializing women's roles. She argued that feminists must clarify that demands for child care are based on *current* needs and the present social distribution of child-rearing responsibilities. This demand can be made, she argued, without universalizing the association of women with both motherhood and the primary responsibility for child care.

Administration

In her discussion of leadership in education, Jackie Blount (1994) provided ideas useful for social work administrators. Blount argued that lists of leadership traits are often devoid of reference to race, gender, or economic class, but that the intended leaders are presumed to be white, male, and middle class. She further asserted that leadership traits, based in rational positivist thinking and considered to be good leadership style, tended to concentrate on making decisions, directing tasks, seeking goals, and directing activities (Blount, 1994). This not only ignores gender biases, but also ignores how socially constructed knowledge and practices are, and how, based on the work of middle-class white males, they conceal bias by claiming value-neutrality. The discourse describes women and leaders as though they were mutually exclusive (Blount, 1994).

Leadership, Blount argued, implies a context-based relationship among people (1994). The leader/follower relationship implies the existence of an intentional, willing relationship. Instead of the traditional bottom-up accountability, by "discourse-privileged persons" (who are typically assumed to be male), leadership ought to be decentered, with leader/follower relationships evolving out of caring, trusting, constant relationships (Blount, 1994). These relationships should entail reciprocity and mutual responsibility. Voices that typically are unheard, she argued, should be incorporated into leadership decision making.

Community Organizing

In this capacity, social workers might help people redefine who has the right to a discourse. They may take gender as a position from which to act politically while simultaneously examining the social construction of gender, the attributes currently assigned to women, and the people who are excluded from the category "woman" because of the term's essentialist definitions.

For example, Anne McClintock cited multiple cases in several cities across the United States in which prostitutes had been raped but rapists had been let off, either because prostitutes were not included in the definition of women, or because rape of a sex worker was not considered possible. In each case, McClintock demonstrated that decisions were based on some variation of "a whore is a whore is a whore"[5] in which "all prostitutes share a common identity that makes them essentially and universally unrapeable" (1992, p. 76). McClintock argued that since rape continues to be perceived as a crime against male property and prostitutes have not given over ownership of their bodies and the earnings they derive from sexual services to a single man, the prostitute is considered to be outside the bounds of (male) law. One of the worst cruelties is that prostitutes are often not allowed to keep their children although

---

5. Quoting Pasadena Superior Court Judge Gilbert C. Alston's 1986 decision in the trial of Daniel Zabuski.

many of the women are working primarily to support their families. McClintock found that in many countries, social workers have the power to remove a prostitute's children to keep them out of "moral danger" (McClintock, 1992, p. 89).[6]

McClintock described the burgeoning activism of prostitutes worldwide. Sex workers are challenging the stigma of practices that are defined as deviant while paying close attention to how prostitutes are being described.

> It seems crucial . . . to remain alert to the nuances and paradoxes of prostitution rather than to patronize prostitutes as embodiments of female sexual degradation or to glamorize them as unambiguous heroines of female revolt. Sex work is a gendered form of work that takes its myriad meanings from the different societies in which it emerges. (McClintock, 1992, p. 94)

Group Work

Joan Laird and Dennis Saleebey each used the construction of meaning in their interventions with groups. Saleebey cited Laird's work (1989) on women in families as an example of working with the cultural interpretation of meaning: "As more and more women tell their own stories and as stories are told about women . . . women's choices for self-construction are enriched and expanded. Women not only begin to connect themselves with other women and to discover new possibilities for their lives, but also have new opportunities to tell the stories of their oppression and of their poverty" (Laird, 1989, pp. 439-440). The groups that Laird was discussing were psychotherapy sessions with families.

Saleebey applied a postmodern framework to task groups in neighborhoods. Describing social work practice as the intersection of meanings, he discussed the use of storytelling as a technique to

---

6. Social work has been ambivalent about involvement with sex workers although there has been some recent social work attention in this area. See for example, Valerie Jenness, (1990). See also Lacey Sloan (1996). *Career contingencies of women who work as topless dancers.* Unpublished PhD Dissertation. University of Texas at Austin. Also, NASW recently considered a platform statement concerning prostitutes and other sex workers but decided against pursuing it for the time being (Lacey Sloan, Personal communication, September 9, 1995).

engage people in a reinterpretation of cultural meaning. Citing Bruner (1990), Saleebey explained that stories either engage normative structures or account for exceptions to that structure. When neither approach fits a given situation, people will create a new story, more suited to their needs.

> Helping the residents in the public housing project construct or enliven alternative stories has, among other things, begun, for some, the process of viewing the "housing project" as a "community" or "neighborhood," where individuals begin to take ownership and transform it, rather than hide behind their doors and wait for the police to come or for the Housing Authority to come up with a new security plan. (Saleebey, 1994, p. 357)

Casework

Patricia Hill Collins (1990) wrote about the power of self-definition for African-American women.

> Black women's lives are a series of negotiations that aim to reconcile the contradictions separating our own internally defined images of self as African-American women with our objectification as the Other. . . . For Black women, constructed knowledge of self emerges from the struggle to reject controlling images and integrate knowledge deemed personally important, usually knowledge essential to Black women's survival. (Collins, 1990, pp. 94-95)

Collins encouraged the use of relationships between black women as well as use of music, literature, and personal writing to "create self-valuations that challenge externally defined notions of Black womanhood" (Collins, 1990, p. 107). Different techniques might appeal to different women: "An individual woman may use multiple strategies in her quest for the constructed knowledge of an independent voice. Like Celie in Alice Walker's *The Color Purple*, some women write themselves freer" (Collins, 1990, p. 112).

Collins (1990) argued that social domination experienced within hegemonic culture is likely to be absent from black women's gatherings, thus providing the social space to speak freely and to construct knowledge of self. A social worker might therefore encourage a woman to use such spaces to negotiate meaning. Collins saw this space as essential for black women's resistance in which they would change the world from one where they merely exist to one over which they have some control, using self-definition as a path to empowerment.

Research

A considerable amount has been written on postmodern feminist research methods. In most instances, there is a common set of recommendations: evaluate the positionality of researchers; eliminate any pretense of objectivity from the research; and attend closely to the ideological power relationships between the researcher and the "subject" of the research. Patti Lather (1991) insisted that encouraging research participants to engage in self-reflection should be given equal weight with generation of empirically grounded knowledge. Reciprocity between researcher and researched is key to such goals. Lather included the following in a list of procedures meant to encourage reciprocity:

- Interviews conducted in an interactive, dialogic manner that requires self-disclosure on the part of the researcher . . .
- Sequential interviews of both individuals and small groups to facilitate collaboration and a deeper probing of research issues . . .
- Negotiating meaning helps build reciprocity. At a minimum, this entails recycling description, emerging analysis, and conclusions to at least a subsample of respondents. A more maximal approach to reciprocity would involve research participants in collaborative efforts to build empirically rooted theory. (1991, pp. 60-61)

Lather described a collective biography method developed by women in Germany. It is a similar approach to that described in Chapter 2 on radical feminist theory, but in this case, the women were interested more in meaning and how it is embedded in cultural narratives. In a unique way, they studied the individual and social construction of the meanings of their bodies "via the investment of parts of the body with a whole range of social and psychological significance" (Lather, 1991, p. 95). They combined consciousness raising with an analysis of the sexualization of women by writing stories.

> Focusing on a particular body part, each woman wrote a story which was then analyzed collectively by tracing how initial opinions and judgments grew out of existent theories and popular knowledge, how, in essence, their reactions were colonized by dominant patterns of thought. (Lathar, 1991, pp. 95-96)

After the group analysis, they each rewrote their stories. Each woman tried to set aside meanings ascribed by the "dominant discourse" so that writing could become a process of change and a way of defending against seeing themselves only as they were defined by others. With the collective biography, the women became objects of their own research, but they also gathered data on the process of challenging dominant meanings (Lathar, 1991).

Chapter 8

Global Feminism

Feminist activists "thought globally" and traveled to each other's countries long before the 1980s and 1990s focus on global feminism. For example, in 1884, Conception d'Arenal traveled from Spain to address the annual meeting of the National Association of Charities and Corrections in the United States, to argue for education and training of women worldwide; and under Mary McLeod Bethune's administration, the National Association of Colored Women's programs fought not only for anti-lynching measures at home, but also focused on the status of women in the Philippines, Puerto Rico, Haiti, and Africa at the turn of the century (Giddings, 1988). Similarly, The Women's International League for Peace and Freedom has been addressing issues of world peace from women's perspectives since 1915 (Donovan, 1985).

Often, those international travelers focused on the complexities of racism, hierarchical nationalism and sexist control over women across time and place. Today the focus tends to be more explicitly directed at the importance of economic factors, although that is *not* the exclusive focus and unlike socialist feminism, promotion of a particular economic system is not the intent.

Examining women's circumstances cross-nationally exposes the considerable effort that goes into the maintenance of oppressive international political systems in their present forms and the many ways in which women are scarified to those systems. The traditional concepts of masculinity and femininity have been surprisingly hard to perpetuate; studying roles which are presented as natural, yet differ so strikingly between and within countries, reveals the ways in which power is exercised, often to the detriment of women (Enloe, 1989). Earlier chapters describe forms of feminism that are based on examination of sex roles, within certain economic and political systems, but here, the principle is applied globally, that is, cross nationally and cross culturally so as to expose and thereby find ways to eliminate oppression of women. This is sometimes a comparative analysis but more often it is an integrative one.

At a conference sponsored by the United Nations Asian and Pacific Centre for Women and Development, held in Bankok, in 1987, attendees defined feminism in terms of two goals:

1. The freedom from oppression for women involves not only equity, but also the right of women to freedom of choice, and the power to control our own lives within and outside the home. Having control over our lives and bodies is essential to ensure a sense of dignity and autonomy for every woman.
2. The second goal of feminism is the removal of all forms of inequity and oppression through the creation of a more just social and economic order, nationally and internationally. This means the involvement of women in national liberation struggles, in plans for national development, and in local and global struggles for change. (Bunch, 1987, p. 302)

This definition is consistent with a global feminist framework. Because of the nascent nature of theoretical concepts in this area, this chapter focuses primarily on global feminism as a framework for analyzing interconnections and interdependencies among countries and as a movement of positive social change for women around the globe.

THE THEORY

In global feminism, women work "across and despite" national borders, rather than as representatives of national entities. This is in recognition that what happens to women in one part of the world is connected to what happens to women quite far away. Global feminists recognize that elimination of women's oppression worldwide, requires joint efforts. As a result of working together, women the world over are learning from each other how to develop a global perspective and they are bringing this perspective back to local feminist movements (Bunch, 1987). Rather than simply comparing how racism, classism and sexism affect women in various societies, they are using a feminist analysis of larger international systems to study the processes by which women are constrained (Enloe, 1989).

There are many complications in organizing globally. One area over which there is disagreement is the place of nationalism. Nationalist efforts are seen by some colonialized women as both an opportunity to work toward the end of colonial domination and as a legitimizing opportunity within their own countries for women to become active internationally (Enloe, 1989). Charlotte Bunch, on the other hand, described nationalism as the ultimate expression of patriarchal domination in which countries fight for control of territory and resources, while justifying aggression in the name of national security (1987). She pointed out that thinking in terms of national interest interferes with the ability to think globally and allows one to ignore or excuse injustices in other parts of the world. When considering the relative merits of this debate, it is important to note that supporters of nationalism often come from colonized countries, while those who oppose nationalism are frequently from countries where active colonization continues to be a part of their national policy.

At present, the debate takes the form of disagreements over "cultural relativism" as opposed to "universalism." Those who support universalism contend that formal international agreements should apply equally to all signatories and any benefits accrued to women under these agreements should be available to all women, regardless of country. Cultural relativists, on the other hand, insist that each country must decide for itself, based on cultural heritage, how women should be treated. Further, cultural relativists argue that applying Western standards of emancipation and condemning discrimination against women is insensitive, ethnocentric and often imperialist in nature (Mayer, 1995).

For example, some Moslem governments argue that Islam requires that patriarchal political structures remain intact.[1] Undeniably, applying international human rights standards to women would profoundly alter legal systems in some countries in the Middle East. But deferring to governments that insist on international tolerance for discrimination against women (for example, denying women the right to work without their husband's permission) is based on cultural relativist principles, and is seen by universalists as misguided (Mayer, 1995). In another example, when a codicil was added to the Treaty of Maastricht to allow Ireland to restrict women's access to abortion in a way that is quite different from other countries covered by the treaty, universalists argued this was a dangerous retreat from universalism (Chowdhury et al., 1994).

While some cultural relativists maintain that demanding similar rights for women and men is disrespectful of Islam, some Muslim women have articulated feminist concerns about inaccurate interpretations of Islam, often in the context of global feminism. Muslim feminists have described Islam as being distorted in ways that justify a wide variety of state-imposed or state-sanctioned oppressive conditions for women. Despite international agreements[2] to eliminate obstacles to women's equality, including those based on social and cultural patterns of a specific country, the United Nations (UN) has accepted the cultural relativist position (Mayer, 1995).

ARAB FEMINISTS: A MULTITUDE OF EXAMPLES OF GLOBAL FEMINIST ISSUES

Differences and similarities among women with some comparable aspects of their histories but different political nationalities are

---

1. In the West, critiques of sexism in religion have come not from global feminists, but primarily from radical feminists (White and Dorbis, 1993). In large part this is because global feminism examines the activities of businesses and nation states, and most Western countries specifically attempt to separate church and state. The same is not true of Islam in the Middle East.

2. For example, the 1979 Convention on the Elimination of All Forms of Discrimination Against Women (CEDAW), a product of the UN Decade for Women (1976-1985). See the discussions of CEDAW by Kaufman and Lindquist (1995), and by Cook (1994).

highlighted in the works of Arab feminists, whose writings are little known in the West. The interplay among religion, colonialism, nationalism, and gender is brought into clear focus in Arab women's struggles. For these reasons, a relatively lengthy focus on Arab women follows.

In the United States, it is African-American women who have most consistently and systematically exploded narrow definitions of feminism. Worldwide, Arab women may now be offering the most complex counterpart to Western feminisms. Study of Arab feminist activities contributes to the dissolution of a definition of either Western *or* Arab feminism as monolithic (Badran and Cooke, 1990).

The Veil

Many of the discussions both by Arab and by Western feminists center on the veil often worn by Arab women. In these discussions, the veil serves as a symbol of many things including tradition, cultural nationalism, religious commitment, and political perspective.

Moghadem calls the dispute over the veil a battle between patriarchy and feminism. Drawing attention to a simple but profound fact, she quoted Fatima Mernissi: "If fundamentalists are calling for a return to the veil, it must be because women have been taking off the veil" (Mernissi, as cited by Moghadam, 1994, p. 15). Wearing of veils involves complex symbolism and changes across time and place, which are often closely connected to reaction against European colonialism—since it was often during periods of Westernization that women stopped wearing the veil. Debates among Arab feminists regarding the veil have been traced back at least as far as the 1890s when Huda Shaarawi, an Egyptian nationalist, participated in arguments about veiling and seclusion of women, noting that the imposition of such practices did not stem from the Quran; rather, Islam guaranteed Muslims rights regardless of gender (Badran and Cooke, 1990).

Veils were not worn uniformly across classes. For example, in nineteenth-century Egypt, middle- and upper-class women veiled, as did lower-class urban women, but peasant women's work often did not allow for a veil to be worn. In some cases, when the veil had been discarded under colonial rule, veiling and seclusion came to be seen by both women and men as a symbol of cultural and national defense; however, it is a custom that requires restraint only of women (Badran and Cooke, 1990).

Temporal and National Differences

Throughout Arab countries, feminist activities varied in time and in focus:

- Egyptian feminism underwent a resurgence in the early 1930s, when feminists organized under the umbrella organization, the Egyptian Feminist Union.
- They were joined by Palestinian women during the Arab revolt in Palestine in the late 1930s. In 1938 and 1944 pan-Arab conferences were held in Cairo and the Arab Feminist Union was formed.
- In response to the creation of the state of Israel, Palestinian feminists withdrew from the feminist struggle and focused on nationalism. They did not actively rejoin Arab feminist movements until the 1970s and 1980s, at which point they tended to focus heavily on both feminism and nationalism.
- For Kuwaiti women, who had relatively more freedom than women in other Arab countries, feminism became quite visible and active.
- In Sudan, the feminist struggle grew out of a nationalist movement in the 1950s.
- Pan-Arab feminism reemerged in the 1980s within the Arab Women's Solidarity Association (AWSA) and many Arab feminists participated in the UN conference in Nairobi in 1985 (Badran and Cooke, 1990).

The rise and fall of Arab feminism has had serious consequences for women. In Algeria, for example, contraceptive policies became closely linked with religious nationalism. Continued suppression of birth control information was supported with the argument that the many men lost in the revolutionary war against France needed to be replaced. Active suppression of birth control resulted in an average birth rate of 7.9 children per woman. When the government determined that a high birth rate was not good for changes in the capitalist structure, birth control policies were reversed, abortion was legalized, and by 1981, families with many children were penalized by tax laws. At no time were these policies connected to supporting the struggles of women. Interestingly, despite the contradictions over time, the policies were often justified on religious grounds (Helie-Lucas, 1990).

In Iran, women participated actively in the revolution in 1979. While they opposed Shah Mohammed Raza Pahlavi as a tyrannical symbol, some were suspicious of revolutionaries' commitment to fundamentalism and of the use of the veil as a sign of solidarity and opposition to the Shah. Just before the celebration of International Women's Day (IWD) in May 1979, Khomeini, who had taken over the leadership of the revolution, announced restrictive measures against women including compulsory veiling and repeal of the Family Protection Law of 1975, which had "restricted polygyny and men's unilateral right to divorce and to child custody" (Tohidi, 1991). Khomeini's actions so enraged the women planning the IWD celebrations that the rally planned for one day turned into a week-long protest. The government's response to feminists was gradual, but severe. By 1991, all women in Iran, including visitors, were required to wear the veil and observe *Hejab*, the complete covering of the body. Violence against those who do not is condoned. Women are now banned from law, agriculture, archeology, and other fields of study; they need their husbands' written permission to work. The minimum legal age for marriage has been reduced from eighteen to nine for girls. Men are again allowed to have multiple wives—including temporary ones. Abortion is again illegal and women convicted of adultery or more than one act of homosexuality can be stoned to death (Tohidi, 1991).

Meanwhile, in Saudi Arabia, the government prohibited all demonstrations by women following a 1990 demonstration against a ban on women driving (Mayer, 1995). Things have not gone well for feminists in Egypt in the 1990s. AWSA was suppressed and then finally dissolved by the Egyptian government in 1991 for disseminating ideas that opposed state policies. An appeal was lost on religious grounds: that AWSA was an offense against Islam in its criticism of marriage and divorce laws (Mayer, 1995).

Feminists may also be losing ground in Turkey where, historically, the secularization of legal and educational systems had contributed to the emancipation of women, to a point comparable to women in the West. In response, the current Islamic fundamentalist movement in Turkey focuses the bulk of its attention on the status of women. The movement is defining Islam primarily in terms of familial and social differentiation of sex roles, with serious repressive implications for women (Toprak, 1994).

Tohidi cautioned Westerners and Arab feminists alike (1) to note the similarities among fundamentalist religions; (2) to actively seek separation of church and state; and (3) to remember that "the women's question should not be relegated to the days after the revolution" (1991, p. 260).

GLOBAL FEMINISM AND ECONOMICS

Global feminism relies heavily on economic perspectives. By recognizing the links between economic policy, government stability, and women's domestic responsibilities, women in Third World countries have spearheaded the global feminist analysis of international debt politics (Enloe, 1989). The World Bank and the International Monetary Fund (IMF) have profound significance as economic lending bodies and as policy formulators. The IMF, when it loans money, has strict requirements as to the internal economic policies of the recipient nation, meant to maximize the likelihood of repayment. Typically included are requirements for wage reductions, cutbacks in public works, reduction in number of government employees, and, ironically, a simultaneous decrease in social services, just when they are needed most (Braidotti et al., 1994; Enloe, 1989). Debt repayment policies call for "structural readjustment." Such policies often lead to exploitation of workers (Acosta, 1994; Sparr, 1994).

Structural readjustment entails a conscious change in the nature of economic relationships in a debtor society. The term usually refers to a move toward a free market economy (Sparr, 1994). Structural readjustment was introduced by the World Bank in 1979. Loans were provided to countries while the countries stabilized prices and then changed their internal economic policies. Within ten years, 25 percent of World Bank lending involved structural adjustment. In poorer countries having heavy debt, this type of lending accounted for more than half of the loans (Chowdhury et al., 1994). Typically, power is shifted away from public sectors and organized labor toward commercial agriculture, private industry, and exports (Chowdhury et al., 1994).

Ultimately, the implementation of policy, which at first glance seems so remote, actually devolves to women. For example, when food subsidies are lowered, the cost of living increases. At the same time, structural readjustment policies require a decrease in wages. Simultaneously, spending on health, educational activities, and social services is curtailed. Women, who are generally responsible for ensuring that families exist on whatever resources are available, suffer disproportionately. Governments entering into restructuring agreements with the IMF are dependent upon women's willingness and ability to conduct themselves according to the policy's dictates (Enloe, 1989).

Structural adjustment policies have had many negative effects on women workers, including deterioration in working conditions, increased wage differentials between women and men, an increase of women in informal as opposed to formal wage sectors, increased poverty of women, an increase in unpaid labor, and a slowing of progress in girls' education. In response to research on the negative effects of women's poverty, and activism on the part of women's and antipoverty groups, the World Bank has changed its policy somewhat and increased its investments in women. In some instances, it has even provided support to activities specifically designed to improve women's status (World Bank, 1995).[3]

Free Trade Zones and the World Market

A Free Trade Zone is an area of a country in which businesses are encouraged to build factories that produce goods for export. Usually, a special arrangement is made by which an authority is created and given the power to negotiate a wide variety of conditions (tax rates, safety and pollution standards, building contracts, etc.) with local,

---

3. Ironically, as of this writing, President Clinton is battling with Republicans over their proposal to dramatically cut U.S. contributions to World Bank loans in the world's seventy-eight poorest countries (Associated Press, October 11, 1995). These monies go to IDA (International Development Association), one of five organizations comprising the World Bank.

foreign, and multinational businesses. This includes setting and implementing labor standards that may differ considerably from the country's usual practices. Sometimes the authority is responsible for recruitment of workers as well (Rosa, 1994).

> The free trade zone is a haven for foreign investment, complete with electricity and other infrastructure and a labor force often housed in nearby dormitories. It is a colonial-style economic order, tailor-made for multinational corporations. Customs-free import of raw materials, components and equipment, tax holidays of up to 20 years and government subsidization of operating costs are some of the enticements to investment. (Fuentes and Ehrenreich, 1982, p. 10)

During the massive global restructuring of capital in the late 1960s, large numbers of women entered the labor force via Free Trade Zones (FTZs) (Rosa, 1994). Annette Fuentes and Barbara Ehrenreich reported that a 1971 survey listed low wage rates as the primary reason corporations gave for choosing other countries for manufacturing. Sound business sense from a corporate perspective perhaps, but what does this mean to employees? Health, safety, wage and benefit requirements, and pollution standards can be avoided by relocating to areas where the need for jobs is desperate enough, and where regulations are minimal and seldom enforced—when they exist (Fuentes and Ehrenreich, 1982). Typically, strategies for reduced cost of production require companies to transfer their production to FTZs. The economic development generally promised to a host country turns out to be premised on workers being and remaining poor since, when labor costs rise, companies threaten to, and sometimes do, move elsewhere (Fuentes and Ehrenreich, 1982).

Women are paid less than men the world over. They become the obvious choice of a company looking for cheap labor (Fuentes and Ehrenreich, 1982).[4] As factories relocate in search of cheap labor, young Third World women constitute the bulk of the labor force. The intersection of sexual, class, and racial ideologies are highlighted in choice and treatment of these workers (Mohanty, 1991).

---

4. Examples of this in the United States are garment sweatshops in the cities and the electronics industry in the area of Silicon Valley, California.

Most of the women are between sixteen and twenty-five years old, with younger workers usually hired in electronics and textile industries where dexterity and eyesight need to be especially good. Older women workers are often employed in food processing, where conditions can be much harder, since the older women are unlikely to find work elsewhere and are therefore less apt to complain. The women often live in overcrowded dormitories and earn subsistence level incomes. Frequently, the working conditions are very dangerous to their health. Sexual harassment is a persistent part of factory work (Fuentes and Ehrenreich, 1982).

Women's vulnerability to unfair labor practices increased in the 1980s with increasingly globalized patterns of investment (Mitter, 1994). In South Korea, women work six-month-long probationary periods at three-fourths of the normal pay rate. It is quite common to be laid off before the "apprenticeship" period ends so the full pay rate is never given. Casual laborers lose access to the benefits and legal rights more often granted permanent workers. The practice is common enough that many of the women workers refer to themselves as "permanent casuals" (Fuentes and Ehrenreich, 1982). Such casualized labor increased markedly during the 1980s. As subcontracting spreads, removing workers further from protection, the frequency of "home work" rises. Although home work is more flexible than factory work, it is also more subject to exploitation (Mitter, 1994). An additional problem is the enmeshment of casual labor with underground economies that provide still fewer avenues for redress by exploited workers.

In wealthier countries, immigrants from poorer countries, rather than indigenous women, usually are recruited into home work (Mitter, 1994). U.S. examples include women from Asia and the Pacific Rim or from Latin America who are recruited into "sweatshops," or hidden garment-manufacturing shops, where women work excessively long hours for less then half of minimum wage, sometimes suffering physical abuse in addition to their economic exploitation. In August and September, 1995, a flurry of newspaper stories in the *Los Angeles Times* (James, 1995), *San Francisco Chronicle* (Business Digest, 1995a; Business Digest, 1995b); and *The Boston Globe* (California subpoenas top retailers, 1995) ran stories on Thai women who were reported to have been held in slave-like conditions, making garments for some of the largest department stores in the United States.

However, not all the employees see the multinationals in a negative light. Export industries sometimes have mixed effects on women. Advancement and job stability may be severely limited, but at the same time, average wages may be high compared to other work available to the women (Sparr, 1994). Brazilian women reported finding wider horizons, opportunity for individualization and independence from family, and the chance for interaction with other women afforded by factory work (Fuentes and Ehrenreich, 1982). Unlike Malaysian women, urban Tanzanian women's status within their families *increased* when they became employed in wage-earning jobs (Sparr, 1994).

Economic Systems and Domestic Labor

The rise in employment of middle-class women in the West, without a corresponding expansion in availability of child care, may have contributed to an increased call for domestic workers, but international debt policies have had a far greater impact on domestic work. Inability to find work at home, coupled with encouragement by their governments for women to work in other countries and send a substantial portion of their wages back home, has led to emigration in search of work—with domestic work often being the only type available. Many Jamaican, Mexican, and Filipino workers end up in Britain, Italy, Singapore, Canada, Kuwait, and the United States "cleaning bathrooms in the country of the bankers" (Enloe, 1989, p. 185). Guest status and ability to work is often dependent upon the goodwill of the employer who must vouch for the domestic worker. The woman's family cannot afford to have her lose her job. In the Philippines, there is an average of five people dependent on the wages sent home by each overseas worker (Enloe, 1989). Fuentes and Ehrenreich (1982, p. 37) summed up the situation of women in the late twentieth-century global economy as follows:

> Crudely put, the relationship between many Third World governments and multinational corporations is like that of a pimp and his customers. The governments advertise their women, sell them and keep them in line for the multinational "johns."

But there are other parties to the growing international traffic in women: Western governments, the World Bank, The International Monetary Fund (IMF) and the United Nations Industrial Development Organization (UNIDO).

The Economics and Control of Sex

The politicization of the intersection of race and sex in the West was clarified and codified in laws such as the 1880s Cantonment Acts. These allowed British colonial police to force women near military bases, usually women of color, to submit to genital examinations to ensure they would not infect British soldiers with venereal diseases. Continued politicization of the intersection of race and sex in the military was evident in the World War II debate about relationships between black American soldiers and white British women. Attempts to control what was seen as a dangerous practice (interracial relationships) included warnings directed at women, proposals to keep African-American soldiers out of Britain, confinement of these soldiers to base, and export of African-American women soldiers to the British bases. Enloe noted that while practices similar to those outlined under the Cantonment Acts continue today,[5] health risks associated with prostitution are only described as a problem in areas where foreign soldiers and the women they are sexually active with are of different races. Pointing to the United Nations World Tourism Organization's forecast that by the year 2000, tourism will be the most important global economic activity, Enloe indicated that global feminists need to closely examine the industry. In Jamaica, for example, as of the mid-1980s, tourism earned more in foreign exchange than sugar. International business travelers are predominantly men, while service workers are generally women (Enloe, 1989).

Organized prostitution, a segment of the tourism industry referred to as the "hospitality industry" employs thousands of women (Fuentes and Ehrenreich, 1982). Enloe quoted a German travel agency's depiction of travel brochures featuring sex with

---

5. Currently, the practices include AIDS testing. For example, Filipino women who work as prostitutes near the U.S. Navy base in Olongapo submit to compulsory AIDS and VD testing twice a month (Enloe, 1989, p. 89).

Thai women as part of the travel package. In the Philippines as well, sex tourism has become crucial to the country's economic survival. Sex tourism is an integral component of worldwide economic policies which ensure that Third World women, in particular, are desperately poor enough to enter prostitution and that chances for escape from the sex industry are virtually nonexistent for those who seek to leave, while working conditions are often deplorable. The industry is often supported by governmental alliances, but without needed health and social services provided to the workers (Enloe, 1989). Connections between economic and sexual exploitation are most evident in forced prostitution. For example, in India, girls are sometimes sold by poverty-stricken families, and in both India and the United States, girls and women running away from forced marriages in the former and physical and sexual abuse in the latter may be forced into the sex trade industry by lack of alternative jobs, safe places to live, etc. (Bunch, 1987).[6]

Economy and Ecology

Women who refer to their work as ecofeminist have been included here when their work takes a global feminist perspective. By that I mean that their concern for the environment is expressed in terms of the control that some nation-states exert over others, and that the theorists focus on how worldwide economic and political policies contribute to the destruction of the environment. Starhawk, (1990, pp. 82-83) an American who refers to her work as ecofeminist, described the connections as follows:

> It is the poor who are forced to work directly with unsafe chemicals, in whose neighborhoods toxic waste incinerators are planned, who cannot afford to buy bottled water and organic vegetables or pay for medical care. Environmental issues are international issues, for we cannot simply export unsafe pesticides, toxic wastes, and destructive technologies without poisoning the whole living body of the Earth. And environmental issues are women's issues, for women sicken, starve, and die from

---

6. For a discussion of presence and absence of coercion in sex work see: Valerie Jenness' work (1990).

toxics, droughts, and famines, their capacity to bear life is threatened by pollution, and they bear the brunt of care for the sick and the dying, as well as for the next generation.

It is at this juncture that ecofeminism overlaps with global feminist theory. Merchant (1990, p. 105) listed as ecofeminist issues: the women's Chipco, sometimes called "tree-hugging" movement in India, in which women seek to protect their fuel resources from lumber companies; the women's Green Belt movement in Kenya, in which massive efforts toward tree planting resulted in more than two million trees being planted in ten years; and Native American women's efforts to protect children who had been exposed to radioactivity from uranium mining.

Ecological problems are described in terms of economic injustices perpetrated by developed (wealthy, mostly Northern hemisphere) countries against undeveloped (economically poor, mostly Southern hemisphere) countries. Structural adjustment programs, when they divert government spending away from health, education, and food subsidies, direct money toward goods that are internationally tradable for foreign currency. In agriculture, foods that are encouraged are those that can be sold rather than consumed locally, and agricultural methods that are unsound ecologically are used to force production of tradable goods. Soils, air, and water become contaminated by chemicals, and deforestation contributes to decreasing biodiversity (Braidotti et al., 1994).

Even as women are required to provide for their families with fewer government supports and less economic access, environmental degradation, particularly in the Southern hemisphere, has accelerated. This has local impacts: it makes fuelwood, animal fodder, and water more scarce in many areas, thus making it more difficult for those women who depended on such items for their families' subsistence. It also has global impacts, contributing to a larger problem of ecological damage (Braidotti et al., 1994).

In the United Nations Conference on Environment and Development (UNCED) 1992 Earth Summit in Rio de Janeiro, governments, the World Bank, and other businesses proposed solutions to environmental crises. The solutions were termed "sustainable development" programs. When ecologists define sustainable development, they indicate policies that differ from present development plans in that they meet current *and future* needs without destroying the environment in the process (Braidotti et al., 1994). This is not what was proposed by governments and businesses at the 1992 Earth Summit. While acknowledging that an environmental crisis existed, the solutions proposed involved doing more of what is already being done: focus on increasing economic growth and increased technological intervention in an effort to manage the natural environment, that is, decrease the say of local people over how their environment should be managed. Braidotti and colleagues argued that technology is often applied ruthlessly and that large-scale projects such as dams typically serve the interest of industrialization and modernization, sacrificing local, rural populations.

Another problem is that the focus on increased production discounts the productivity of both women and the environment.

> A stable and clean river is not a productive resource in this view. It needs to be "developed" with dams to become productive. Women, sharing the river as a commons to satisfy the water needs of their families and society, are thus not involved in productive labor. When they are replaced by man's engineering, water management and water use become productive activities. Natural forests are unproductive according to Western patriarchy. (Shiva, 1990, p. 191)

Waring (1988) called such systems of accounting for what counts as work "applied patriarchy." Tasks are added as though women were doing nothing previously; the environment is degraded, making women's work more difficult to perform, yet the increased economic resources remain inaccessible to women. Global feminists argue instead that local control is important as is recognition of differential effects of environmental policy on women and on members of different classes and ethnic groups (Braidotti et al., 1994). They have recommended a number of alternatives to the ecologically damaging structural adjustment programs, for example, providing women access to public sector services such as water, electricity, health care, education, and transportation or implementing programs such as the *structural transformation* proposed by The Economic Commission for Africa (ECA). The alternative strategy relies on human-centered economic recovery, with full input from the general population in the design, implementation, and monitoring of the programs. In this vein, the African Charter for Popular Participation in Development (1990) called for international support of indigenous efforts toward participation in political and economic decisions of their countries. African women have argued for incorporation of women's concerns in economic adjustment programs, providing for basic needs, such as child care, education, and employment. They also proposed that women's bureaus be added to economic ministries to review proposed legislation and programs in terms of their potential impact on women (Elabor-Idemudia, 1994).

SEXUAL VIOLENCE, GENDER, AND WAR

Rape is frequently a condition of international disputes. Witness the rape of German women by Russian soldiers in World War II, while at the same time, "comfort women," mostly Korean, but also Filipino, Chinese, Indonesian, and some Dutch women, as hostages of the Japanese army, were moved from battlefield to battlefield to motivate and reward Japanese soldiers. Many Bengali women were raped during war of independence from Pakistan. Uncharacteristically, the war in Boznia-Herzegovina drew international attention to rape. In this case, rape was used as part of a campaign of "ethnic cleansing" committed by Serbs against Bosnian Muslim women (Copelon, 1995).[7] This time rape was not discounted as "poor discipline" on the part of needy soldiers who had momentarily lost control, as it often tends to be described. It was recognized around the world for the heinous crime it is. In part, this occurred because of the clear attention drawn to the role of ethnicity in selection of victims. Although Serbs certainly were not the only ones guilty of rape, they seemed more willing to enunciate their purposes. Additionally, given the lack of attention and outrage usually accorded to wartime rape, the situation in Boznia appeared unique. It wasn't (Copelon, 1995).

---

7. The attempt was to decrease the contribution of Bosnian Muslim's to the gene pool by holding women captive and forcing them to bear children who were considered genetically superior by virtue of their Serbian paternity.

Rape has long been a weapon of war used, as in Boznia-Herzego-vina, to destabilize populations and dilute ethnic and racial identity. The parallels between genocide, where people are destroyed based on their identity as a people, and rape, where a woman is degraded and abused based on her identity as a woman, intersect in the genocidal rape of women, as in Bosnia. The contempt for and dehumanization of Muslim women were clarified in that war (Copelon, 1995).[8]

But the attention to rape in global feminism is not limited to genocidal rape, as in Bosnia. Global feminists have pointed out that the killing, torture, and inhumane treatment during time of war, which are forbidden by The Geneva Conventions, do not specify rape as a similar crime. Nor is rape recognized as a form of torture. This is because of the failure to recognize gender as a category of persecution. While it is important to acknowledge that religion, ethnicity, and gender were *all* used in selection of Bosnian Muslim women as targets, it is essential to also recognize that when women are raped simply as women, it should still be cause for international outrage (Copelon, 1995), and nation states should still be held accountable (Bunch, 1995).

CRITIQUE

Global feminists, particularly those whose work focuses on eco-logical problems, sometimes demonize technological development. Certainly there is much to be learned from societies in which technology is at a minimum, but the solution to our ecological crisis does not lie in technology avoidance, nor did women's problems originate with the advent of technology. As Eisler (1990) pointed out, not all technological tools kill and oppress. In many instances, appropriate technology reduces the burden of manual labor for women (Elabor-Idemudia, 1994).

As with other forms of feminism, it is a mistake here too, to see women as only passive victims. Women have been active in resisting

---

8. In America, a very similar thing occurred when "enslaved African women in the southern United States were raped as property to produce babies who were then bartered, sold, and used as property" (Copelon, 1995, p. 205).

oppressive global economic and development policies, and they have planned and provided for themselves despite the loss of resources. Enloe (1989) argued against describing global economic policy solely in terms of bad behavior on the part of businessmen; this ignores the complicity of some "respectable" women (Enloe's example was Margaret Thatcher) and fails to accurately depict how international systems operate with women functioning as the "glue" that holds the system together. It also discounts some of the very real economic needs of women that *are* being met when women obtain employment and even minimal economic self-sufficiency for the first time even when initial employment occurs in a Free Trade Zone.

For Muslim women, decisions about whether to wear the veil have not been made simply at the whim of Westerners who discouraged it *or* Islamic fundamentalists who insisted on it. Women have been agents in their own decisions whether to wear the veil or not. Although sometimes they had more choice than at other times, decisions about whether to wear the veil involve a complex interplay of actual religious beliefs, a utilitarian use of a religious symbol to assert separation from colonial rule, an interest in promoting women's emancipation, and a way of distinguishing themselves from nationals of more or less progressive Islamic countries.

Bunch (1987) asserted that global feminism exists through worldwide feminist activity and thought. There *is* a lack of central doctrine and organization. But, according to Bunch, it is more than made up for by a fundamental questioning of social organization, viewed from the perspectives of women within varying cultures. The test is in the action. Rather than getting caught up in trying to define a single cohesive theory that will apply to all cultures and nation-states, the point is to develop *a global perspective*, allowing feminism to diversify and expand, while still maintaining a focus on perspectives offered by women (Bunch, 1987).

There is much left to be done. What we do in the United States affects women in other parts of the world. Bunch (1987) gave as an example the fight by U.S. women to eliminate harmful birth control devices. This struggle is only successful if the device is eliminated, rather than withdrawn from the United States only to be used on women in other countries. It is the responsibility of U.S. feminists to change the way the United States exercises power in the world, specifically in regard to military aggression, foreign aid and trade policies, nuclear and chemical contamination, support of traffic in women, and use of women internationally as a cheap labor pool (Bunch, 1987).

Citizenship and immigration laws, which serve to define insiders and outsiders (Mohanty, 1991), also need feminist attention. Laws defining who may enter and under what circumstances, control not only entry but also racial definitions. For example, the "yellow peril" stereotype operating in the 1800s was closely connected to immigration laws (resulting from hearings on Chinese prostitution) that allowed immigration officers the latitude to determine whether women entering from China, Japan, and Mongolia were criminals who would engage in immoral behavior or were people with good character. The stereotype was transformed to the "model minority" when immigration laws changed to a quota system that welcomed Asian professionals with technical and specialized training (Mohanty, 1991). Applying a global feminist perspective to U.S. and other immigration laws could help eliminate racism in the laws' direct and indirect effects on women.

In sum, global feminism provided an important lens with which to analyze the connections among seemingly unrelated problems experienced by women in different parts of the world.

APPLICATION OF GLOBAL FEMINISM TO SOCIAL WORK PRACTICE

Policy

Rosenthal (1991) argued that the task of the international social worker is facilitation of indigenous self-sufficiency. A global feminist would take more of an *inter*dependent stand. The interrelationship among social welfare issues in developing countries and those in the United States is reflected in such work as the provision of social services to refugees in the United States (Rosenthal, 1991) and social workers' attempts to address the effects of U.S. workers' unemployment (Jones, 1992) when companies move jobs to other parts of the world.

In some cases, work in other countries might be similar to what needs to be done in the United States. For example, international social work practitioners might work for decriminalization of prostitution, abolition of discrimination against women in education, in employment, and in access to health care. In other cases, the work would be distinct: the Mexican battered women's movement benefited from maintaining international ties, but direct application of practices used in industrialized countries would not be feasible. For example, the housing shortages and lack of telephones make the shelter and hot-line models ineffectual for cross-cultural transfer of service models (Cox, 1992).

Administration/Organizations

There are a number of international organizations focusing on ecofeminist issues including the Women's Environmental and Development Organization's (WEDO) and the World Women's Congress for a Healthy Planet (Abzug, 1994). The example reviewed here is that of a system of local organizations that work on problems described by global feminist theorists.

Kumudhini Rosa works with women employees in Free Trade Zones in Sri Lanka. Often, the women have moved some distance from their families. Religious organizations work to integrate the women into the activities of the villages near the FTZ, and they work to educate the women about their rights. Some of the organizations provide boarding houses with space available where the women can meet to discuss issues and to socialize. Christian and Buddhist organizations have formed an alliance to help the women stop the sexual harassment they experience at work. Former FTZ factory workers started a very popular women's center that offers legal, medical, educational services, and job skills training. It also provides instruction on women's rights. Rosa pointed out, however, that these organizations work for, and on behalf of, women. Continued progress would mean encouraging the development of organizations initiated by the women workers themselves, rather then by religious groups (Rosa, 1994).

Community Organizing

Chowdhury and colleagues described the United Nations International Women's Year (1975) and Decade for Women (1976-1985) as phenomenally helpful ways of nourishing global connections among women. By providing the resources for organizing to women who otherwise would not have had access to them, the UN, (perhaps unwittingly, Chowdhury et al. implied) promoted the development of feminist theorizing and organizing. The UN did this by creating international forums for action that highlighted women and provided the means by which women could gather and compare data. Perhaps most importantly, the UN provided a mechanism by which women could hold their governments accountable for injustices suffered by women. Chowdhury and colleagues suggested that the three UN women's conferences (in Mexico City in 1975, Copenhagen in 1980, and Nairobi in 1985) raised the global connections among women to a qualitatively different level (Chowdhury et al., 1994, p. 9). That work continued in Beijing in 1995.

Maria Suarez Toro (1995) pointed out that using formal international strategies is only one way of organizing for positive social change for women on a global scale. Another approach is to organize on a grassroots level, the women who are negatively affected by international policies. Toro argued that most gains for women have emerged from women's struggles in their own communities. Additionally, when women organize themselves they can more quickly move beyond women-as-victims thinking. The methods Toro recommended for organizing women to combat the political violence in Central America included consciousness raising, or encouraging women to think first about how their rights have been violated, and working with them to analyze international policies and how they pertain to women. In the process, women would be encouraged to discuss their fears as well as their enthusiasm for participating in change processes, and they would provide support and encouragement to each other to continue their social change activities. Based on their analysis of the problems and needs, the women would then formulate strategies and plans for action on multiple levels: local, national, and international. Toro also recommended that Central American women form regional networks to share experiences and agendas and influence each others' work.

Group Work

Patricia Robin Herbst (1992) described a group she provided to Cambodian women survivors of torture. The group consisted of women who had escaped rural Cambodia during the Pol Pot regime (1975-1979) by walking through the jungles into Thailand. After living for several years in refugee camps, the women and their children had resettled in Chicago. Language, American customs, city living, unfamiliar foods, strange transportation systems, and lack of access to money all provided significant obstacles, complicated immeasurably by histories of torture and loss.

Clinicians at the Marjorie Kolver Center, one of five centers in the United States that work with survivors of torture, provided an oral history group to interested survivors. Group members worked with an interpreter and a clinician to provide histories of their pasts, in part to emphasize that their lives incorporated but were not the equivalent of their experience with torture. In the process, the women described their experiences with the Khmer Rouge[9], in part, to heal themselves and in part, to educate others in hopes that such a thing would not happen again. Herbst (1992) described striking positive changes in the women after they had the opportunity to tell their stories and express their rage.

Casework and Research

In this example, case work and research are discussed together. Casework is used differently here than in other sections of the book. The "case" is a country and the research is a project described in a book which is astonishing for the extent and quality of the global feminist work. In *Women and Politics Worldwide*, forty-three nation-states are represented by articles from indigenous women, reporting data on the political subordination of women and, importantly, on women's political engagement in each of their countries.

What made this study different from other studies of comparative politics was: (1) the focus on women; (2) the not-unexpected confirmation of women's status—women's political status, access, and influence is less than men's in every country studied; (3) the attention

---

9. The Khmer Rouge was a revolutionary organization headed by Saloth Sar (Pol Pot). The regime was responsible for the imprisonment, torture, and deaths of hundreds of thousands of Cambodian men, women, and children between April 17, 1975 and January 7, 1979. The regime is the subject of the movie, *The Killing Fields*.

to activism outside of formal politics, in part, as a recognition of women's exclusion from formal politics, but also in acknowledgment of the accomplishments made outside of formal systems; and (4) the specific attention to global feminism (Chowdhury et al., 1994). The book describes the process and results of a nine-year research project that contributes enormously to our understanding of women's situations and perspectives and interrelationships around the globe.

In sum, as this chapter and indeed the entire book illustrates, neither Western nor Third World feminisms are monolithic schools of analysis. The media image of the whole of feminism, particularly Western feminism, as limited to a few eccentrics, or to those who wish to join the corporate boardroom has been used against not only the broad range of women in the West who are concerned about feminism and its interaction with other forms of oppression, but also against women who are organizing elsewhere (Bunch, 1987). Presented as an aberration of elite Western women, who are unconcerned with all but their own narrow interest group, Western feminism is reduced to a narrow form of conservative, liberal feminism and portrayed as disinterested in survival issues (Bunch, 1987). The image continues to be used against feminists and at times has proven to be an effective divisive tool. Contrary to that image, feminist responses to injustice against women have taken many forms.

Chapter 9

Conclusions

Feminists will probably continue to disagree about feminist theories and how best to apply them to social work practice. Disconcerting though that may be, disharmony is more likely to promote the ongoing development of theories that are mindful of women's differences as well as similarities. Still, to return to a point raised in the Introduction, theories that contradict each other can sometimes lead to actions that are at cross purposes, and so it is important to be aware of contradictions.

This chapter highlights the distinctions and parallels among the theories. Starting with a summary sentence meant to articulate the gist of each theory, I highlight the dissimilarities among the branches. In the next section, I describe four social issues: alcohol problems, battering, women's employment, and sex work from each of several contrasting theoretical perspectives. In each case, speaking as a proponent of that theory, I describe how the problem would be viewed, and I list recommendations for intervention that fall within that framework. Then I briefly discuss the solutions to the problems proposed by the differing theories. In the final section, I outline some of the questions left unanswered by feminist theories.

Liberal feminism argues that, based on gender, women are unfairly denied equal access to society's resources. **Radical feminism** argues that society is psychologically structured on male needs, that to maintain that order women's needs are subjugated, and that the fabric of society must be fundamentally altered. **Lesbian feminism** challenges the organization of society around both heterosexual and male dominance and the ongoing enforcement of that arrangement. **Cultural feminism** holds that women are more peaceful, cooperative, and nurturing than men, probably because women reproduce and nurture the species. **Ecofeminism** is the application of women's culture to efforts toward peace and ecology. **Socialist feminism** blames the economics of capitalism in combination with patriarchy for women's subordinate position in society. **Womanism** defines sexism as one of multiple, interlocking systems of oppression functioning simultaneously and interdependently, inextricable from each other theoretically or experientially. **Postmodern feminism** argues that, since *woman* is a socially defined and inherently distorting term, which cannot be defended on empirical or theoretical grounds, we have no reason to think females have an inherent nature or role. Thus, social organization rooted in gender is based on an invented concept. **Global feminism** seeks to explain the interconnectedness of disparate feminist struggles by examining how worldwide economic factors combine with national histories of colonialism, religion and culture to oppress women.

EXAMPLES OF CONTRASTING VIEWS WITHIN FEMINISMS

These examples provide contrasting approaches to problem definition and problem solving. To make the points clearer, I exaggerated the differences among the theories. The boundaries are less distinct in real life than they are in these theoretical exercises. Once again, I want to caution the reader that these are my formulations. There will probably be feminists who espouse each of these theories who would disagree with the distinctions and potential solutions I suggest here.

Alcohol Problems

Cultural Feminism

It may not be clear where alcohol problems in women come from, but since it is women's nature to develop in the context of relationships, treatment should focus on connections between women. If a spiritual approach is used to help women recover, it should center on feminist spirituality, perhaps with a focus on the goddess, since praying to a male deity may be incongruent with women's sense of a healing, nurturing power as female. Women with alcohol problems would recover best in a woman-only program that employs an all-woman staff and focuses on the nurturing aspects of women's nature. Political change will occur naturally as more and more women heal, recognize the need for more attention to women's ways of knowing and conducting the business of the world, and with the inner strength they gain through recovery, become more able to assume positions of power, to which they will bring women's perspective.

Radical Feminism

Because of sexist assumptions about proper roles, women are overdiagnosed with alcohol problems, even when they simply drink moderately. We need to stop pathologizing women who step outside prescribed roles. Occasionally, however, women do develop problems with alcohol. These seemingly "private" alcohol problems are one way of coping with stress induced by living in a patriarchal society in which women have inadequate access to power over their own lives. To decrease alcohol problems in women, sexism needs to be eliminated from society. Consciousness-raising groups would help women put their problems in context politically and help women heal the psychological damage done to them by sexism. The groups would also provide a format in which women could make plans and take action to alter the sexist structures contributing to their alcohol problems.

Liberal Feminism

Women develop alcohol problems for exactly the same reasons, perhaps even at similar rates, as men do. Because the alcohol treatment industry is accustomed to thinking of alcoholism as a man's problem, women's problems with alcohol tend to be underdiagnosed. The primary changes that are needed to correct this situation are for women's alcoholism to be diagnosed more readily and for treatment to be made as available to women who need it as it is to men. Since alcohol problems are alcohol problems, regardless of who has them, no major changes would need to be made in treatment settings. Therefore, there is no reason why women cannot be accommodated immediately if providers will simply pay attention to the need. Minor accommodations might include acknowledgment of women's child care responsibilities and ideally, some assistance with helping women plan their child care arrangements during treatment.

Solutions

<u>Cultural</u>
- connections between women
- woman-only programs
- feminist spirituality
- political change will take care of itself

<u>Radical</u>
- eliminate sexism
- narrow the definition of alcohol problems
- stop pathologizing women who drink
- consciousness raising groups
- plan and execute fundamental political change

<u>Liberal</u>
- broaden the definition of alcohol problems
- expand case-finding efforts to women
- open men's treatment programs to women
- help women meet their child care needs

Discussion

The varying emphasis on political activism may not be a problem since different women could focus their energies differently and still make some headway. The most serious problems here would be the disagreements over whether women could be adequately served in male-modeled programs and whether case finding should be expanded to include more women who need help or narrowed to avoid overpathologizing women who drink.

Battering

Lesbian Feminism

Our culture is a violent one in which we learn to settle disputes with violence instead of by more peaceful means. People sometimes express their frustration through violent attempts to control others, and frustration with sexism and heterosexism may contribute to violence in lesbian relationships. Thinking of battering only in terms of men battering women fails to acknowledge how women can also internalize violent means of problem solving. Seeing violence as male behavior obscures lesbian battering and prevents lesbians from getting the help they need. As much as lesbians might like to avoid any new reasons for heterosexist people to denigrate lesbian communities, hiding such a serious problem can make matters worse.

What is needed instead is for lesbians to have access to shelters and other services for battered women. While lesbian-only services might be preferable, they are impractical, given the small numbers of women who would need the services and the likelihood that funders would not be willing to provide for a group held in contempt by society. Furthermore, creating separate services could inadvertently contribute to replication of heterosexism, with services for lesbians being funded less adequately, resulting in lower quality services than those provided to heterosexual women. The best way to change society is not to accept segregation, but to force service systems to acknowledge lesbians and the possibility of lesbianism and change to accommodate their needs. This would also provide a helpful model to heterosexual women: although they may or may not choose to partner with women, they do not have to accept society's constrictions on women's roles.

Womanism

Woman battering is a function of rage inappropriately vented at women. Violence against women is unlikely to be seen as a serious social problem. It is particularly unlikely to be taken seriously if the abused woman is a woman of color. This is complicated by the inability of poor women to access needed resources to escape violent victimization. Shelters for battered women have been successful, of late, in their outreach to women of color and have included more diverse groups among their service recipients, but the model is still primarily a white one.

What is needed is joint consideration of race, class, and gender issues. Service providers must consider the increased likelihood that an African-American man who is arrested for battering will be mistreated by the criminal justice system. In encouraging women to hold their batterers responsible, providers must realize that while this is necessary, it is unlikely to be done in a fair or reasonable way by the criminal justice system. Additionally, while pro-arrest may have been found to serve as a deterrent for future battering for white men, the same policy may simply add to the increasing numbers of African-American men in jail without providing a batterer the opportunity for rehabilitation.

The issue needs to be considered in a sociological perspective. Injuring African-American women is always unacceptable. At the same time, rage felt by black men in American society is perfectly reasonable. These two facts need to be considered together so that responses simultaneously attack the reasons for, and the inappropriate expression of, rage. Dismantling affirmative action and other gains made by African Americans must be stopped. The backlash against black progress needs to be reversed. At the same time, programs for battered women must help women focus first on their safety and right to freedom from abuse, and second, on ways to change black communities to decrease male violence against women without dividing the community along gender lines.

The increased risk of a battered woman of color losing custody of her children must be acknowledged and stopped. Women of color are caught in a reprehensible system of integrated oppressions that often forces them to choose between continuing to live with battering or risking loss of child custody, while jailing their partners in a criminal justice system that is likely to mistreat men of color. Dissolution of this complex web of oppression is more likely to occur if social action is an integral component of services in which both battered women and the staff who serve them are actively engaged. Social action against racism, sexism, and classism cannot be peripheral activities of the staff reserved for times when more day-to-day needs are met. At the same time, the combined effects of racism, sexism, and battering can be devastating to African-American women's spirits; thus, social action alone is insufficient. Intrapersonal healing, often of a spiritual nature, must also be a component of intervention.

Liberal Feminism

Battering results from a variety of problems, including the ways that women and men are socialized, with women socialized to be passive and men to be aggressive. Women and men learn that their respective sex roles are limited, and sometimes the limitations are rigid, with men being required to provide economically but constrained from expressing fears and inadequacies. Women are prevented from having equal access to sources of income and other resources that might lighten men's load and increase women's self-esteem and sense of competence. In addition, women learn to be compliant with men's expectations, and men learn to control women. This imbalance occasionally gets out of control. Both women and men suffer personally from this, with women often physically bearing the brunt of the problem.

The solution is, in part, to resocialize both women and men. Women need to be taught that they do not deserve to be victimized by domestic violence. They can be assertive and insist on safety and respect. Men need to learn that violence is not acceptable, even if it is socially condoned, and to use assertiveness in place of aggression.

To protect a woman and children, and to help teach a man that he needs to learn different ways of expressing himself, it is often necessary, at least initially, to use the criminal justice system. Once a woman is taught that she has the right to assert herself and insist on protection, she can use restraining orders and similar measures to reinforce the message that the man's behavior needs to change. If he refuses to learn new behaviors and continues to abuse her, he should be punished by being sent to jail. Since the criminal justice system has been slow to recognize these needs, it is often necessary to lobby for new laws, including "pro-arrest" policies, in which a spouse who perpetrates domestic violence is arrested automatically, even if the injured spouse is not able to assert herself, or himself, by signing a complaint.

Radical Feminism

Woman-battering is a logical outgrowth of a misogynist society in which women are disrespected and are forced to be dependent on men. To end battering, we need a massive reorganization of society so that violence against women will no longer be tolerated and women will no longer be economically and psychologically dependent on men. In the interim, to help battered women escape from their batterers, an underground system of safe houses needs to be maintained.

To begin to heal from the terrible psychological and physical wounds of male battering, women need some time away from men. Since legal systems are also misogynist and tend to blame women for their battering, it is not useful to depend on the legal system's protection. The system typically fails to protect women, anyhow, and fails to account for the fact that leaving is sometimes the most dangerous thing a woman can do since that is when a large portion of women are seriously injured or killed. If a woman decides to pursue legal protection, however, she needs support and advocates who will accompany her to appointments and remind both her and the legal system that the problem is violent sexism, not any fault of hers.

The goal should be to escape permanently. This will require economic and psychological liberation from her batterer/oppressor, from oppressive social and economic systems that kept her trapped, and from her internalization of oppressive messages. More immediately, she will need help finding a place to live and a job that will support her and any children she has. Sometimes, safety will require her to move from safe house to safe house until she finds a permanent location where she can be free from the batterer.

Solutions

Lesbian Feminism
- open "straight" women's shelters to lesbians
- avoid ghettoization of separate services
- force society to acknowledge and accommodate lesbians
- stop defining battering as male-only behavior
- examine how society produces violence

Womanism
- services must focus simultaneously on race, gender, and class issues, and work toward changing all three, not just talking about them in counseling
- expect some women of color to want to protect themselves in different ways than mainstream white women might want

- help women of color focus on ways to heal their community from all forms of violence, including violence against women
- attention to child custody issues should be an integral component of services
- address the psychological results of oppression, including spirituality in intervention

Liberal Feminism

- use the criminal justice system as a source of funding and to help women protect themselves
- lobby to make the criminal justice system more responsive to women
- assertiveness training for women and men to help change inappropriately socialized behaviors
- teach men that violence is not acceptable and that they will be punished for it
- define domestic violence as a family issue so it will not be dismissed as applying only to women
- avoid inflammatory issues so as to increase funding opportunities

Radical Feminism

- keep women away from the influence of all men during the initial psychological healing
- do not depend on the legal system since it is designed to serve the patriarchy and thus can never meet women's needs
- avoid criminal justice funding as the money will lead to co-optation and redefinition of services
- strengthen the focus on *woman* abuse and the misogyny inherent in choice of target
- help liberate the woman psychologically and economically so she can escape permanently
- continue to develop the underground system of safe houses for women

Discussion

Few people will argue for separate battered women's services for lesbians, primarily because of practicality rather than philosophical issues. How openly services to lesbians should be acknowledged and marketed is contentious, depending on whether you are trying to change society to acknowledge and accommodate lesbians or trying to keep lesbians in a low profile to maintain funding. Using the criminal justice system as a source of funding has economic benefits, but feminists are conflicted about whether violence against women should be treated as different than other kinds of violence and how much that funding source will negatively alter the mission of the shelter movement.

Problem definition raises a multitude of disagreements because of the clear differences that each perspective suggests in how to approach the problem. Defining the problem as family violence holds family members responsible (although liberal feminists will point out that men are more responsible given their—usually—greater size and control) and suggests fixing the family and perhaps looking for ways women can return home safely. Defining the problem as misogyny holds individual men and sexist social structures responsible and suggests changing society, getting battered women away from men, and discouraging women from returning to their batterers. Defining the problem as an outgrowth of a complex matrix of oppressive structures suggests that getting women away from men, while essential in the short term, will do little to solve the problems that bring such large numbers of women to shelters in the first place.

Employment Issues: Pay, Child Care, and Sexual Harassment

Liberal Feminism

Despite equal qualifications, in terms of education, employment history, and skills, women are discriminated against in the workplace and are often refused jobs based on their gender rather than their qualifications. This is due to employer's biases about women's capacity to do high quality work or to make a commitment to their careers. Women are also underpaid, compared to similarly qualified men, and women are unfairly passed over for advancement more often than men are. They are economically restricted by a "glass ceiling" that limits how far women are likely to be promoted. Women need legislation that will ensure equal pay for equal work and that will help eliminate the glass ceiling.

Women in the workplace are also disadvantaged by lack of consideration of child care arrangements. Although they are still primarily responsible for children, they are not provided the flexibility needed for sometimes unpredictable child care needs, nor are they compensated for the high cost of child care. Since equality in child-rearing has not been achieved yet and is not desired by some families, we need programs that compensate women for their extra responsibilities, for example, "cafeteria-style" benefit packages by which women who need financial help with child care or access to company child care services can choose the option that best meets their needs, in lieu of other benefits.

Those women who choose to have both a career and children need a wider variety of options for work arrangements. For example, a "mommy track" should be available to them by which they can opt for increased job flexibility and varying responsibilities, based on their family's needs. This would allow women with children to balance their responsibilities without being seen as less committed to their work. At the same time, it would allow women who choose not to have children to be seen more clearly as career women who are willing to devote the extra time needed for rapid advancement in the corporate world. It is important to eliminate the "glass ceiling" in employment so that women can rise to their full career potential in terms of promotion and the accompanying economic, status, and power compensations.

Sexual harassment, which makes the workplace less conducive to women's mental, economic, and sometimes physical well-being, should be eliminated. We need legislation ensuring that individuals who are guilty of sexual harassment, will be held accountable for their behavior. We also need training programs to teach women that they deserve to be treated more respectfully and to train women to be more assertive in responding to sexual harassment. Men should also be trained to be sensitive to the perceptions of women regarding sexual harassment, so that they understand that what a man may see as flattery, a woman may perceive as harassment. It is crucial for men to be taught that it is unacceptable to suggest that women trade sexual favors for career advancement. When women are guilty of sexual harassment, they too should be held accountable. Gender-blind policies should be written so that employees are provided with the means to file complaints and seek redress regardless of the gender of either the employer or employee.

Womanism

Problems in women's employment vary considerably by race and gender. College-educated black women who are employed full-time year-round have achieved parity with white women, but college educations and full-time year-round work are less often available to women of color than to white women. Black women have consistently had a higher labor force participation rate than white women, but unemployment is still of great concern, as black women who participate in the labor force are twice as likely to be unemployed as white women (Working women in the USA, 1993). Joblessness is especially high for black and Hispanic teenage girls. For waged workers, race and class differentials are striking. While nearly half of white male waged workers earn $10 or more per hour, only a third of black male workers earn that much. Women still tend to be employed in service and administrative support jobs (Women's Action Coalition, 1993), and black women are still less likely than white women to be employed in white-collar work. The major need in this area is to move more black women into employment that provides a living wage.

Many women have inadequate access to child care; the situation is compounded by the greater likelihood of black women to have insufficient salaries to pay for child care expenses. Poor women are often forced to leave their children unattended while they work, but women of color are more likely to have their children taken away as a result—since leaving the children alone is not defined as a social problem—thus, society fails to provide for its children. It is defined instead as personal neglect on the part of the employed mother (who would be criticized for her laziness if she gave up her job to care for her children). What is needed is more publicly funded after-school programs and increased monies for Head Start and other pre-school programs to make quality child care more readily available to poor families and families of color. Since flexibility in family roles is common in black families, employers should be encouraged to provide both male and female parents flexible schedules to accommodate the emergency needs of their children.

Sexual harassment on the job is a serious problem for a black woman, and it is accompanied by a greater likelihood that if she reports it, she will not be believed. This is true even if she is a professional woman with stature and respect, as was seen in discussions surrounding the Clarence Thomas Supreme Court hearings. Anita Hill's testimony that Thomas had engaged in long-term sexual harassment, and the Senate's unbelieving response, provided an example of the intersection of racism and sexism. If Thomas had been a white man, it is unlikely that the accusations of a black woman would have been taken seriously enough to even allow her testimony since racism makes black women's "virtue" automatically suspect. It is also less likely that such behavior on the part of a white man, whether sexual harassment was suspected or confirmed, and whether the female accuser was black or white, would have been cause to consider loss of the appointment.

Similarly, if Hill had been a *poor* black woman, instead of a highly educated academic, accusing a black man in Thomas' social position, the combination of her race and lower social class might have prevented her accusations from being made public. On the other hand, if Hill had been a white woman, accusing a black man of sexual harassment, negative stereotypes of black male sexuality and myths about black male desire would have made the testimony more believable to the white male senators. Under those circumstances, it is unlikely Thomas would have been appointed. When a black man was accused by a black woman of similar social class, however, the accusations were made public but were discounted, and Thomas was appointed.

What needs to happen is for work against racism, classism, and sexism to be redoubled, and for those who would pit racism against sexism to learn from the Thomas/Hill hearings that trying to solve only one of the problems would not be possible since racism, sexism, and classism are so interwoven and interdependent as to be the same problem—the assumption that one group should be allowed to trample on the needs of another.

Socialist Feminism

Women as a group are relegated to second-class status in the workforce. In addition, fields that have been traditionally occupied by women are more grossly underpaid than traditionally male fields so that when women perform work that is comparable in skill, responsibility, etc., to "men's work," the women are not paid comparable wages. This is because a capitalist economic structure, by nature, ensures that business owners will exploit workers, and sexism dictates that women will be exploited to an even greater extent than men. Besides gross underpayment in the workforce, women's productive and reproductive activities in the home are devalued and unwaged, even though capitalism depends on women's free home labor for survival and availability of its workers. What needs to happen is socialization of the labor market so that profits are shared by workers. New models of worker-owned businesses are a step in the right direction. In addition, either childrearing and housework should be socialized, or wages should be paid by the state to those who are engaged in this work, in recognition of the role that such labor plays in making workers available to meet the market's demand for laborers.

For example, child care should be seen as a public rather than a private good. Those who raise children are taking on the responsibility of producing the next generation and preparing new citizens for the state. This work should be honored and rewarded generously. State-supported, high quality child care should be available to all, and child care workers should be well paid. Family allowances should be provided by the state to any parent who is raising a child to help lighten the financial burden of this task, on which society depends for its continuation.

Male control of women's labor is reproduced in the workforce, thus making it easier for men to sexually harass women with impunity. Since men are more likely to be employers and control women's source of income, women remain vulnerable to loss of wages through dismissal if they protest against sexual harassment. The demise of sexual class systems in the labor force, the equitable distribution of profits from the products of labor, and provision of state-supported child care will remove the necessity for women to pair with men as an income-pooling unit, thus freeing women to make their choice to be partnered or not based on interest and desire rather than on capitalist and patriarchal forces. In addition, when women's labor is no longer controlled by men at home or in the workforce, sexual harassment will disappear as women, no longer comprising a subordinate class, will be free to refuse to accept such behavior.

Solutions

Liberal Feminism
- equal pay for equal work
- optional "mommy track"
- provide everyone equal access to the workplace through gender-blind and race-blind policy
- employer provided or subsidized child care
- eliminate the "glass ceiling"
- gender-blind policies to eliminate and punish sexual harassment

Womanism
- strengthen affirmative action for people of color and women
- raise the income floor
- provide publicly supported neighborhood child care
- increase funding to Head Start
- concerted, ongoing efforts to eliminate racism and sexism from the workplace
- teach employers and employees about the futility of trying to pit racism against classism or against sexism

Socialist Feminism
- either wages for housework or a significant restructuring of both the means of production and the means of reproduction so that women and working-class men will no longer be exploited
- worker-owned businesses
- socialized child care for workers
- good pay for child care workers
- redistribute power in the workplace so that men will no longer have the power to get away with sexual harassment

Discussion

There is not much disagreement about women's need to earn more for the work they do, but feminists disagree over whether the focus should be on the income ceiling or the income floor. It may be possible to do both, however, as they are not mutually exclusive goals or inherently at cross purposes. The major disagreements are over whether to admit women to the workplace with minor or moderate adjustments to accommodate them or to radically restructure the workplace as we know it, to better focus on diverse needs. There is also disagreement over whether capitalism is capable of responding adequately to workers' needs. Finally, there is disagreement over whether sexual harassment is a problem of male power, a complex problem that intersects race, class, and gender, or power inherent in capitalist patriarchal employment structures. Solutions would be at cross purposes here if socialist feminists are aiming for elimination of capitalism while womanists are trying to eliminate racism and sexism from capitalist systems and liberal feminists are seeking gender- and race-blind policies that downplay the influence of race and sex.

Sex Work

Liberal Feminism[1]

Women who engage in sex work are stigmatized and oppressed for the work they do; their occupation is used as an excuse to ostracize and mistreat them. They are denied needed health and social services because they are seen as undeserving of society's resources. When sex workers' organizations lobby for changes in policies that are harmful to them, they are typically ignored and disparaged.

Sex workers are subjected to sexual and physical violence and exploitation by customers, pimps, and often by police as well. When they are assaulted, sex workers often find little or no support from the criminal justice system. This is in part because of their illegal status as workers and in part because of puritanical attitudes that portray sex work as immoral and the women who engage in it as bringing victimization on themselves by virtue of their job.

Sex workers are held criminally liable for their work, with legal sanctions designed to prevent them from earning a livelihood in their occupation. Given the limited options women have for making

---

1. I want to acknowledge Lacey Sloan for patiently explaining to me her liberal feminist position on sex work.

sufficient money to support themselves and their families, it is wrong for women in the sex-trade industry to face prosecution for work which is often more lucrative than other options. Periodically, regulations of sex work are expanded, with the expressed intent of controlling or eliminating the work. Instead, such regulations tend to further restrict women's rights to health, safety, autonomy, and self-determination, without diminishing the extent of sex work.

It is both unrealistic and unnecessary to attempt to eliminate sex work. People object to the work based on moral, health, feminist, or other grounds. These arguments tend to assume women engage in sex work for a limited number of reasons. The opposite is true. There are many reasons women enter the industry, including a free choice based on preference for the work, a limited number of options available to them, the chance to earn a higher income, and sometimes, coercion. Singling out only one reason for sex work misses the complexity of the industry and leads to misguided, if well-meaning, policy.

What is needed is decriminalization so that all women have the option to engage in whatever work suits them. Decriminalization would make sex work more similar to other occupations in that safety and health regulations could then apply to sex work—as they do in other industries. Workers would have legal recourse if employers engaged in forced, unfair, or unsafe labor practices (such as requiring women to work without condoms). Additionally, sex workers should have access to health and social services including assistance in leaving the industry, if that is what a woman chooses. Sex workers are no different from other women workers. They need to be treated with dignity and respect; they should have an equal opportunity to meet their basic needs.

Radical Feminism

Sex work exploits women and is both a symptom and a reinforcer of the dehumanization and objectification of women. Sex work is institutionalized victimization, created by a patriarchal society to commodify sex, keep women in a subordinate position, and allow men to abuse women. Sex work is based in an institutionalized definition of women as valuable primarily for their sexuality, and it contributes to the framework that allows all women to be treated as sexual objects, rather than as human beings.

Women engage in sex work because they are forced into it by economic pressures, coercion, or violent means. They do not freely choose prostitution or any other form of sex work. Rather, sex work exists on a continuum of coercion, in which women experience everything from being manipulated into unwanted sexual activities to outright rape. Pimp-controlled prostitution is, essentially, female sexual slavery.

The patriarchy does not recognize prostitution as coercion but sees sex workers as seducers, masochists, and nymphomaniacs who are contrasted with honorable women (Jaggar, 1983) who would never choose such work. Because of these definitions, customers, who also are breaking the law when they engage in prostitution, are not arrested. Only the women are harassed and fined by police and the courts.

If women genuinely had other options by which they could support themselves, they would not participate in sex work as the work is dangerous: many women are abused and even killed within the industry or when they try to leave it. This exploitation is not caused by the way the work is structured. Rather, it is in the nature of the work. Sex workers are in an inherently powerless position due to the structure of patriarchy.

What is needed is an end to all forms of prostitution. Women who are trying to escape the industry should be provided with shelters and the means to escape. Education, training, and good jobs should be made available to all women so that they are never forced into prostitution. With redistribution of economic resources, women would no longer need to do sex work. Men who choose to frequent prostitutes should be arrested and publicly named so that women will know which men are objectifying women this way. Sex workers, however, should not be prosecuted for their victimization.

Postmodern Feminism

There are many valid perspectives on sex work. It is important to remember that women experience quite different realities, depending on their position in society. The street prostitute does not experience sex work in quite the same way as the escort or professional masseuse. The lap dancer has a different perception of sex work than the stripper on stage. Likewise, these jobs will not be experienced in the same way by women of color as by white women. Lesbians and bisexual women in the sex industry will have different perspectives than heterosexual women. Women whose entry into the trade was forced will experience a different reality than those who entered the work voluntarily.

The problem in defining sex work and determining how to respond to the needs of women in the industry has resulted from working within an essentialized notion of women that fails to acknowledge positionality. Both the varying positions of women in the industry as well as the relative positions of workers and purchasers of sex services need to be taken into account. Because women have not been allowed to control the discourse of sex work, the work has been misunderstood; it has been viewed only from a patriarchal frame of reference. The language of prostitution has organized the sex trade industry in ways that create cultural practices that primarily benefit men and fail to meet women's needs. Language that allows women to be defined in ways that exclude sex workers from the definition of "woman" make sex workers more vulnerable to abuse, particularly gender-based abuses like rape and loss of children due to being labelled "morally unfit" mothers.

Women must participate in the deconstruction of sex work as a monolithic industry experienced similarly by all workers. They must also construct a definition of sex workers as valuable people, entitled to self-definition. Women's choices for self-construction must be extended by encouraging them to tell their stories about sex work, their entry into it, and the meanings the work holds for them. Every woman's perspective should be valued equally since each woman will construct a story that holds meaning for her. What is needed is a continuum of approaches to assist women and eliminate the abuses in the industry. The continuum should be defined by those who work in the sex industry.

Global Feminism

Race, sex, and nationality intersect in the political definitions and conduct of sex work. More powerful countries organize aspects of the sex industry to meet the needs of certain of their citizens without regard for women from less powerful countries. For example, sex tourism is an international industry that meets the needs of some members of wealthy nations by sacrificing women whose countries are under the economic control of international monetary agencies and donor countries. Debtor countries are dependent on the income produced by sex trade and are thus forced to participate in the industry.

In another example, sexual interactions between people who are nationals of different countries, and perceived as racially distinct, are sometimes controlled by governments. This was evident in World War II attempts to separate African-American soldiers from white British women and in the more recent practice of forcing Filipino sex workers near the U.S. Navy base in Olongapo to submit to compulsory AIDS and venereal disease testing (Enloe, 1989).

Women are unlikely to have input into the control of sex work, often have few alternatives to participation in the industry, and cannot afford to leave it since they commonly have families dependent upon them for support. The women's governments are also unlikely to assist them, as debtor countries frequently are already unable to meet the demands for debt repayment and cannot afford to lose whatever influx of money, however meager, results from women working in the sex industry.

Women in the sex industry need alternative forms of work so they do not have to remain in sex work. Additionally, sex tourism, which sacrifices the women of one nation to the men of another, needs to be eliminated. International monetary policies must change so that repayment agreements are flexible enough to avoid forcing women into sex work. The notion of distinct races, with a hierarchy of value placing caucasians at the top, needs to be eliminated first from policy and next from political and social interactions. Finally, those women who remain in the sex industry must be provided health services that are designed to benefit them, rather than focused on the presumed needs of their customers.

Solutions

Liberal Feminism
- decriminalization of sex work
- improved working conditions
- protection of the civil rights of sex workers
- application of usual health and safety regulations to the sex work industry

- health and social service benefits normally associated with the workplace
- assistance in leaving the industry if that is what a woman chooses
- equality in employment, generally, so that women who choose to leave sex work can get jobs that pay as well as sex work

Radical Feminism
- elimination of sex work
- prosecution of customers
- public naming of customers
- elimination of social definitions of women as sex objects
- no more harassment of sex workers by police
- shelters and outreach to women so they can escape the industry
- redistribution of economic resources so women won't have to do sex work

Postmodern Feminism
- expand the definition of woman to include sex workers
- honor many points of view–from those who were forced into sex work to those who freely chose it
- eliminate the patriarchal discourse from sex work
- deconstruct the essentialist notion of sex work as a monolithic industry; recognize different parts of the industry will need different responses
- encourage sex workers to tell their many stories from multiple positions within the industry
- provide a continuum of approaches to respond to the different perspectives of women in sex work

Global Feminism
- do away with sex tourism
- provide more alternative sources of employment to women, with particular attention to women from economically poor countries
- rewrite international monetary policies to decrease the likelihood that individual women or nations will depend on sex trade
- eliminate all policies that support the notion of distinct races or racial hierarchies
- provide health services that meet the needs of sex workers, as defined by the workers

Discussion

The most obvious problem is whether to work toward prohibition or decriminalization, that is, whether to increase or decrease regulation, prosecution, and control of the sex work industry. Second, it is unclear whether the entire industry should be treated the same or whether certain segments of it, such as sex tourism, should be eliminated. Another point of departure is that sex workers who want to stay in the industry contest the idea of punishing customers and are particularly opposed to publishing customer's names; it would eliminate, or at least seriously curtail, their prospects for work. Feminists agree, however, that sex workers should not be prosecuted or harassed, that they should have better access to health services, and that the services should be of benefit to the workers, rather than focusing only on the needs of customers. Whether those services are designed around the needs of the workers in a strengthened, worker-controlled sex industry or provided in ways that encourage women to leave the industry is hotly debated.

Postmodern feminism's positionality provides little help here. If the point of view of women who have been forced into sex work and want the industry eliminated is equally as valid as the point of view of women who chose to do the work and want the industry strengthened, it is difficult to choose a direction for policy or services.

In sum, there are some problems on which feminists must decide what theory and direction to take. Not all feminisms work well together and failing to take that into account might mean feminists are working against each other's efforts.

A FEW FEMINIST INSIGHTS

What feminists have learned about women and their various situations are:

1. *Things Are Not Always What They Seem.* Culturally defined perceptions of women and their roles are generally distorted by such social factors as race, class, sexuality, and physical ability. The image of *woman* is generally one that describes the

prescribed idealized role of only the most dominant group, and generally does not accurately reflect them very well either.

2. *Things Have Not Always Been This Way.* Women's situations vary across time and place, with roles, constraints and definitions of capacity changing in dynamic relationships with medical, technological, social, political, and economic conditions.

3. *Things Do Not Have To Be This Way.* The world as it exists is not predetermined by immutable forces. Women can change things. It is because this is so that we experience so much resistance in our efforts toward feminist goals.

4. *Clashes Among Theories Are Inevitable.* When theories are being developed to reflect the situations and needs of over half the human race, it is highly unlikely that theoretical outlooks will coincide.

This review of some of the major divisions in feminist theory has highlighted a few of the disputed arenas. The theories help answer philosophical and political questions to a number of key dilemmas. Several theorists have attempted to reduce the debates to a single, conclusive question: Are we the same as, or different from, men? Perhaps the following discussion could also be reduced that way, but an alternative view is that there are five basic questions of which sameness versus difference is one.

It seems clear that women are not inherently alike in any fundamental respect other than a capacity for most, at a certain period of their lives, to give birth. For those women who choose to do so, at that time in their lives, pregnancy and childbirth often, but not always, have a significant impact on the way they live their lives. The social reality of responsibility for child care still falls primarily on women, so providing for adequate child care arrangements will continue to be of primary interest to many women. The need to expand state and federal funding for child care seems clear. Socialization and various forms of oppression *do* shape women's lives in ways that are often similar, and women *do* tend to focus more on relationships and interconnectedness than men generally do. But socialization and oppression do not produce a world of clones, nor do they eliminate the capacity of individual women to shape their responses to life. While general tendencies can be observed and shown to be socially and statistically significant, they can never predict with certainty the response of an individual. Generalized, socially created limits should not be accepted as justification for the continued limitations placed on women. To return to the Sears case, discussed in Chapter 1, a problem related to the present discussion was: if in fact, discrimination against women had occurred, at what point did it happen? Was it in socialization patterns that constrained women or in employers' decisions? If it was the former, could Sears reasonably be held responsible? If it was a combination, how much responsibility should Sears bear?

A second general question for feminists concerns unity versus diversity among women; that is, should women be organized as a single group, *as women*, or should the focus be on diversity? Again, it seems prudent to make a decision based on the needs that are at hand. It does appear, however, that separate organizations for women who share a particular circumstance or history can be an effective precursor and parallel to coalitions. Feminists have learned to value the complexities that diversity allows, and the strength of large numbers will often be the determinant of success-ful political campaigns. The problems of how to work successfully with people who are very different and how to equalize power differentials in working relationships, when some groups continue to have the privilege of extricating themselves from the working relationships and returning to a culture of dominance, will be an ongoing, painful struggle. To expect fear of difference to disappear is unrealistic, yet this does not excuse women—particularly those who are in positions of relative power—by virtue of their sexual orientation, class, race, etc. from learning to work closely with women who are dissimilar. Both unity via large coalitions and sepa-ratism through smaller groups of women who share important social characteristics are needed. Either one alone may be unrealis-tic and ineffective.

The third issue, closely related to the second, is autonomy versus community. This seems the simplest dilemma to solve—intellectually, at least. We are not autonomous individuals; humans are interdepen-dent. While some level of self-sufficiency is necessary and a sense of self as unique is valuable, in the West in particular, we need to balance our sense of autonomy with the strength we gain from inter-

connectedness. Fortunately, one of the positive patterns in the socialization of women is that we usually learn to value relationship.

The fourth question concerns single versus multiple issues. It
seems like a false dichotomy. Human needs and issues are as inter-
connected as humans are. Attention to a particular issue *as part of a
comprehensive analysis* makes sense. Needs such as child care,
health care, employment, education, and housing often must be
dealt with separately, but none can be *completely* separated from the
others, nor would there be any reason to think that a plan for child
care would not *contradict* a plan for employment, for example, if
the two were not considered together.

Finally, must an issue be specifically relevant to women alone or
to women *as women* to constitute a woman's issue? This is a more
difficult question to answer. At first glance, it would appear that any
issue can be construed as a woman's issue and that it would be an
enormous mistake to limit ourselves to a particular sphere of topics
on which women should be heard. But if everything effects every-
body and all issues are everyone's issues, what is the rationale for
calling a problem a woman's issue? However, it is often the case
that problems which seem unrelated to gender *do* affect women and
men differently. For example, lack of sufficient public transportation is problematic for many people, regardless of gender. But if
women are less able to afford cars and more likely to be sexually
harassed on unsafe buses and trains, public transportation becomes
a woman's issue.

WHERE DO WE GO FROM HERE?

There are still recurring efforts (despite postmodern feminists'
excellent critiques of generalized, essentialist arguments) to identify
a single elegant theory about women the world over, as though
reduction to simplicity would make feminist theory more authentic,
more incontrovertible, or more legitimate. It would not. The theories
are complex and evolving, in part because women's lives and situations continue to unfold in "endless variety and monotonous similarity," to again quote Gayle Rubin. Increased understanding of the
similarities and complexities have had an impact on the theories. The
initial liberal ideas of Western women *were* narrow. This review has

demonstrated, however, that narrowness is no longer characteristic of either liberal feminism or the aggregate of feminist thought.

Our tasks are to continue working toward social changes that will eliminate the oppressions experienced by women, to recognize that women's needs will sometimes conflict, to continue to develop feminist theories, and to incorporate them into social work, that is, to build a feminist future.

Appendix A:
A Bibliography
of Psychoanalytic Feminism

Allen, Jeffner. (1993). Poetic politics: How the Amazons took the Acropolis. In S. Wolfe and J. Penelope (Eds.). *Sexual practice, textual theory: Lesbian cultural criticism*. Cambridge, MA: Blackwell, pp. 307-321.

Barrett, Michele. (1992). Psychoanalysis and feminism: A British sociologist's view. *Signs, 17*(2), 455-467.

Bowlby, Rachel. (1992). *Still crazy after all these years: Women, writing, and psychoanalysis*. London and New York: Routledge.

Brennan, Teresa. (1989). (Ed.). *Between feminism and psychoanalysis*. London: Routledge.

Burack, Cynthia. (1994). *The problem of the passions: Feminism, psychoanalysis and social theory*. New York: New York University Press.

Chodorow, Nancy. (1978/1993). Gender, personality and the sexual sociology of adult life. In A. Jaggar and P. Rothenberg (Eds.). *Feminist frameworks: Alternative theoretical accounts of the relations between women and men, 3rd ed*, pp. 414-424.

Chodorow, Nancy. (1989). *Feminism and psychoanalytic theory*. Cambridge, MA: Polity.

Chodorow, Nancy. (1995). Gender as personal and cultural construction. *Signs, 20*(3), 516-544.

Cixous, Hélène. (1975/1992). The laugh of the Medusa. Excerpted in M. Humm (Ed.). *Modern feminisms: Political, literary and cultural*. New York: Columbia University Press, pp. 196-202.

Deutsch, Helene. (1932/1951). *Psycho-analysis of the neuroses*. London: Hogarth Press; Institute of Psycho-analysis.

Dinnerstein, Dorothy. (1976). The mermaid and the minotaur. Excerpted in M. Humm (Ed.). *Modern feminisms: Political, literary and cultural*. New York: Harper and Row.

Doane, Janice L. (1992). *From Klein to Kristeva: Psychoanalytic feminism and the search for the "good enough" mother.* Ann Arbor, MI: University of Michigan Press.

Elliot, Patricia. (1990). *From mastery to analysis: Theories of gender in psychoanalytic feminism.* Ithaca, NY: Cornell University Press.

Flax, Jane. (1990). *Thinking fragments: Psychoanalysis, feminism, and postmodernism in the contemporary West.* Berkeley, CA: University of California Press.

Flax, Jane. (1993). *Disputed subjects: Essays on psychoanalysis, politics, and philosophy.* New York and London: Routledge.

Gallop, Jane. (1982). *The daughter's seduction: Feminism and psychoanalysis.* Ithaca, NY: Cornell University Press.

Glassgold, Judith. (1995). *Lesbians and psychoanalysis: Revolutions in theory and practice.* New York: Free Press.

Grosz, Elizabeth, A. (1990). *Jacques Lacan: A feminist introduction.* Sydney and Boston, MA: Allen and Unwin.

Holmlund, Christine. (1991). The lesbian, the mother, the heterosexual lover: Irigaray's recodings of difference. *Feminist Studies, 17*(2), 283-309.

Horney, Karen. (1973). *Feminine psychology.* New York: W. W. Norton.

Irigaray, Luce. (1977/1992). The sex which is not one. Excerpted in M. Humm (Ed.). *Modern feminisms: Political, literary and cultural.* New York: Columbia University Press, pp. 204-210.

Irigaray, Luce. (1982). *Speculum of the other woman.* Ithaca, NY: Cornell University Press.

Klein, Melanie. (1975). *The writings of Melanie Klein.* New York: Delacorte Press.

Kristeva, Julia. (1980/1993). *Desire in language: A semiotic approach to literature and art.* New York: Columbia University Press.

Kurzweil, Edith. (1995). *Freudians and feminists.* Boulder, CO: Westview Press.

Luepnitz, Deborah Anna. (1988). The family interpreted: Psychoanalysis, feminism, and family therapy. New York: Basic Books.

Marecek, Jeanne and Hare-Mustin, Rachel. (1991). A short history of the future: Feminism and clinical psychology. *Psychology of Women Quarterly, 15*(4), 521-537.

Marks, Elaine and de Courtivron, Irene. (Eds.), *New French Feminisms*. New York: Schocken Books.

Miller, Jean Baker. (1976). *Toward a new psychology of women*. Boston, MA: Beacon Press.

Minsky, Rosalind. (1990). "The trouble is it's ahistorical": The problem of the unconscious in modern feminist theory. *Feminist Review, 36*(4).

Mitchell, Juliet. (1974/1984). On Freud and the distinction between the sexes. In Juliet Mitchell (Ed.). *Women: The longest revolution*. London: Virago Press, pp. 219-232.

Mitchell, Juliet. (1974). *Psychoanalysis and feminism*. New York: Vintage Books.

Mitchell, Juliet. (1982/1984). Freud and Lacan: Psychoanalytic theories of sexual difference. In Juliet Mitchell (Ed.). *Women: The longest revolution*. London: Virago Press, pp. 248-277.

Salecl, Renata. (1994). *The spoils of freedom: Psychoanalysis and feminism after the fall of socialism*. London and New York: Routledge.

Sayers, Janet. (1986). *Sexual contradictions: Psychology, psychoanalysis and feminism*. London: Tavistock Publications.

Sayers, Janet. (1991). *Mothers of psychoanalysis: Helene Deutsch, Karen Horney, Anna Freud, Melanie Klein*. 1st American ed. New York: W.W. Norton.

Sprengnether, Madelon. (1990). *The spectral mother: Freud, feminism, and psychoanalysis*. Ithaca, NY: Cornell University Press.

Appendix B:
Additional Bibliographies
of Feminist Writings

Africans

Mikell, Gwendolyn. (1995). African feminism: Toward a new politics of representation. *Feminist studies, 21*(2), 405-427.

Oduyoye, Mercy Amba. (1995). *Daughters of Anowa: African women and patriarchy.* Maryknoll, NY: Orbis Books.

Ogundipe-Leslie, Molara. (1994). *Re-creating ourselves: African women & critical transformations.* Trenton, NJ: Africa World Press.

Walker, Alice and Parmar, Pratibha. (1994). *Warrior marks: Female genital mutilation and the sexual binding of women.* London: Jonathan Cape.

Asian and Pacific Island Women

Asian Journal of Women's Studies. Seoul, Korea: Ewha Woman's University Press. Vol. 1 (1995).

Asian Women United of California. (1989). *Making waves: An anthology of writings by and about Asian American women.* Boston, MA: Beacon Press.

Barlow, Tani (Ed.). (1994). *Gender politics in modern China: Writing and feminism.* Durham, NC: Duke University Press.

Fugimora-Fanselow, Kumiko and Kameda, Atsuko. (1994). *Japanese women: New feminist perspectives on the past, present and future.* NY: The Feminist Press at The City University of New York.

Geok-Lin; Lim, Shirley; Tsutakawa, Mayumi; and Donnelly, Margarita (Eds.). (1990). *The forbidden stitch: An Asian-American women's anthology.* Corvalis, OR: Calyx Books.

Jacka, Tamara. (1994). Countering voices: An approach to Asian and feminist studies in the 1990s. *Women's studies international forum, 17*(6), 663-672.

Kumar, Nita. (1994). *Women as subjects: South Asian histories.* Charlottesville, VA: University Press of Virginia.

Minh-Ha, Trinh T. (1991). *When the moon waxes red.* New York: Routledge.

Shah, Sonia. (1994). Presenting the blue goddess: Toward a national pan-Asian feminist agenda. In Karin Aguilar-San Juan (Ed.). *The state of Asian America: Activism and resistance in the 1990s.* Boston, MA: South End Press.

The Women of South Asian Descent Collective. (1993). *Our feet walk the sky: Women of the South Asian diaspora.* San Francisco, CA: Aunt Lute.

Latinas

Alarcóne, Norma; Castro, Rafaela; Peréz, Emma; Riddel, Adaljiza Sosa; and Zavella, Patricia (Eds.). *Chicana critical issues.* Berkeley, CA: Third Woman Press.

Bergmann, Emilie L. (1990). *Women, culture, and politics in Latin America.* Berkeley, CA: University of California Press.

de la Torre, Adela and Pesquera, Beatríz (Eds.). (1993). *Building with our own hands: New directions in Chicana Studies.* Berkeley, CA: University of California Press.

Fernández, Roberta (Ed.). (1994). *In other words: Literature by Latinas of the United States.* Houston, TX: Arte Público Press.

Fisher, Jo. (1989). *Mothers of the disappeared.* Boston, MA: South End Press.

Frontiers, 14(2). (1994). Special Issue: Chicana Identity.

Hardy-Fanta, Carol. (1993). *Latina politics-Latino politics: Gender, culture and political participation in Boston.* Philadelphia, PA: Temple University Press.

Küppers, Gaby (Ed.) (1994). *Compañeras: Voices from the Latin American women's movement.* London: Latin American Bureau.

Latina: A journal of ideas. (1993). New York: Heresies Collective.

Nash, June and Safa, Helen. (1985). *Women and change in Latin America.* South Hadley, MA: Bergin and Garvey.

Scholarship by and about Las Mujeres (Chicanas, Latinas, Puertor-riquenos, Cubananas) in the United States. (1990). Minneapolis, MN: University of Minnesota. Center for Advanced Feminist Studies.

Trujillo, Carla (Ed.). (1991). *Chicana lesbians: The girls our mother warned us about*. Berkeley, CA: Third Woman Press.

Native American Women

Allen, Paula Gunn. (1986/1992). *The sacred hoop: Recovering the feminine in American Indian tradition*. Boston, MA: Beacon Press.

Allen, Paula Gunn. (1989). *Spider Woman's granddaughters: Traditional tales and contemporary writing by Native American women*. Boston, MA: Beacon Press.

Allen, Paula Gunn. (1991). *Grandmothers of the light: A medicine woman's source book*. Boston, MA: Beacon Press.

Brant, Beth (Ed.). (1988). *A gathering of spirit: A collection by North American Indian Women*. Ithaca, NY: Firebrand.

Chrystos. (1994). She said they say. In Joseph Bruchac (Ed.). *Returning the gift: Poetry and prose from the First North American Native Writers' Festival*. Tucson, AZ: The University of Arizona Press, pp. 78-79.

Emberley, Julia. (1993). *Thresholds of difference: Feminist critique, native women's writings, postcolonial theory*. Toronto: University of Toronto Press.

Frontiers, 6(3). (1982). Special Issue: Native American women. (See especially Lyle Koehler's Native women of the Americas: A bibliography, pp. 73-101.)

Hanson, Wynne (1980). The urban Indian woman and her family. *Social Casework, 6*(8), 476-483.

LaFromboise, Theresa D., Heyle, Anneliese M., and Ozer, Emily J. (1990). Changing and diverse roles of women in American Indian cultures. *Sex Roles, 22*(7-8), 455-476.

Maracle, Brian. (1994). *Crazywater: Native people speak on addiction and recovery*. Toronto: Penguin.

Yazzie-Shaw, Carole. (1994). Back in those days. In Joseph Bruchac (Ed.). *Returning the gift: Poetry and prose from the First*

North American Native Writers' Festival. Tucson, AZ: The University of Arizona Press, pp. 330-337.

Women of Color: Multicultural Anthologies and Additional Works

Adams, Diane L. (1995). *Health issues for women of color: A cultural diversity perspective*. Thousand Oaks, CA: Sage Publications.

Albrecht, Lisa and Brewer, Rose. (1990). *Bridges of power: Women's multicultural alliances*. Philadelphia, PA: New Society Publishers.

Amott, Teresa and Matthaei, Julie. (1991). *Race, gender and work: A multicultural economic history of women in the United States*. Boston, MA: South End Press.

Anzaldua, Gloria (Ed.). (1990). *Making face, making soul: Haciendo Caras*. San Francisco, CA: Aunt Lute Books.

Bayne-Smith, Marcia. (1995). *Redefining health care: Issues for women of color*. Thousand Oaks, CA: Sage Publications.

Comas-Diaz, Lillian and Greene, Beverly (Eds.). *Women of Color: Integrating ethnic and gender identities in psychotherapy*. New York: The Guilford Press.

Du Bois, Ellen and Ruiz, Vickie (Eds.). *Unequal Sisters*. New York: Routledge, Chapman and Hall.

Glancy, Diane, and Truesdale, C. W. (Eds.). (1994). *Two worlds walking: Short stories, essays, & poetry by writers with mixed heritages*. New York: New Rivers Press.

Moghadam, Valentine (Ed.). (1994). *Identity politics and women: Cultural reassertions and feminisms in international perspective*. San Francisco, CA: Westview Press.

Mohanty, Chandra, Russo, Ann and Torres, Lourdes (Eds.). *Third World women and the politics of feminism*. Bloomington, IN: Indiana University Press.

Moraga, Cheri. and Anzaldua, Gloria (Eds.). (1983). *This bridge called my back: Writings by radical women of color*. New York: Kitchen Table: Women of Color Press.

Schuler, Margaret (Ed.). (1992). *Freedom from violence: Women's strategies from around the world*. New York: United National Development Fund for Women.

Silvera, Makeda (Ed.). (1991). *Piece of my heart: A lesbian of color anthology.* Toronto: Sister Vision Woman of Color Press.

Women with Disabilities

Browne, Susan, Connors, Debra, and Stern, Nancy. (1985). *With the power of each breath: A disabled women's anthology.* Pittsburgh, PA: Cleis Press.

Cottone, Laura Perkins and Cottone, R. Rocco. (1992). Women with disabilities: On the paradox of empowerment and the need for a trans-systemic and feminist perspective. *Journal of Applied Rehabilitation Counseling, 23*(4), 20-26. Special Issue: Women with Disabilities.

Fowler, Carol; O'Rourke, Barbara; Wadsworth, John; and Harper, Dennis. (1992). Disability and feminism: Models for counselor exploration of personal values and beliefs. *Journal of Applied Rehabilitation Counseling, 23*(4), 14-19.

Hannaford, Susan. (1985). *Living outside inside: A disabled woman's experience: Towards a social and political perspective.* Berkeley, CA: Canterbury Press.

Hillyer, Barbara. (1993). *Feminism and disability.* Norman, OK: University of Oklahoma Press.

Morris, Jenny (Ed.). (1989). *Able lives: Women's experience of paralysis.* London: The Women's Press.

Morris, Jenny. (1992). "Us" and "them"? Feminist research, community care and disability. *Feminist Research, 33*(3), 22-39.

Morris, Jenny. (1993). Feminism and disability. *Feminist Review, 43,* 57-70.

Saxton, Marsha and Howe, Florence. (1987). *With wings: An anthology of literature by and about women with disabilities.* New York: The Feminist Press at The City University of New York.

Silvers, Anita. (1995). Reconciling equality to difference: Caring (F) or justice for people with disabilities. *Hypatia, 10*(1), 30-55.

Thomson, Rosemarie Garland. (1994). Redrawing the boundaries of feminist disability studies. *Feminist studies, 20*(3), 583.

Wendell, Susan. (1989). Toward a feminist theory of disability. *Hypatia, 4*(2), 104-124.

Glossary

Chicana Cultural Nationalism. While supporting feminism, this position maintains allegiance to a sense of national consciousness, with an emphasis on preservation of Chicano culture. It downplays the role of patriarchy in Chicano culture.

Chicana Cultural Nationalist Feminism. This stance supports a profound change in gender relationships while retaining other traditional values of Chicano culture.

Colonization. The process of usurping another group's land and its resources, for example, when Europeans claimed ownership of Native Americans' lands; the process of claiming the right to control of another's life and the benefits of that person's labor.

Cultural relativism. The belief that each culture or country must decide for itself, based on cultural heritage, how women should be treated.

Deconstruction. The process of analyzing the cultural and ideological construction of meanings and social orders.

Difference. A postmodern term: a system by which meaning is created through contrast, with a positive definition dependent upon the negation of something else that has been presented as its opposite. Difference assumes binary oppositions such as unity/diversity, universality/specificity.

Discourse. A structure of statements, terms, categories, and beliefs that may be expressed in organizations and institutions. To understand a discourse, one must first know who is speaking, who has the "right" or is considered qualified to use that particular discourse.

Dual Systems theorists. These theorists examine systems of oppression separately, as parallel but often interacting systems, for example, sexism and capitalism or sexism and heterosexism.

Enlightenment. Eighteenth-century movement that advocated the substitution of rationalism for then-traditional social, religious, and political values that assigned privilege to members of the church and to royalty.

Essentialism. The assumption that all members of a group, in this case women, share certain characteristics and that while individuals and subgroups may vary in important or essential ways, they are the same.

Exchange-value goods. Goods produced with the intent of even exchange for other needed goods.

Family wage system. A system that assumes one adult in a family–generally a man–supports an entire family on a single salary while another adult–generally a woman–performs day-to-day survival functions for the entire family, thereby freeing wage earners to devote most of their time to waged work.

Free Trade Zone. This is an area of a country in which businesses are encouraged to build factories that produce goods for export. Usually, a special arrangement is made by which an authority is created and given the power to negotiate a wide variety of conditions (tax rates, safety and pollution standards, building contracts, etc.) with local, foreign and multinational businesses. This includes setting and implementing labor standards, which may differ considerably from the country's usual practices. Sometimes the authority is responsible for recruitment of workers as well.

Hegemony. The dominant cultural definition, in this case, of the status and roles of women.

Historical materialism. The theory of economic relations as the determinant force of social organization and development.

Individualization. Explaining problems in terms of aspects which are peculiar to single persons; failing to examine the consequence of social conditions for individuals; assumption that values and duties reside within individuals rather than within social systems.

Language. In postmodern terms, language is a system that not only constructs meaning, but also organizes cultural practices. Words, whether spoken or written, lack fixed and intrinsic meanings, so that one must always know the context, the speaker and the social processes that contributed to the use of words to understand their meaning and the social structures they derive from and, in turn, support.

Lesbian. Someone who calls herself a lesbian; "a woman whose sexual/affectional preference is for women, and who [has] thereby rejected the female role on some level, . . . she may or may not embrace a lesbian-feminist political analysis (Bunch, 1987, p. 198).

Liberals:

Egalitarian liberal or Welfare liberal. A position that assigns to the state the responsibility for balancing some of the relative advantages held by individuals by providing social services (e.g., legal services, school loans, food stamps, low-cost housing, government-funded health insurance) to disadvantaged individuals, to help them obtain a fair share of resources.

Libertarian liberal or Classical Liberal. A position that assigns to the state (1) the protection of civil liberties such as property ownership, voting rights, and freedom of speech; and (2) the protection of equal opportunity for individuals, without interference with the free market.

Matrix of oppression. A complex, interlocking system of social structures that constrict people on multiple levels; interpersonally, socially, and politically. The constrictions are based on multiple characteristics, for example, gender, race, sexual orientation, and class. The systems of oppression are dependent on each other for effective, hierarchical social control.

Means of production refers to the organizational system by which goods are produced and resources are distributed. In capitalism, production systems (for example, factories) are owned by private individuals who retain profits from the sale of goods. This is contrasted with state-owned or worker-owned businesses, in which any profit from labor is distributed among laborers or to society as a whole.

Meritocracy. A system by which people are rewarded based on their accomplishments.

Metalanguage of race. According to the *Merriam Webster's Collegiate Dictionary*, 10th edition, a metalanguage is a language used to explain another language. In the metalanguage of race, we discuss race and racial differences with a language in which race hierarchies are so intrinsic that even in a discussion of racial issues, the racism in our terms is often invisible.

Metaphysical dualism. The belief that mind and body are separate substances, independent of each other and knowable separately.

Mother right. Matriarchy–descent and inheritance are traced through the mother.

Nominalism. The notion that all abstract terms are simply convenient tools of language or thought, existing as names only, without corresponding realities.

Ontology. The description of the nature of being and reality.

Oppression. Oppressed people are . . . "confined and shaped by forces and barriers which are . . . systematically related to each other in such a way as to . . . restrict or penalize motion in any direction . . . a network of systematically related barriers, no one of which would be a hindrance . . . but which, *by their relations to each other*, are as confining as the solid wall of a dungeon" (Frye, 1983, pp. 4-5, emphasis added).

Pluralism. According to the *Merriam Webster's Collegiate Dictionary*, 10th edition, pluralism is a state of society in which members of diverse ethnic, racial, religious, or social groups maintain an autonomous participation in and development of their traditional culture or special interest within the confines of a common civilization.

Political solipsism. The intellectual commitment to the individual as functioning with needs that stand in opposition to, and separate from, all others (Tong, 1989).

Positionality. The situation of a speaker, defined in terms of the speaker's level of power and institutional context.

Psychoanalytical feminism. A theory which holds that we need to deconstruct the socially assigned meanings of biology, sex, and nature and explore the experience of subjugation to understand the psychology and personalities of women.

Queer theory. A theory that examines oppressions which are based on sexuality, sexual identification, and sexual orientation. It contests socially assigned sex and gender role constrictions.

Separatism. A broad range of activities and approaches to building solidarity among an oppressed group. The continuum of feminist separatism encompasses everything from providing a women-only intervention group to living on women's land and interacting solely with women in work and day-to-day existence.

Structural adjustment. Entails a conscious change in the nature of economic relationships in a debtor society–usually a move toward a free market economy.

Structural transformation. Relies on human-centered economic recovery, with full input from the general population in the design, implementation, and monitoring of the programs.

Surplus value goods. These are products intended to be sold for more than they are worth in order to accumulate capital.

Sustainable development programs. When ecologists define sustainable development, they indicate policies that differ from present development plans in that they meet current and future needs without destroying the environment in the process.

Systems of domination. Based on the concept of a matrix of domination, it assumes that oppression operates in different ways for different people. For example, a white, middle-class lesbian with disabilities will experience several interlocking oppressions, but that cluster or system of oppressions will be different from the cluster experienced by an able-bodied, working-class, Native American heterosexual woman.

Transcendentalism. Romanticism: Countering the liberal posture that government was needed to protect people, transcendentalists held that people were inherently capable of unfolding and developing in a positive direction when unimpeded by interference from society or government (Donovan, 1985).

Unified systems theorists. These theorists explain oppression in terms of a single, overarching system with multiple facets, such as sex, class, and race oppressions; the facets intersect in varied ways within the single system.

Universalism. In global feminism, universalism refers to the belief that all women, regardless of country, should be free from gender-based constrictions. Formal international agreements to end oppression of women should apply equally to all women.

Use-value goods. Production of goods meant to satisfy immediate human needs.

Virgin. "The word 'virgin' did not originally mean a woman whose vagina was untouched by any penis, but a free woman, one not betrothed, not married, not bound to, not possessed by any man. It meant a female who is sexually and hence socially her own person. In any universe of patriarchy, there are no virgins in this sense . . . . Hence Virgins must be unspeakable, thinkable only as negations . . . . Radically feminist lesbians have claimed positive virginity and have been inventing ways of living it out, in creative defiance of patriarchal definition of the real, the meaningful" (Frye, 1992, p. 133).

Woman-identified woman. A feminist who adopts a lesbian-feminism ideology and enacts that understanding in her life, whether she is a lesbian sexually or not (Bunch, 1987, p. 198).

References

Abbott, Ann. (1994). A feminist approach to substance abuse treatment and service delivery. *Social Work in Health Care, 19* (3/4), 67-83.

Abbott, Sydney and Love, Barbara. (1977). *Sappho was a right-on woman.* New York: Stein and Day.

Abramowitz, Mimi (1988). *Regulating the lives of women: Social welfare policy from Colonial times to the present.* Boston, MA: South End Press.

Abzug, Bella. (1994). Forward. Braidotti, R., Charkiewicz, E., Häusler, S. and Wieringa, S. (1994). *Women, the environment and sustainable development: Towards a theoretical synthesis.* London: Zed Books and INSTRAW (United Nations International Research and Training Institute for the Advancement of Women).

Acosta, Gladys. (1994). Where next? Feminism and the New World Order. In Gaby Küppers (Ed.). *Compañeras: Voices from the Latin American women's movement.* London: Latin American Bureau, pp. 167-172.

Alcoff, Linda. (1988). Cultural feminism versus post-structuralism: The identity crisis in feminist theory. *Signs: Journal of Women in Culture and Society, 13*(3), 405-436.

Al-Hibri, Azizah. (1981). Capitalism is an advanced state of patriarchy: But Marxism is not feminism. In Lydia Sargent (Ed.). *Women and revolution: A discussion of the unhappy marriage of Marxism and feminism.* Boston, MA: South End Press, pp. 165-194.

Allen, Paula Gunn. (1990). The woman I love is a planet; The planet I love is a tree. In Irene Diamond and Gloria Orenstein (Eds.). *Reweaving the world: The emergence of ecofeminism.* San Francisco, CA: Sierra Club Books, pp. 52-57.

Allen, Paula Gunn. (1991). *Grandmothers of the light: A medicine woman's sourcebook.* Boston, MA: Beacon Press.

Alpert, Jane. (1973). Mother right: A new feminist theory. *Ms.,* August.

Alyn, Jody and Becker, Lee. (1984). Feminist therapy with chronically and profoundly disturbed women. *Journal of Counseling Psychology, 31*(2), pp. 202-208

Ashbury, Jo-Ellen. (1987). African-American women in violent relationships: An exploration of cultural differences. In Robert Hampton (Ed.). *Violence in the Black family: Corretales and consequences.* Lexington, MA: Lexington Books, pp. 89-105.

Associated Press. (October 11, 1995). *Clinton defends economic plan.* [On-line]. Available: clari.news.usa.gov.white house.

Atkinson, Ti-Grace. (1974). *Amazon odyssey.* New York: Links Books.

Badran, Margot and Cooke, Miriam (Eds.). (1990). *Opening the gates: A century of Arab feminist writing.* Bloomington, IN: Indiana University Press.

Balser, Diane. (1987). *Sisterhood and solidarity: Feminism and labor in modern times.* Boston, MA: South End Press.

Beasley, Chris. (1994). *Sexual economyths: Conceiving a feminist economics.* New York: St. Martin's Press.

Benston, Margaret. (1970). The political economy of women's liberation. In Leslie Tanner (Ed.). *Voices from women's liberation.* New York: Signet, pp. 279-291.

Bepko, Claudia. (1989) Disorders of power: Women and addiction in the family. In Monika McGoldrick, Carol Anderson, and Froma Walsh. (1989). *Women in families: A framework for family therapy.* New York: W. W. Norton & Company, Inc., pp. 406-426.

Berryman-Fink, Cynthia and Venderber, Kathleen. (1985). Attributions of the term feminist: A factor analytic development of a measuring instrument. *Psychology of Women Quarterly, 9,* pp. 51-64.

Blount, Jackie. (1994). One postmodern feminist perspective on educational leadership: And ain't I a leader? In Spencer Maxcy (Ed.). *Postmodern school leadership: Meeting the crisis in educational administration.* Westport, CT: Praeger, pp. 47-59.

Bograd, Michele. (1988). *Feminist perspectives on wife abuse.* Newbury Park, CA: Sage.

Bradford, Judith and Ryan, Caitlin. (1987). *The national lesbian health care survey: Final report.* Washington, DC: National Lesbian and Gay Health Foundation.

Braidotti, Rosi; Charkiewicz, Ewa; Häusler, Sabine; and Wieringa, Saskia. (1994). *Women, the environment and sustainable development: Towards a theoretical synthesis.* London: Zed Books and INSTRAW (United Nations International Research and Training Institute for the Advancement of Women).

Brandwein, Ruth. (1986). A feminist approach to social policy. In Nan Van den Berg and Lynn Cooper (Eds.). *Feminist visions for social work.* Silver Spring, MD: NASW, pp. 250-261.

Brewer, Rose. (1993). Theorizing race, class and gender: The new scholarship of Black feminist and Black women's labor. In Stanlie James and Abena Busis (Eds.). *Theorizing black feminisms: The visionary pragmatism of black women.* New York: Routledge, pp. 13-30.

Brown, Elsa Barkley. (1990). Womanist consciousness: Maggie Lena Walker and the Independent Order of Saint Luke. In Ellen Du Bois and Vickie Ruiz (Eds.). *Unequal sisters.* New York: Routledge, pp. 208-223.

Brownmiller, Susan. (1975). *Against our will.* New York: Bantam.

Budapest, Z. (1986). *The holy book of women's mysteries.* San Francisco, CA: Harper & Row.

Bunch, Charlotte. (1987). *Passionate politics: Feminist theory in action.* New York: St. Martin's Press.

Bunch, Charlotte. (1993). Women's subordination through the lens of sex/gender and sexuality: Radical feminism. In Alison Jaggar, and Paula Rothenberg (Eds.). *Feminist frameworks: Alternative accounts of the relations between women and men. Third Edition.* New York: McGraw-Hill, pp. 174-178.

Bunch, Charlotte. (1995). Transforming human rights from a feminist perspective. In Julie Peters and Andrea Wolper (Eds.). *Women's rights, human rights: International feminist perspectives.* New York: Routledge, pp. 11-17.

Burden, Diane and Gottlieb, Naomi. (1987). Women's socialization and feminist groups. In Claire Brody (Ed.). *Women's therapy groups: Paradigms of feminist treatment.* New York: Springer Publishing, pp. 24-39.

Burnham, Linda and Louie, Miriam. (1985). The impossible marriage: A Marxist critique of socialist feminism. *Line of March: A Marxist-Leninist Journal of Rectification,* 17, Spring.

Business Digest. (1995a). Sweatshop links probed. *San Francisco Chronicle,* August 10, D, 2:3.

Business Digest. (1995b). Sweatshop suit filed. *San Francisco Chronicle,* August 11, B, 2:3.

Calhoun, Cheshire. (1994). Separating lesbian theory from feminist theory. *Ethics, 104,* pp. 558-581.

California subpoenas top retailers in sweatshop investigation. (1995). *Boston Globe,* August 16, 46:1.

Cameron, Barbara. (1983). "Gee, you don't seem like an Indian from the reservation." In Cheri Moraga and Gloria Anzaldua (Eds.). *This bridge called my back: Writings by radical women of color.* New York: Kitchen Table: Women of Color Press, pp. 46-52.

Canzoneri Klipfel, Linda. (1994). The political economy of male violence against women. University at Buffalo, School of Social Work. Unpublished manuscript.

Carse, Alisa. (1995). Pornography: An uncivil liberty? *Hypatia, 10*(1), 155-182.

Cavin, Susan. (1985). *Lesbian origins.* San Francisco: Ism Press.

Childers, Mary and hooks, bell. (1990). A conversation about race and class. In Marianne Hirsch and Evelyn Fox Keller (Eds.). *Conflicts in feminism.* New York: Routledge.

Chowdhury, Najma; Nelson, Barbara; Carver, Kathryn; Johnson, Nancy; and O'Loughlin, Paula. (1994). Redefining politics: Patterns of women's political engagement from a global perspective. In Barbara Nelson and Najma Chowdhury (Eds.). *Women and politics worldwide.* New Haven, CT: Yale University Press, pp. 3-24.

Christian, Barbara. (1985). *Black feminist criticism.* New York: Pergamon.

Christian, Barbara. (1988). The race for theory. *Feminist Studies, 14*(1), 67-79.

Christian, Barbara. (1989). But who do you really belong to? *Women's Studies, 17,* 17-23.

Cixous, Hélène. (1981). The laugh of the medusa. In Elaine Marks and Irene de Courtivron, (Eds.). *New French Feminisms.* New York: Schocken Books, pp. 245-264.

Clarke, Cheryl. (1983). Lesbianism: An act of resistance. In Cheri Moraga and Gloria Anzaldua (Eds.). *This bridge called my back: Writings by radical women of color.* New York: Kitchen Table: Women of Color Press, pp. 128-137.

Cocks, Joan. (1984). Wordless emotions: Some critical reflections of radical feminism. *Politics and Society, 13*(1):29.

Collins, Patricia Hill. (1990). *Black feminist thought: Knowledge, consciousness and the politics of empowerment.* Boston, MA: Unwin Hyman.

Comas-Diaz, Lillian. (1994). An integrative approach. In Lillian Comas-Diaz and Beverly Greene (Eds.). *Women of Color: Integrating ethnic and gender identities in psychotherapy.* New York: The Guilford Press, pp. 287-318.

Combahee River Collective. (1983). The Combahee River Collective statement. In Barbara Smith (Ed.). *Home girls: A black feminist anthology.* New York: Kitchen Table: Women of Color Press, pp. 272-282.

Cook, Rebecca. (1994). State accountability under the Convention on the Elimination of All Forms of Discrimination Against Women. In Rebecca Cook (Ed.). *Human rights of women: National and international perspectives.* Philadelphia, PA: University of Pennsylvania Press, pp. 228-256.

Copelon, Rhonda. (1995). Gendered war crimes: Reconceptualizing rape in time of war. In Julie Peters and Andrea Wolper (Eds.). *Women's rights, human rights: International feminist perspectives.* New York: Routledge, pp. 197-214.

Cox, Elizabeth (1992). The Mexican battered women's movement and the case for internationalism. *Response, 14*(3), 2-4.

Cuomo, Christine (1994). Ecofeminism, deep ecology, and human population. In Karen Warren (Ed.). *Ecological feminism.* London: Routledge, pp. 88-105.

Dalla Costa, Mariarosa and James, Selma. (1975). *The power of women and the subversion of the community.* Bristol, England: Falling Wall Press.

Daly, Mary. (1968/1985). *The church and the second sex.* Boston, MA: Beacon Press.

Daly, Mary. (1978). *Gyn/ecology: The metaethics of radical feminism.* Boston, MA: Beacon Press.

Davion, Victoria. (1994). Is ecofeminism feminist? In Karen Warren (Ed.). *Ecological feminism.* London: Routledge, pp. 8-28.

Davis, Angela. (1990). *Women, culture, & politics.* New York: Vintage Books.

d'Eaubonne, Françoise. (1974). *Le Féminisme ou la Mort,* Paris: P. Horay.

de Beauvoir, Simone. (1981). Introduction to the second sex. In Elaine Marks and Irene de Courtivron (Eds.). *New French Feminists.* New York: Schocken Books, pp. 99-106.

de Lauretis, Teresa. (1990). Upping the anti (sic) in feminist theory. In Marianne Hirsch and Elizabeth Fox Keller (Eds.). *Conflicts in feminism.* New York: Routledge, pp. 255-270.

DiNitto, Diana. (1995). *Social welfare: Politics and public policy.* 4th ed. Boston, MA: Allyn & Bacon.

DiStefano, Christine. (1990). Dilemmas of difference: Feminism, modernity, and postmodernism. In Linda Nicholson (Ed.). *Feminism/Postmodernism.* New York: Routledge, Chapman & Hall.

Donovan, Josephine. (1985). *Feminist theory: The intellectual traditions of American feminism.* New York: Frederick Ungar Publishing.

Drake, Susan. (1992). Personal transformation: A guide for the female hero. *Women and Therapy, 12,*(3), 51-65.

Dworkin, Andrea. (1988). *Letters from a war zone.* New York: E. P. Dutton.

Dworkin, Andrea. (1989). *Pornography: Men possessing women.* New York: E. P. Dutton.

Dworkin, Andrea. (1993). The real pornography of a brutal war against women. *Los Angeles Times,* September 5, M, 2:5.

Dworkin, Andrea. (1995). In Nicole Brown Simpson's words. *Los Angeles Times,* January 29, M, 1:3.

Echols, Alice. (1989). *Daring to be bad: Radical feminism in America 1967-1975.* Minneapolis, MN: University of Minnesota Press.

Eisenstein, Hester. (1983). *Contemporary feminist thought.* Boston, MA: G. K. Hall & Company.

Eisenstein, Zillah. (1981). *The radical future of liberal feminism.* Boston, MA: Northeastern University Press.

Eisler, Riane. (1987). *The chalice and the blade: Our history and our future.* San Francisco, CA: Harper & Row.

Eisler, Riane. (1990). The Gaia tradition and the partnership future: An ecofeminist manifesto. In Irene Diamond and Gloria Orenstein (Eds.). *Reweaving the world: The emergence of ecofeminism.* San Francisco, CA: Sierra Club Books, pp. 23-34.

Elabor-Idemudia, Patience. (1994). Nigeria: Agricultural exports and compensatory schemes: rural women's production resources and quality of life. In Pamela Sparr (Ed.). *Mortgaging women's lives: Feminist critiques of structural adjustment.* London: Zed Books, pp. 134-164.

Elshtain, Jean. (1982). Feminist discourse and its discontents: Language, power and meaning. In Nanerl Keohane, Michelle Rosaldo and Barbara Gelpi (Eds.). *Feminist Theory: A critique of ideology.* Chicago: University of Chicago Press, pp. 127-146.

Engels, Frederick. (1972). *The origin of the family, private property and the state.* New York: International Publishers.

Enloe, Cynthia. (1989). *Bananas, beaches and bases: Making feminist sense of international politics.* Berkeley, CA: University of California Press.

Faderman, Lillian. (1981). *Surpassing the love of men: Romantic friendship and love between women from the Renaissance to the present.* New York: William Morrow and Company.

Faderman, Lillian. (1992). *Odd girls and twilight lovers: A history of lesbian life in twentieth century America.* New York: Penguin.

Faludi, Susan. (1991). *Backlash: The undeclared war against American women.* New York: Crown Publishers.

Farwell, Marilyn. (1993). The lesbian literary imagination. In Susan Wolfe and Julia Penelope (Eds.). *Sexual practice, textual theory: Lesbian cultural criticism.* Cambridge, MA: Blackwell, pp. 66-84.

Federn, Ernst. (1992). From psychoanalysis to clinical social work: An evolutionary process. *Clinical Social Work Journal, 20*(1), 9-16.

Ferguson, Ann and Folbre, Nancy. (1981). The unhappy marriage of patriarchy and capitalism. In Lydia Sargent (Ed.). *Women and revolution*. Boston: South End Press, pp. 313-338.

Figuera-McDonough, Josephine. (1994). Family policies: The failure of solidarity and the costs of motherhood. *The Journal of Applied Social Sciences, 18*(1), Special Issue: Feminist thought, social policy and social work practice, 41-54.

Firestone, Shulamith. (1970). *The dialectic of sex*. New York: Bantam.

Flax, Jane. (1990). Postmodernism and gender relations in feminist theory. In Linda Nicholson (Ed.). *Feminism/Postmodernism*. New York: Routledge, Chapman & Hall, pp. 39-62.

Flexner, Eleanor. (1959/1971). *Century of Struggle*. New York: Atheneum.

Foucault, Michel. (1972). *The archaeology of knowledge and the discourse on language*. New York: Pantheon.

Foucault, Michel. (1980). *The history of sexuality: Volume 1: An introduction*. New York: Vintage Books.

Fraser, Nancy and Nicholson, Linda. (1990). Social criticism without philosophy: an encounter between feminism and postmodernism. In Linda Nicholson (Ed.). *Feminism/Postmodernism*. New York: Routledge, Chapman & Hall, pp. 19-38.

French, Marilyn, (1985). *Beyond power: On women, men, and morals*. New York: Ballentine Books.

Friedan, Betty. (1963). *The feminine mystique*. New York: Dell.

Frye, Marilyn. (1983). *The politics of reality: Essays in feminist theory*. Trumansburg, NY: The Crossing Press.

Frye, Marilyn. (1992). *Willful virgin: Essays in feminism 1976-1992*. Freedom, CA: The Crossing Press.

Fuentes, Annette and Ehrenreich, Barbara. (1982). *Women in the global factory*. Boston, MA: South End Press.

Gage, Matilda Joslyn. (1893). *Woman, church and state*. Chicago, IL: C.H. Kerr & Co.

Garcia, Alma. (1990). The development of Chicana feminist discourse. In Gloria Anzaldua (Ed.). *Making face, making soul: Haciendo Caras*. San Francisco, CA: Aunt Lute Books, pp. 418-431.

Gary, Lisa Tieszen. (1991). Feminist practice and family violence. In Mary Bricker-Jenkins, Nancy Hooyman, and Naomi Gottlieb (Eds.). *Feminist social work practice in clinical settings,* Newbury Park, CA: Sage Publications, pp. 19-32.

Fuller, Margaret. (1843). *Woman in the nineteenth century.* New York: Greeley & McElrath.

Giddings, Paula. (1988). *When and where I enter.* New York: Bantam.

Gilligan, Carol. (1982). *In a different voice: Psychological theory and women's development.* Cambridge, MA: Harvard University Press.

Gilligan, Carol. (1995). Hearing the difference: Theorizing connection. *Hypatia, 10*(2), 120-127.

Gimbutas, Marija. (1982). *The goddesses and gods of old Europe.* Berkeley, CA: University of California Press.

Goffman, Erving. (1963). Stigma: Notes on the management of spoiled identity. New York: Simon & Schuster.

Gottlieb, Naomi; Burden, Dianne; McCormick, Ruth; and Nicarthy, Ginny. (1983). The distinctive attributes of feminist groups. *Social Work with Groups, 6*(3/4), 81-93.

Griffin, Susan. (1971). Rape: The all-American crime. *Ramparts, 10,* 26-35.

Griffin, Susan. (1978). *Woman and nature: The roaring inside her.* New York: Harper & Row.

Griffin, Susan. (1979). *Rape: The power of consciousness.* San Francisco, CA: Harper & Row.

Grimshaw, Jean. (1986). *Philosophy and feminist thinking.* Minneapolis, MN: University of Minnesota Press.

Groves, Patricia and Schondel, Connie. (1994). Lesbian couples who are survivors of incest: Groupwork using a feminist perspective. Paper presented at the Sixteenth Annual Symposium of Social Work with Groups. Hartford, CT: October 27-30.

Gunther, Pat. (1986). A rural and lesbian perspective on feminist practice. In Mary Bricker-Jenkins and Nancy Hooyman (Eds.). *Not for women only.* Silver Spring, MD: National Association of Social Workers, pp. 88-100.

Guy-Sheftall, Beverly. (1993). A black feminist perspective on transforming the academy: The Case of Spelman College. In

Stanlie James and Abena Busis (Eds.). *Theorizing black feminisms: The visionary pragmatism of black women.* New York: Routledge, pp. 77-89.

Hamilton, Cynthia. (1990). Women, home, and community: The struggle in an urban environment. In Irene Diamond and Gloria Orenstein (Eds.). *Reweaving the world: The emergence of ecofeminism.* San Francisco, CA: Sierra Club Books, pp. 215-222.

Harding, Sandra. (1990). Feminism, science and the anti-enlightenment critiques. In Linda Nicholson (Ed.). *Feminism/postmodernism.* New York: Routledge, pp. 83-106.

Hartmann, Heidi. (1981). The unhappy marriage of Marxism and feminism: Towards a more progressive union. In Lydia Sargent (Ed.). *Women and revolution.* Boston, MA: South End Press, pp. 1-42.

Hartsock, Nancy. (1979). Feminist theory and the development of revolutionary strategy. In Zillah Eisenstein (Ed.). *Capitalist patriarchy and the case for socialist feminism.* New York: Monthly Review Press, pp. 56-77.

Hartsock, Nancy. (1987). The feminist standpoint: Developing the ground for a specifically feminist historical materialism. In Sandra Harding (Ed.). *Feminism and methodology.* Bloomington, IN: Indiana University Press.

Helie-Lucas, Marie-Aimee. (1990). Women, nationalism and religion in the Algerian struggle. In Margot Badran and Miriam Cooke (Eds.). *Opening the gates: A century of Arab feminist writing.* Bloomington, IN: Indiana University Press.

Herbst, Patricia Robin. (1992). From helpless victim to empowered survivor: Oral history as a treatment for survivors of torture. *Women and Therapy, 13*(1-2), 141-154.

Hess, K.; Langford, Jean; and Ross, Kathy. (1988). Comparative separatism. In Sarah Hoagland and Julia Penelope (Eds.). *For lesbians only: A separatist anthology.* London: Onlywomen Press, pp. 125-131.

Higgonbotham, Elizabeth. (1992). African-American women's history and the metalanguage of race. *Signs, 17*(2), 251-274.

Higginbotham, Elizabeth. (1993). *Righteous discontent: The women's movement in the Black Baptist Church, 1880-1920.* Cambridge, MA: Harvard University Press.

Hoagland, Sarah. (1988). *Lesbian ethics.* Palo Alto, CA: Institute for Lesbian Studies.

hooks, bell. (1981). *Ain't I a woman: Black women and feminism.* Boston, MA: South End Press.

hooks, bell. (1984). *Feminist theory: From margin to center.* Boston, MA: South End Press.

hooks, bell. (1990). *Yearning: Race, gender and cultural politics.* Boston, MA: South End Press.

hooks, bell. (1993). *Sisters of the yam: Black women and self-recovery.* Boston, MA: South End Press.

Hooyman, Nancy and Cunningham, Rosemary. (1986). An alternative administrative style. In Nan Van Den Berg and Lynn Cooper (Eds.). *Feminist visions for social work,* Silver Spring, MD: NASW, pp. 163-186.

Hooyman, Nancy and Gutiérrez, Lorraine. (1994). Introduction to feminist thought, social policy and social work practice. *Journal of Applied Social Services, 18*(1), 2-4.

Hudson-Weems, Clenora. (1993). *Africana womanism: Reclaiming ourselves.* Troy, MI: Bedford Publishers.

Hull, Gloria T.; Scott, Patricia Bell; and Smith, Barbara (Eds.). (1982). *But some of us are brave.* New York: The Feminist Press.

Ianello, Kathleen. (1992). *Decisions without hierarchies: Feminist interventions in organization theory and practice.* New York: Routledge.

Isserman, Maurice. (1995). A brief history of the American Left. [On-line]. Available: http://ccme–mac4.bsd.uchicago.edu/DSA-Lit/History.html.

Jaggar, Allison. (1983). *Feminist politics and human nature.* Totowa, NJ: Rowman and Allanheld.

James, Ian. (1995). Freed Thai workers file lawsuit. *Los Angeles Times,* September 6, B, 3:1.

Javors, Irene. (1990). Goddess in the metropolis: Reflections on the sacred in an urban setting. In Irene Diamond and Gloria Orenstein (Eds.). *Reweaving the world: The emergence of ecofeminism.* San Francisco, CA: Sierra Club Books, pp. 211-214.

Jenness, Valerie. (1990). From sex as sin to sex as work: COYOTE and the reorganization of prostitution as a social problem. *Social Problems, 37*(3), 403-420.

Jo, Bev. (1981). Female only. In Sarah Hoagland and Julia Penelope (Eds.). *For lesbians only: A separatist anthology.* London: Onlywomen Press, pp. 74-75.

Johnston, Jill. (1973). *Lesbian nation: The feminist solution.* New York: Simon & Schuster.

Jones, Loring. (1992). His unemployment and her reaction: The effects of husbands' unemployment on wives. *Affilia, 7*(1), 59-73.

Jordan, Judith; Kaplan, Alexandra; Miller, Jean Baker; Stiver, Irene; and Surrey, Janet. (1991). *Women's growth in connection: Writings from the Stone Center.* New York: The Guilford Press.

Joseph, Gloria. (1981). The incompatible menage á trois: Marxism, feminism and racism. In Lydia Sargent (Ed.). *Women and revolution.* Boston, MA: South End Press.

Joseph, Gloria and Lewis, Jill. (1981). *Common differences: Conflicts in black and white feminist perspectives.* Boston, MA: South End Press.

Kanuha, Valli. (1994). Women of Color in battering relationships. In Lillian Comas-Diaz and Beverly Greene (Eds.). *Women of Color: Integrating ethnic and gender identities in psychotherapy.* New York: The Guilford Press, pp. 428-454.

Kaufman, Natalie and Lindquist, Stefanie. (1995) Critiquing gender-neutral treaty language: The convention on the Elimination of All Forms of Discrimination Against Women. In Julie Peters and Andrea Wolper (Eds.). *Women's rights, human rights: International feminist perspectives.* New York: Routledge, pp. 114-125.

Kennedy, Elizabeth and Davis, Madeline. (1994). *Boots of leather, slippers of gold: The history of a lesbian community.* NY: Penguin Books.

Kenney, Janet and Tash, Donna. (1992). Lesbian childbearing couples' dilemmas and decisions. *Health Care for Women International, 13,* 209-219.

Kessler-Harris, Alice. (1990). Equal Employment Opportunity Commission v. Sears, Roebuck and Company: A personal account / Alice Kessler-Harris. In Ellen Du Bois and Vickie Ruiz (Eds.). *Unequal Sisters.* New York: Routledge, Chapman & Hall, pp. 432-446.

King, Ynestra. (1990). Healing the wounds: Feminism, ecology, and the nature/culture dualism. In Irene Diamond and Gloria Orenstein (Eds.). *Reweaving the world: The emergence of ecofeminism.* San Francisco, CA: Sierra Club Books, pp. 106-121.

Kirsh, Barbara. (1987). Evolution of consciousness raising groups. In Claire Brody (Ed.). *Women's therapy groups: Paradigms of feminist treatment.* New York: Springer Publishing, pp. 43-54.

Kisner, Arlene (Ed.). (1972). *Woodhull & Claflin's Weekly: The lives and writings of notorious Victoria Woodhull and her sister Tennessee Claflin.* Washington, NJ: Times Change Press.

Kitzinger, Celia. (1987). *The social construction of lesbianism.* London: Sage.

Kitzinger, Celia and Perkins, Rachel. (1993). *Changing our minds: Lesbian feminism and psychology.* New York: New York University Press.

Koedt, Anne. (1973). Lesbianism and feminism. In Anne Koedt, Ellen Levine, and Anita Rapone (Eds.). *Radical Feminism.* New York: Quadrangle Books, pp. 246-258.

Kramer, Terry. (1983). The diary as a feminist research method. *Newsletter of the Association for Women in Psychology,* 3-4.

Kravetz, Diane. (1986). Women and mental health. In Nan Van Den Berg and Lynn Cooper (Eds.). *Feminist visions for social work.* Silver Spring, MD: NASW, pp. 101-127.

Kravetz, Diane and Jones, Linda. (1991). Supporting practice in feminist service agencies. In Mary Bricker-Jenkins, Nancy Hooyman, and Naomi Gottlieb (Eds.). *Feminist social work practice in clinical settings,* Newbury Park, CA: Sage Publications, pp. 233-249.

Kristeva, Julia. (1980). Woman can never be defined. In Elaine Marks and Irene deCourtivron (Eds.). *New French Feminisms.* New York: Schocken Books.

Lahar, Stephanie. (1991). Ecofeminist theory and grassroots politics. *Hypatia, 6*(1), 28-45.

Laird, Joan. (1989). Women and stories: Restorying women's self-constructions. In Monica McGoldrick, Carol Anderson, and Froma Walsh (Eds.). *Women in families: A framework for family therapy.* New York: W. W. Norton, pp. 427-450.

Lambert, Susan. (1994). A day late and a dollar short: Persistent gender differences amid changing requirements for organizational advancement. *The Journal of Applied Social Sciences, 18*(1), 89-108.

Lather, Patti. (1991). *Getting smart: Feminist research and pedagogy with/in the postmodern.* New York: Routledge.

Leiberman, Alice and Davis, Liane. (1992). The role of social work in the defense of reproductive rights. *Social Work, 37*(4), 365-371.

Lewin, Ellen. (1993). *Lesbian mothers: Accounts of gender in American culture.* Ithaca, NY: Cornell University Press.

Lim, Ginny. (1983). Wonder woman. In Cheri Moraga and Gloria Anzaldua (Eds.). *This bridge called my back: Writings by radical women of color.* New York: Kitchen Table: Women of Color Press, pp. 25-26.

Locke, John. (1977). Second treatise on civil government. In Samuel Stumpf (Ed.). *Philosophy: History and Problems.* Second edition. New York: McGraw-Hill, pp. 202-207.

Lorde, Audre. (1979/1983). The master's tools will never dismantle the master's house. In Cheri Moraga and Gloria Anzaldua (Eds.). *This bridge called my back: Writings by radical women of color.* New York: Kitchen Table: Women of Color Press, pp. 98-101.

Lorde, Audre. (1984). *Sister outsider.* Freedom, CA: The Crossing Press.

Lorde, Audre. (1990). I am your sister: Black women organizing across sexualities. In Gloria Anzaldua (Ed.). *Making face, making soul: Haciendo Caras.* San Francisco, CA: Aunt Lute Books, pp. 321-325.

Lovibond, Susan. (1989). Feminism and postmodernism. *New Left Review, 178,* 5-28.

Luker, Kristen. (1984). *Abortion and the politics of motherhood.* Berkeley, CA: University of California Press.

MacKinnon, Catherine. (1993). *Only words.* Cambridge, MA: Harvard University Press.

Mainardi, Pat. (1976). The politics of housework. In Kathryn Paulsen and Ryan Kuhn (Eds.). *Woman's almanac.* Philadelphia, PA: J.B. Lippincott, pp. 313-315.

The many faces of feminism. (1994). *Ms. 5,* (1), 33-64.

Mariechild, Diane. (1981). *Mother wit: A feminist guide to psychic development.* Trumansburg, NY: The Crossing Press.

Marks, Elaine and de Courtivron, Irene (Eds.). (1981). Introduction. *New French Feminisms.* New York: Schocken Books.

Marx, Karl. (1932). *Capital, The Communist Manifesto and other writings.* New York: The Modern Library.

Marx, Karl (1977). *Capital: A critique of political economy, Volume one.* New York: Vintage Books.

Mascia-Lees, Frances; Sharpe, Patricia; and Cohen, Colleen. (1989). The postmodernist turn in anthropology: Cautions from a feminist perspective. *Signs, 15*(1), 7-33.

Mayer, Ann Elizabeth (1995). Cultural particularism as a bar to women's rights: Reflections on the Middle Eastern experience. In Julie Peters and Andrea Wolper (Eds.). *Women's rights, human rights: International feminist perspectives.* New York: Routledge, pp. 176-188.

McClintock, Anne. (1992). Screwing the system: Sexwork, race, and the law. *Boundary 2, 19*(2), 70-95.

Merchant, Carol. (1990). Ecofeminism and feminist theory. In Irene Diamond and Gloria Orenstein (Eds.). *Reweaving the world: The emergence of ecofeminism.* San Francisco, CA: Sierra Club Books, pp. 100-105.

Mernissi, Fatima. (1987). *Beyond the veil: Male-female dynamics in modern Muslim society.* Bloomington and Indianapolis, IN: Indiana University Press.

Milkman, Ruth. (1985). Women workers, feminism and the labor movement since the 1960's. In Ruth Milkman (Ed.). *Women, work and protest: A century of U.S. women's labor history.* Boston, MA: Routledge & Kegan Paul.

Millett, Kate. (1969). *Sexual politics.* New York: Ballentine Books.

Minow, Martha. (1990). Adjudicating differences: Conflicts among feminist lawyers. In Marianne Hirsch and Evelyn Fox Keller (Eds.). *Conflicts in feminism.* New York: Routledge, pp. 149-163.

Mitchell, Juliet. (1973). *Woman's estate.* New York: Vintage Books.

Mitchell, Juliet. (1975). *Psychoanalysis and feminism: Freud, Reich, Laing and women.* New York: Vintage Books.

Mitter, Swasti. (1994). On organising women in casualized work: A global overview. In Sheila Rowbotham and Swasti Mitter (Eds.).

Dignity and daily bread: New forms of economic organizing among poor women in the Third World and the First. London: Routledge, pp. 14-52.

Moghadam, Valentine. (1994). Introduction: Women and identity politics in theoretical and comparative perspective. In Valentine Moghadam (Ed.). *Identity politics and women: Cultural reassertions and feminisms in international perspective.* San Francisco, CA: Westview Press, pp. 3-26.

Mohanty, Chandra. (1991). Cartographies of struggle. In Chandra Mohanty, Ann Russo, and Lourdes Torres (Eds.). *Third World women and the politics of feminism.* Bloomington, IN: Indiana University Press, pp. 1-47.

Molina, Papusa. (1990). Recognizing, accepting and celebrating our differences. In Gloria Anzaldua (Ed.). *Making face, making soul: Haciendo Caras.* San Francisco, CA: Aunt Lute Books, pp. 326-331.

Morgan, Robin. (1978). *Going too far.* New York: Random House.

Naples, Nancy. (1991). A socialist feminist analysis of the Family Support Act of 1988. *Affilia, 6*(4), 23-38.

Nes, Janet and Iadicola, Peter. (1989). Toward a definition of feminist social work: A comparison of liberal, radical, and socialist models. *Social Work, 34*(1), 12-21.

Nestle, Joan (1981). Butch-Fem relationships: Sexual courage in the 1950's. *Heresies 3,* 4(12), 100-109.

Nicholson, Linda. (Ed.). (1990). *Feminism/postmodernism.* New York: Routledge.

Nuccio, Kathleen and Sands, Roberta. (1992). Using postmodern feminist theory to deconstruct "phallacies" of poverty. *Affilia, 7*(4), 26-48.

NWSA. (1990). *NWSA Directory of Women's Studies Programs, Women's Centers, and Women's Research Centers.* College Park, MD: National Women's Studies Association.

Ogunyemi, Chikwenye. (1985). Womanism: The dynamics of the contemporary black female novel in English. *Signs, 11*(1), 63-80.

Papachristou, Judith. (1976). *Women together.* New York: Knopf.

Patterson, Charlotte. (1992). Children of lesbian and gay parents. *Child Development, 63*(5), 1025.

Patterson, Charlotte. (1994). Lesbian and gay couples considering parenthood: An agenda for research, service, and advocacy. *Journal of Gay and Lesbian Social Services, 1*(2), 33-55.

Payne, Carol. (1973). Consciousness raising: A dead end? In Anne Koedt, Ellen Levine, and Anita Rapone (Eds.). *Radical Feminism.* New York: Quadrangle Books, pp. 282-284.

Penelope, Julia (1990). The lesbian perspective. In Jeffner Allen, (Ed.). *Lesbian philosophies and cultures,* Albany, NY: State University of New York Press, pp. 89-108.

Pesquera, Beatriz and Segura, Denise. (1993). There is no going back: Chicanas and feminism. In Norma Alarcóne, Rafaela Castro, Emma Peréz, Adaljiza Sosa Riddel, and Patricia Zavella (Eds.). *Chicana critical issues.* Berkeley, CA: Third Woman Press, pp. 95-115.

Phelan, Shane. (1994). *Getting specific: Postmodern lesbian politics.* Minneapoli, MN: University of Minnesota Press.

Plaskow, Judith. (1979). The coming of Lilith: Toward a feminist theology. In Carol Christ and Judith Plaskow (Eds.). *Womanspirit rising: A feminist reader in religion.* San Francisco, CA: Harper & Row, pp. 198-209.

Plaskow, Judith. (1990). *Standing again at Sinai: Judaism from a feminist perspective.* San Francisco, CA: Harper & Row.

Plumwood, Val. (1991). Nature, self, and gender: Feminism, environmental philosophy, and the critique of rationalism. *Hypatia, 6*(1), 3-27.

Radicalesbians. (1994). The woman-identified woman. In Miriam Schneir (Ed.). *Feminism in our time: The essential writings, World War II to the present.* New York: Vintage Books, pp. 160-167.

Ramsey, Karen and Parker, Martin. (1992). Gender, bureaucracy and organizational culture. In Mike Savage and Anne Weitz (Eds.). *Gender and bureaucracy.* Cambridge, MA: Blackwell Publishers, pp. 253-276.

Reagon, Bernice. (1983). Coalition politics: Turning the century. In Barbara Smith (Ed.). *Home girls: A black feminist anthology.* New York: Kitchen Table: Women of Color Press.

Reinhartz, Shulamit. (1992). *Feminist methods in social research*: New York: Oxford University Press.

Remafedi, Gary. (1990). Fundamental issues in the care of homosexual youth. *Medical Clinics of North America, 74*(5), 1169-1179.

Rich, Adrienne. (1979a). Disloyal to civilization. *Chrysalis, 7,* 9-27.

Rich, Adrienne. (1979b). *On lies, secrets, and silence.* New York: W. W. Norton.

Rich, Adrienne. (1980). *Compulsory heterosexuality and lesbian experience.* Denver, CO: Antelope Publications.

Richie, Beth. (1985). Battered black women: A challenge for the Black community. *Black Scholar, 16,* 40-44.

Roach, Catherine. (1991). Loving your mother: On the woman–nature relation. *Hypatia, 6*(1), 46-59.

Robinson, Kristen. (1991). Gay youth support groups: An opportunity for social work intervention. *Social Work, 36*(5), 458-459.

Rodrique, Jessie. (1990). The black community and the birth-control movement. In Ellen Du Bois and Vickie Ruiz (Eds.). *Unequal sisters.* New York: Routledge, pp. 333-344.

Rosa, Kumudhini. (1994). The conditions and organisational activities of women in Free Trade Zones: Malaysia, Philippines and Sri Lanka, 1970-1990. In Sheila Rowbotham and Swasti Mitter (Eds.). *Dignity and daily bread: New forms of economic organizing among poor women in the Third World and the First.* London: Routledge, pp. 73-99.

Rosenthal, Beth. (1991). Social workers' interest in international practice in the developing world: A multivariate analysis. *Social Work, 36*(3), 248-252.

Rubin, Elizabeth. (1992). Female development: How to operationalize what we know. *Women and Therapy, 12*(3), 67-80.

Rubin, Gayle. (1974). The traffic in women: Notes on the "political economy" of sex. In Michelle Rosaldo and Louise Lamphere (Eds.). *Woman, culture and society.* Stanford, CA: Stanford University Press.

Russell, Julia (1990). The evolution of an ecofeminist. In Irene Diamond and Gloria Orenstein, (Eds.). *Reweaving the world: The emergence of ecofeminism.* San Francisco, CA: Sierra Club Books, pp. 223-230.

Saleebey, Dennis. (1994). Culture, theory and narrative: The intersection of meanings in practice. *Social Work, 39*(4), 351-359.

Salleh, Ariel. (1993). Class, race, and gender discourse in the ecofeminism/deep ecology debate. *Environmental Ethics, 14,* 225-244.

SAMOIS (1981/1987). *Coming to power.* Boston, MA: Alyson Publications.

Sancier, Betty. (1981). Beyond Advocacy. In Ann Weick and Susan Vandiver (Eds.). *Women, power, and change.* Washington, DC: National Association of Social Workers, pp. 186-196.

Saulnier, Christine Flynn. (1994). *Alcohol problems and marginalization: Social group work with lesbians and black women.* Ann Arbor, MI: University of Michigan Press.

Saulnier, Christine Flynn. (1996). Images of the twelve step model, and sex and love addiction in an alcohol intervention group for black women. *Journal of Drug Issues, 26*(1), 95-123.

Schneir, Miriam. (1994). *Feminism in our time: The essential writings, World War II to present.* New York: Vintage Books.

Scott, Joan. (1990). Deconstructing equality-versus-difference: Or, the uses of poststructuralist theory for feminism. In Marianne Hirsch and Elizabeth Fox Keller (Eds.). *Conflicts in feminism.* New York: Routledge, pp. 134-148.

Shanley, Kate. (1984/1988). Thoughts on Indian feminism. In Beth Brant (Ed.). *A gathering of spirit: A collection by North American Indian women.* Ithaca, NY: Firebrand Books, pp. 213-215.

Shiva, Vandana. (1990). Development as a new project of Western patriarchy. In Irene Diamond and Gloria Orenstein (Eds.). *Reweaving the world: The emergence of ecofeminism.* San Francisco, CA: Sierra Club Books, pp. 189-200.

Slicer, Deborah. (1994). Wrongs of passage. In Karen Warren (Ed.). *Ecological feminism.* London: Routledge, pp. 29-41.

Sloan, Lacey. (In review). The debate over sex work: Toward a unified policy. University at Buffalo, SUNY, School of Social Work.

Sloan-Hunter, Margaret. (1988). The issue is woman identification. In Sarah Hoagland and Julia Penelope (Eds.). *For lesbians only: A separatist anthology.* London: Onlywomen Press, pp. 147-148.

Smith, Barbara. (1986). Some home truths on the contemporary black feminist movement. In Nan Van Den Berg and Lynn Cooper (Eds.). *Feminist visions for social work,* Silver Spring, MD: NASW, pp. 45-60.

Smith, Barbara and Smith, Beverly. (1983). Across the kitchen table. In Cheri Moraga and Gloria Anzaldua (Eds.). *This bridge called my back: Writings by radical women of color (2nd ed.)*. New York: Kitchen Table: Women of Color Press, pp. 113-127.

Sparr, Pamela. (1994). What is structural adjustment? In Pamela Sparr (Ed.). *Mortgaging women's lives: Feminist critiques of structural adjustment*. London: Zed Books, pp. 1-12.

Stanfield, John H. II (1994). Ethnic modeling in qualitative research. In Norman Denzin and Yvonna Lincoln (Eds.). *Handbook of qualitative research,* Thousand Oaks, CA: Sage, pp. 175-188.

Stanley, Liz. (1990). Recovering women in history from feminist deconstructionism. *Women's Studies International Forum, 13*(1/2), 151-157.

Stanton, Elizabeth Cady. (1895/1898). *The woman's Bible.* New York: European Pub. Co.

Starhawk. (1990). Power, authority, and mystery: Ecofeminism and earth-based spirituality. In Irene Diamond and Gloria Orenstein (Eds.). *Reweaving the world: The emergence of ecofeminism.* San Francisco, CA: Sierra Club Books, pp. 73-86.

Stone, Merlin. (1976). *When God was a woman.* New York: Harcourt Brace Jovanovich.

Tohidi, Nayereh. (1991). Gender and Islamic fundamentalism. In Chandra Mohanty, Ann Russo, and Lourdes Torres (Eds.). *Third World women and the politics of feminism.* Bloomington, IN: Indiana University Press, pp. 251-265.

Tong, Rosemarie. (1989). *Feminist thought: A comprehensive introduction.* San Francisco, CA: Westview Press.

Toprak, Binnaz. (1994). Women and fundamentalism: The case of Turkey. In Valentine Moghadam (Ed.). *Identity politics and women: cultural reassertions and feminisms in international perspective.* San Francisco, CA: Westview Press, pp. 293-306.

Toro, Maria Suarez. (1995). Popularizing women's human rights at the local level: A grassroots methodology for setting the international agenda. In Julie Peters and Andrea Wolper (Eds.). *Women's rights, human rights: International feminist perspectives.* New York: Routledge, pp. 189-194.

Townes, Emilie. (1993). *Womanist justice, womanist hope.* Atlanta, GA: Scholars Press.

Trebilcot, Joyce. (1994). *Dyke ideas: Process, politics, daily life.* Albany, NY: State University of NY Press.

Trujillo, Carla. (1993). Chicana Lesbians. In Norma Alarcóne, Rafaela Castro, Emma Peréz, Adaljiza Sosa Riddel, and Patricia Zavella (Eds.). *Chicana critical issues.* Berkeley, CA: Third Woman Press, pp. 117-125.

Truth, Sojourner. (1970). The women want their rights. In Linda Tanner (Ed.). *Voices from women's liberation.* New York: The New American Library, p. 73.

Tully, Carol. (1994). To boldly go where no one has gone before: The legalization of lesbian and gay marriages. *Journal of Gay and Lesbian Social Services 1,* (1), 73-87.

Uribe, Virginia. (1994). Project 10: A school-based outreach to gay and lesbian youth. *High School Journal, 77*(1 and 2), 108-112.

Walker, Alice. (1983). *In search of our mothers' gardens.* San Diego, CA: Harcourt Brace Jovanovich.

Waring, Marilyn. (1988). *If women counted: A new feminist economics.* London: Macmillan.

Weaver, Hilary. (In press). Indigenous people in a multicultural society: Issues of identity, assimilation, and multiculturalism. University at Buffalo, SUNY, School of Social Work.

Weedon, Chris. (1987). *Feminist practice and poststructuralist theory.* New York: Basil Blackwell, Inc.

Weems, Renita. (1988). *Just a sister away: A womanist vision of women's relationships in the Bible.* San Diego, CA: Lura Media.

Wetzel, Janet Wood. (1986). A feminist world view conceptual framework. *Social Casework, 67*(3), 167-173.

White, Cindy and Dobris, Catherine. (1993). A chorus of discordant voices: Radical feminist confrontations with patriarchal religions. *The Southern Communications Journal, 58*(3), 239-246.

Wilcox, Clyde. (1990). Black women and feminism. *Women and Politics,* 10(3), 65-84.

Willis, Ellen. (1989). Forward. In Alice Echols, *Daring to be bad: Radical feminism in America 1967-1975.* Minneapolis, MN: University of Minnesota Press.

Withorn, Ann. (1994). Helping ourselves. In Peter Conrad and Rochelle Kern (Eds.). *The sociology of health and illness: Critical perspectives.* New York: St. Martin's Press, pp. 441-449.

Wittig, Monique. (1985). *Les Guerilleres.* Boston, MA: Beacon Press.

Wittig, Monique. (1988a). The straight mind. In Sarah Hoagland and Julia Penelope (Eds.). *For lesbians only: A separatist anthology.* London: Onlywomen Press, pp. 431-438.

Wittig, Monique. (1988b). One is not born a woman. In Sarah Hoagland, and Julia Penelope (Eds.). *For lesbians only: A separatist anthology.* London: Onlywomen Press, pp. 439-447.

Wolfe, Janet. (1987). Cognitive-behavioral therapy for women. In Claire Brody (Ed.). *Women's therapy groups: Paradigms of feminist treatment.* New York: Springer Publishing, pp. 163-173.

Wollstonecraft, Mary. (1792/1967). *A vindication of the rights of woman.* Charles Hagelman (Ed.). New York: W.W. Norton.

Women's Action Coalition. (1993). *WAC stats: The facts about women.* New York: The New Press.

Working women in the USA. (1993). *Women's International Network News, 19*(1), 69.

The World Bank: A global partnership for development. (1995). [On-line]. Available: www.worldbank.org. News release # 95/01.

Yamada, Mitsuye. (1983). Asian Pacific American women and feminism. In Cheri Moraga and Gloria Anzaldua (Eds.). *This bridge called my back: Writings by radical women of color.* New York: Kitchen Table: Women of Color Press, 71-75.

Young, Iris. (1981). The unhappy marriage of Marxism and feminism: Towards a more progressive union. In Lydia Sargent (Ed.). (1981). *Women and revolution: A discussion of the unhappy marriage of Marxism and feminism.* Boston, MA: South End Press, pp. 1-42.

Zaretsky, Eli. (1973/1986). *Capitalism, the family, and personal life.* New York: Harper & Row.

Zavella, Patricia. (1993). The politics of race and gender: Organizing Chicana cannery workers in Northern California. In Norma Alarcóne, Rafaela Castro, Emma Peréz, Adaljiza Sosa Riddel, and Patricia Zavella (Eds.). *Chicana critical issues.* Berkeley, CA: Third Woman Press.

Index

Page numbers followed by the letter "n" indicate notes.